D1351501

PUBLICITY RIGHTS AND IMAGE

Academics and practitioners are currently divided on the issues involved in permitting and regulating the commercial exploitation of publicity. 'Publicity' is the practice of using an individual's name, image and reputation to promote products or to provide media coverage, often in gossip magazines and the tabloid press. This book provides a theoretical and multi-jurisdictional review of the nature of publicity practice and its appropriate legal regulation. The book includes a detailed exploration of the justifications advanced in favour of publicity rights and those that are advanced against. Removing the analysis from any one jurisdiction, the book examines current academic and judicial perspectives on publicity rights in a range of jurisdictions, drawing out similarities and differences, and revealing a picture of current thinking and practice which is intellectually incoherent. By then clearly defining the practice of publicity and examining justifications for and against, the author is able to bring the nature and shape of the right of publicity into much sharper focus.

The book includes a careful consideration of possible limits to any right of publicity, the potential for assigning publicity rights or transferring them post mortem, and whether defences can be offered. The author concludes by arguing for a publicity right which provides a degree of protection for the individual but which is significantly curtailed to recognise valid competing interests.

This is a work which will be of interest to academics and practitioners working in the field of publicity, privacy and intellectual property.

Publicity Rights and Image

Exploitation and Legal Control

GILLIAN BLACK

·H A R T·
PUBLISHING

OXFORD AND PORTLAND, OREGON
2011

Published in the United Kingdom by Hart Publishing Ltd
16C Worcester Place, Oxford, OX1 2JW
Telephone: +44 (0)1865 517530
Fax: +44 (0)1865 510710
E-mail: mail@hartpub.co.uk
Website: http://www.hartpub.co.uk

Published in North America (US and Canada) by
Hart Publishing
c/o International Specialized Book Services
920 NE 58th Avenue, Suite 300
Portland, OR 97213–3786
USA
Tel: +1 503 287 3093 or toll-free: (1) 800 944 6190
Fax: +1 503 280 8832
E-mail: orders@isbs.com
Website: http://www.isbs.com

British Library Cataloguing in Publication Data

Data Available

ISBN: 978-1-84946-054-5

Typeset by Columns Design Ltd, Reading
Printed and bound in Great Britain by
TJ International Ltd, Padstow, Cornwall

Jeeves: *It has been my experience, sir, that the normal person enjoys seeing his or her name in print, irrespective of what is said about them. I have an aunt, sir, who a few years ago was a martyr to swollen limbs. She tried Walkinshaw's Supreme Ointment and obtained considerable relief – so much so that she sent them an unsolicited testimonial. Her pride at seeing her photograph in the daily papers in connexion with descriptions of her lower limbs before taking, which were nothing less than revolting, was so intense that it led me to believe that publicity, of whatever sort, is what nearly everyone desires.*

From *Carry On, Jeeves* by PG Wodehouse. First published 1925, this edition published by Penguin Books, London, 1999, page 23.

Acknowledgements

This account of publicity rights and image is based upon my PhD thesis, 'A Right of Publicity in Scots Law', completed at the University of Edinburgh in 2009. Since then it has been updated and revised, most notably to turn the focus from Scots law to a wider, a-jurisdictional review. My thanks are due to many people who have provided invaluable assistance, support and friendship during the research and writing of both the thesis and this book. In particular, I would like to thank my supervisors, Professor Hector MacQueen and Professor Charlotte Waelde, and the following friends and colleagues: Professor John Blackie, Mr Paul Carlyle, Professor Fraser Davidson, Ms Lindsey Henderson, Professor Chris Himsworth, Professor Sir Neil MacCormick, Ms Laura Macgregor, Mr Jim McLean, Dr Claudio Michelon, Professor Niamh Nic Shuibne, Professor Ken Reid, Professor Niall Whitty and Mr Scott Wortley. The present work also benefits from the comments of my PhD examiners, Professor Joe Thomson, Ms Hazel Carty, and Professor Graeme Laurie, and I would like to thank them for their time and for putting me through my paces in the viva.

It is fair to say that publicity rights are capable of creating much controversy—arguably much greater than one would expect from a right which frequently (though not exclusively) concerns prima donna celebrities and celebrity-exploiting corporations, to paraphrase Baroness Hale in *Campbell v MGN.* I would therefore like to emphasise that the views expressed in this work are entirely my own, and do not reflect the views of all, or indeed many, of the people to whom I have extended my thanks. I am of course entirely responsible for any errors.

Richard Hart and his staff have been incredibly enthusiastic and supportive and I would like to thank them for their work in turning my manuscript into a book. I am delighted to join the Hart catalogue.

In addition to academic and professional support, I have also been fortunate to have had the encouragement of my family: my parents, Colin and Lynda Davies, and my siblings, Denise Barison and Ross Davies.

One person above all others, however, has helped throughout my PhD and the subsequent work on this text—my thanks and love go to my husband Callum for his unfailing love and support.

Gillian Black
Edinburgh, 27 July 2010

A Note on URLs

All URLs cited were correct as at 27 July 2010.

A Note on Case Citations

Case citations in footnotes have been given with reference to the official Law Reports where possible. The neutral citation (if one exists) for these cases has also been included in the case list. Other cases have been cited by the relevant volume of law reports, such as FSR, or by their neutral citation, where available. Unreported cases have been cited by neutral citation.

Several recent cases (including, notably, *Douglas v Hello!* and *Irvine v Talksport*) have raised different issues on appeal from the issues debated in, and decided by, the lower courts. For accuracy, the case citation given on each occasion will refer to the case report for the relevant issue under discussion, rather than the case report for the highest court involved in the litigation. By way of example, *Douglas v Hello!* raised issues of privacy when it was heard in the Court of Appeal and issues of commercial confidence in the House of Lords. The Court of Appeal citation will therefore typically be used when referring to the privacy elements of the case, while the House of Lords citation will be used when referring to the commercial aspects of the litigation.

Contents

Acknowledgements		vii
A Note on URLs		viii
A Note on Case Citations		viii
List of Journal Abbreviations		xiii
Table of Cases		xv
Table of Legislation		xix

1		The Power of Image: Introducing Publicity Rights	1
	I.	Introduction	1
	II.	Tracing the Development of Publicity Practice	2
	III.	The Scope of this Project	5

Part I	**Understanding Publicity: Theory and Practice**	**9**

2		The Theory of Image and Publicity Rights	11
	I.	The Legal Landscape	11
	II.	The 'Publicity as Property' Approach	12
	III.	Publicity as a Subset of Personality Rights	16
	IV.	Appropriation of Personality	19
		A. Appropriation of Personality	19
		B. Character Merchandising	22
	V.	A Fourth Way: Privacy and Publicity	25
	VI.	Cross-Overs and Conclusions	27

3		The Exploitation of Image and Publicity	30
	I.	Introduction	30
	II.	The Dual Classification Part 1: The Use Approach	32
		A. Examining Publicity Uses	32
		B. The Tripartite Classification of Uses	35
		C. The Paradigm Publicity Use Cases	39
		D. Authorised and Unauthorised Use	42
	III.	The Dual Classification Part 2: The Subject Matter Approach	44
		A. Identifying the Subject Matter	44
		B. The Underlying Element: Reputation	48
	IV.	Analysis of Contracts for Publicity Exploitation	53
	V.	Conclusion	58

4   Privacy as a Basis for Protecting Publicity Rights   60
    I.   Introduction   60
    II.   The Right to Privacy in the UK   61
        A. Introduction   61
        B. Breach of Confidence   63
        C. A Reasonable Expectation of Privacy   64
        D. Freedom of Expression   69
        E. Summary   71
    III.   Publicity as a Privacy Right   72
        A. Introduction   72
        B. The Need for a Confidential Relationship or a
           Reasonable Expectation of Privacy   73
        C. Private Information: Invasion versus Dissemination   73
        D. Defences to Privacy Infringements   75
        E. Positive Exploitation   76
           i. Waiving the Right to Privacy   76
        F. Exploiting Publicity by Licensing a Privacy Right:
           Douglas v Hello!   78
    IV.   Conclusion   81

Part II   Justifying Publicity Rights   83

5   Justifying Publicity Rights: Setting the Scene   85
    I.   Introduction   85
    II.   Benefits and Harms: Identifying the Interests at Stake   87
        A. The Dual Interests in Publicity Literature   88
        B. The Dual Interests in Publicity Practice   92
        C. The Economic and Dignitarian Interests in Other
           Areas of Law   94
        D. Dignitarian and Economic Interests: Mutually Exclusive
           or Mutually Compatible?   95
    III.   Accepting Three Rebuttals of Publicity Rights   96

6   Order, Autonomy and Efficiency: Justifying a Right of Publicity   102
    I.   Advancing Justifications for Publicity Rights   102
    II.   Ordering the Chaos   103
    III.   The Dignitarian Rationale for Publicity   107
        A. Autonomy and Dignity   107
        B. The Significance of Image for Autonomy   109
        C. Autonomy and Dignity in the Context of Publicity   110
        D. Denial of Autonomy and Dignity in Publicity   112
        E. Autonomy and Dignity in the Economic Interest   116
        F. Waiver of Autonomy and Dignity in Persona?   117
        G. Summary   118

IV.	The Economic Rationale for Publicity	119
	A. Economic Efficiency	119
	B. Identifying the Social Asset	120
	C. Over-Consumption of Persona Leading to Tragedy?	121
	D. Allowing Net Positive Externalities	124
	E. Maximising Efficiency through a Balance of Rights	125
	F. Summary	126
V.	Two Further Objections Considered	127
	A. The Argument from Free-Riding	127
	B. The Argument from Wealth Distribution	129
VI.	The Alternative Question	131
VII.	Conclusion	133
7	The Competing Interests	134
I.	Introduction	134
II.	Freedom of Expression	134
III.	Creative and Communicative Use	138
IV.	Conclusion	141
8	The Nature of Publicity Rights	142
I.	Introduction	142
II.	Identifying the Individual	142
III.	Inalienability and the Property Status of Publicity	145
IV.	Publicity as a Monopoly	147
V.	The Likelihood of Legislation	150
VI.	Conclusion	151
Part III	**Shaping Publicity Rights**	**153**
9	The Scope of Publicity Rights: Formation, Duration and Transfer	155
I.	Introduction	155
II.	Formalities	156
	A. Labour or Creativity	156
	B. Registration	157
III.	Duration	160
	A. Introduction	160
	B. Duration in Life	161
	C. Post Mortem Duration	162
IV.	Transmission and Transferability	167
	A. Transfer of the Right in Life: Assignation and Licensing	168
	B. Transmission of the Right Post Mortem	170
10	The Permitted Uses of Persona	171
I.	Introduction	171
II.	Private Use	171
III.	Freedom of Expression	171

IV.   Public Policy   172
V.   Public Interest   173
VI.   Fair Dealing   177
VII.   Parody   178
VIII. Other Possible Permitted Uses   180

11 Remedies for Breach of Publicity Rights   182
I.   Introduction   182
II.   Preventing Unauthorised Use   182
III.   Redressing Unauthorised Use: Damages   184
       A. Introduction   184
       B. The Notional Licence Fee   185
       C. Additional Damages   190
       D. Account of Profits   190
       E. The Calculation of the Award   191
       F. Windfalls   192
IV.   Other Disposals   193
V.   Remedies for Authorised Users   194

12 Conclusion   196

Appendix 1   199

Bibliography   200

Index   215

List of Journal Abbreviations

Cardozo Arts and Ent LJ	Cardozo Arts and Entertainment Law Journal
Cal L Rev	California Law Review
Colum-VLA JL & Arts	Columbia-VLA Journal of Law & the Arts
Cornell L Rev	Cornell Law Review
CILSA	Comparative and International Law Journal of Southern Africa
CLJ	Cambridge Law Journal
DePaul-LCA J Art & Ent L	DePaul-LCA Journal of Art and Entertainment Law
Edin LR	Edinburgh Law Review
EHRLR	European Human Rights Law Review
EIPR	European Intellectual Property Review
EJCL	Electronic Journal of Comparative Law
Ent LR	Entertainment Law Review
Fordham Intell Prop Media and Ent LJ	Fordham Intellectual Property, Media & Entertainment Law Journal
Harv L Rev	Harvard Law Review
Hastings LJ	Hastings Law Journal
ICCLR	International Company and Commercial Law Review
IPQ	Intellectual Property Quarterly
ISLR	International Sports Law Review
JBL	Journal of Business Law
J Legal Stud	Journal of Legal Studies
Law & Contemp Problems	Law & Contemporary Problems
LA L Rev	Louisiana Law Review
LQR	Law Quarterly Review
MLR	Modern Law Review
New Eng L Rev	New England Law Review

PL	Public Law
UCLA Ent L Rev	UCLA Entertainment Law Review
TMR	Trademark Reporter
Tulane L Rev	Tulane Law Review
U Brit Colum L Rev	University of British Columbia Law Review
U Ill L Rev	University of Illinois Law Review
Va L Rev	Virginia Law Review
Yale JL & Human	Yale Journal of Law and the Humanities

Table of Cases

A v B and C [2002] 2 All ER 545, [2002] EWCA Civ 337 .... 27, 64
Arsenal v Reed [2003] 3 All ER 865 AC, [2003] EWCA Civ 696 38
Ashdown v Telegraph Group [2002] Ch 149, [2001] 4 All ER 666, [2001] EWCA
    Civ 1142 138
Athans v Canadian Adventure Camps Ltd (1977) 17 OR (2d) 425 46
Attorney General v Blake [2001] 1 AC 268 .... 186, 189
Attorney-General v Guardian Newspapers (No 2) [1990] 1 AC 109 .... 63, 79
Aubry v Les Editions Vice-Versa Inc [1998] 1 SCR 591 .... 11, 51

Bette Midler v Ford Motor Company 849 F 2d. 460 (9th Cir 1988) 47, 103
Byron v Johnston (1816) 2 Mer 29 (reported at 35 English Reports, 851) 3

Campbell v MGN Ltd [2004] 2 AC 457, [2004] UKHL 22 .... 63, 64, 68–70, 72, 75, 107,
                                                    135, 137, 180
Carson v Here's Johnny Portable Toilets Inc 698 F 2d 831 (6th Cir 1983) 47
CC v AB [2006] EWHC 3083 (QB) 27, 64, 67
Chester v Afshar [2005] 1 AC 134, [2004] 4 All ER 587, [2004] UKHL 41 .... 174, 184
Clark v Freeman (1848) 11 Beav 112 (reported at 50 English Reports 759) 3
Common Services Agency v Scottish Information Commissioner [2008] 1 WLR 1550,
    [2008] UKHL 47 26

*David Murray (by his litigation friends Neil Murray and Joanne Murray) v (1) Express
    Newspapers Plc and (2) Big Pictures (UK) Ltd* [2007] EWHC 1908 (Ch), [2007]
    EMLR 583 74
*David Murray (by his litigation friends Neil Murray and Joanne Murray) v Big Pictures
    (UK) Ltd* [2008] 3 WLR 1360, [2008] EWCA Civ 446 .... 26, 27, 63, 64, 68, 69
Donaldson v Beckett (1774) 2 Bro PC 129 148
Douglas v Hello! (No 3) [2003] 3 All ER 996, [2003] EWHC (Ch) 786 .... 39, 79, 93
Douglas v Hello! (No 3) [2006] QB 125, [2005] 4 All ER 128, [2005] EWCA Civ 595 ... 2,
         21, 26, 30, 40, 54, 63, 66, 70, 79, 93, 103, 130, 175, 188, 189, 195
Douglas v Hello! (No 3), reported as *OBG & Others v Allan & Others* [2008] 1 AC 1,
    [2007] 4 All ER 545, [2007] UKHL 21 .... 1, 22, 31, 40, 48, 73, 78, 79, 80, 81, 93, 185
Douglas v Hello! [2003] 1 All ER 1087, [2003] EWHC (Ch) 55
Douglas v Hello! [2003] EWHC (Ch) 2629 40
Durant v Financial Services Authority [2004] FSR 28, [2003] EWCA Civ 1746 26

Elvis Presley Trade Marks [1997] RPC 543 .... 21, 23, 24
Elvis Presley Trade Marks [1999] RPC 567 41
Experience Hendrix v PPX Enterprises [2003] 1 Comm All ER 830, [2003] EWCA Civ 323
    .... 185, 186, 189

General Tire and Rubber Company v Firestone Tyre and Rubber Company Ltd [1075] FSR
273 .... 186, 187

Haelan Laboratories v Topps Chewing Gum Inc 202 F 2d 866 (2nd Cir
1953) 2, 5, 12, 13, 15, 77, 78, 103, 149, 169
Her Majesty's Printer & Stationer v Messrs Bell & Bradfute, and Others (1790) Mor 8316
Hinton v Donaldson (1773) Mor 8307 148
HJ (Iran) v Secretary of State for the Home Department [2010] UKSC 31 .... 121, 177
Hosking & Hosking v Simon Runting & Anor [2004] NZCA 34 .... 66, 68, 69
Howlett v Holding [2006] EWHC 41 (QB) 74

In Re American Greeting Corporation's Application [1984] 1 WLR 189 (HL) 23, 24, 41
In re S (a child) [2005] 1 AC 593, [2004] UKHL 47 .... 69, 70, 135
Irvine v Talksport Ltd [2003] EMLR 6 188
Irvine v Talksport Ltd [2003] 2 All ER 881, [2003] EWCA Civ 423 ...... 2, 5, 21, 23, 30, 40,
53, 55, 73, 93, 103, 123, 137, 187
Irvine v Talksport Ltd [2002] 1 WLR 2355, [2002] 2 All ER 414, [2002] EWHC 367
(Ch) 36, 38, 40, 41, 49, 53, 55, 80, 93
Irvine v Talksport Ltd [2002] EWHC 539 187

Jane Austen Trade Mark [2000] RPC 879 .... 21, 23, 41
John v Associated Newspapers Ltd [2006] EWHC 1611 (QB), [2006] EMLR 27 68

Kaye v Robertson [1991] FSR 62 31

Laugh it Off Promotions CC v South African Breweries International (Finance) BV 2006
(1) SA 144 (CC) 33, 138, 140, 179, 180
Lord Browne of Madingley v Associated Newspapers Limited [2008] 1 QB 103, [2007]
EWCA Civ 295 .... 64, 67, 176
Lyngstad v Anabas Products Ltd [1977] FSR 62 .... 23, 24, 31, 41, 73

Martin v McGuiness 2003 SLT 1424, [2003] ScotCS 96 74
McCulloch v Lewis A May (1948) 65 RPC 58 .... 24, 41, 47
McKennitt v Ash [2008] QB 73, [2006] EWCA Civ 1714 .... 27, 64, 67, 68, 70, 175
Mirage Studios v Counter-Feat Clothing Company Ltd [1991] FSR 145 .... 23, 24, 41,
47, 142
Morrison v Robertson 1908 SC 332 160
Mosley v News Group Newspapers Ltd [2008] EWHC 1777 (QB) 27, 64, 66, 67, 68, 70,
71, 74, 75, 107, 111, 136, 173, 175, 184, 185, 190
Mosley v News Group Newspapers Ltd [2008] EWHC 687 (QB) 66, 186

Pavesich v New England Life Insurance Co (1905) 50 SE 68 .... 5, 51
Peck v The United Kingdom (App no 44647/98) (28 January 2003), [2003] ECHR 44,
(2003) 36 EHRR 41 .... 64, 65
Pell Frischmann Engineering Ltd v Bow Valley Iran Ltd [2009] UKPC 45 189

Reklos and Davourlis v Greece (App no 1234/05) (Judgment of 15 April 2009) 64, 68,
74, 75, 109, 110, 111
Roberson v Rochester Folding Box Co (1902) 171 NY 538 .... 5, 51

Table of Cases

Shogun Finance Ltd v Hudson [2004] 1 AC 119, [2003] UKHL 62 160

Tavener Rutledge Ltd v Trexapalm Ltd [1975] FSR 479 .... 24, 41
Terry v Persons Unknown [2010] EWHC 119 (QB) 64, 183
Theakston v MGN Ltd [2002] EWHC 137 (QB), [2002] EMLR 22 .... 67, 175

Von Hannover v Germany (App no 59320) (24 June 2004), (2005) 40 EHRR 1 ..... 64, 65, 70

W v Edgell [1990] Ch 359 175
Wackenheim v France, UN Human Rights Committee Communication No 854/1999, of 15 July 2002 109
Wainwright v Home Office [2004] 2 AC 406, [2003] UKHL 53 .... 62, 74
Ward v Scotrail Railways Ltd 1999 SC 255, [1998] ScotCS 81 74
White v Samsung Electronic America Inc 971 F.2d 1395 (9th Cir 1992) 47, 99, 180
Wilkie v McCulloch 1822–1824 2S (SC) 413 .... 3, 47
William Grant & Sons Ltd v Glen Catrine Bonded Warehouse Ltd 2001 SC 901, 2001 ScotCS 116
Williams v Hodge (1887) 4 TLR 175 3
Wombles Ltd v Wombles Skips Ltd [1975] FSR 488 .... 23, 24, 41
Wood v Commissioner of Police for the Metropolis [2009] EWCA Civ 414 ... 61, 64, 65, 74, 75, 111
Wrotham Park Estate Co v Parkside Homes Ltd [1974] 1 WLR 798 .... 185, 186, 189

X v BBC 2005 SLT 796, [2005] ScotCS CSOH 80 .... 27, 64, 65

Zacchini v Scripps-Howard Broadcasting Company (1977) 433 US 562 .... 33, 35

Table of Legislation

Council of Europe

Convention for the Protection of Human Rights and Fundamental Freedoms, Rome, 4.XI.1950 .... 25, 62, 69
Convention for the Protection of Human Rights and Fundamental Freedoms, Rome, 4.XI.1950, article 8 .... 25, 26, 62, 63, 64, 65, 69, 71, 76–78, 108, 109–10, 112
Convention for the Protection of Human Rights and Fundamental Freedoms, Rome, 4.XI.1950, article 10 .... 69, 71, 134–38, 140, 171–72, 181
Council of Europe Resolution 1165, 26 June 1998 .... 63, 194

United Kingdom

Compensation Act 2006 194
Consumer Protection from Unfair Trading Regulations 2008 SI 2008/1277 100
Copyright and Related Rights Regulations 2003 SI 2003/2498 177
Copyright Designs and Patents Act 1988 .... 35, 78, 94, 148, 149, 161, 174, 177, 190

Data Protection Act 1998 .... 26, 39
Defamation Act 1996 194

Human Rights Act 1998 .... 5, 25, 27, 61–63, 74, 135, 137

Patents Act 1977 .... 148, 156, 161
Protection from Harassment Act 1997 62
Public Interest Disclosure Act 1998 .... 173, 174, 175

Trade Marks Act 1994 .... 148, 156, 161

United States

American Law Institute's Restatement of the Law Second, Torts Volume 3, St Paul, Minn, 1977 .... 14, 20, 22, 26
American Law Institute's Restatement of the Law Third, Unfair Competition, St Paul, Minn, 1995 .... 14, 20, 117, 128

Florida: The Regulation of Trade, Commerce, Investments and Solicitations, ch 540 s 08 .... 45, 165

Illinois: Right of Publicity Act (765 ILCS 1075) 14, 45, 166
Indiana: IC 32–36. Article 36: Publicity 14, 45, 165, 166

Kentucky: Kentucky Acts 1984, 391.170: Commercial Rights to Use of Names and
Likenesses of Public Figures 14, 45, 165

Massachusetts: General Law, Part III, Title I, Chapter 214, Section 3A: Unauthorized Use
of Name, Portrait or Picture of a Person; Injunction Relief; Damages; Exceptions
.... 45

Nevada: Right of Publicity, NRS 597.770–597.810 .... 45, 165
New York: Civil Rights, Article 5: Right of Privacy 45

Oklahoma: Stat tit 12, paras 1448–49 .... 14, 45, 166

Rhode Island: Title 9, Chapter 9–1, Section 28: Action for Unauthorized Use of Name,
Portrait or Picture 45

State of Washington: Chapter 63.60 RCW Personality Rights, sections 010–080 .... 14, 45

Germany

The German Civil Code, Bürgerlichen Gesetzbuches, translated into English and
published online by the Federal Ministry of Justice, Bundesministerium der
Justiz (www.gesetze-im-internet.de/englisch_bgb/englisch_bgb.html#
Section%20823) 19, 112

1

The Power of Image:
Introducing Publicity Rights

I. Introduction

The celebrity image is a cultural lode of multiple meanings, mined for its symbolic resonances and, simultaneously, a floating signifier, invested with libidinal energies, social longings, and political aspirations.[1]

T HE IMAGE OF any individual in general—and of celebrities in particular—can be a powerful instrument, whether used to add to our shared cultural experience, to pass political comment, to raise awareness of social issues, to promote goods or services, or simply to illustrate the latest gossip and tittle-tattle. One consequence of the social use and versatility of personal image is the price that it can command: Catherine Zeta Jones and Michael Douglas sold their wedding photographs to OK! magazine for £1 million in 2000,[2] while David Beckham was allegedly paid $20 million in 2007 for his Emporio Armani advertising deal.[3] The market for personal images—or indeed, for any signifiers of the individual—can be referred to as publicity practice. In turn, the *practice* of publicity leads to the desire for *legal* control over use of image.

Courts and legal commentators, however, have struggled to identify and agree a common legal response to publicity. Confusion ranges from terminology to taxonomy. How should we refer to the practice of 'buying' and 'selling' image or reputation or gossip? Is it image rights, character merchandising, personality rights or publicity rights? How should we analyse the rights or assets in question?

---

[1] RJ Coombe, 'Author/izing the Celebrity: Publicity Rights, Postmodern Politics, and Unauthorized Genders' (1991–92) 10 *Cardozo Arts & Ent LJ* 365, 365.

[2] *Douglas v Hello!* [2008] 1 AC 1.

[3] Evidence of such deals can be hard to come by: online articles and blogs give this figure for the Emporio Armani deal. (www.adpunch.org/entry/david-beckham-signs-underwear-deal-for-giorgio-armani/). For a more general comment on the commercial value of such deals, see D Westfall and D Landau, 'Publicity Rights as Property Rights' (2005–06) 23 *Cardozo Arts and Ent LJ* 71, 73, fn 3.

Do breaches raise issues of publicity, privacy,[4] breach of confidence,[5] goodwill,[6] property rights[7]—or nothing at all? Should legal development be influenced by concerns for personal dignity and autonomy or economic considerations, or both?

Any review of publicity rights thus comes up against a considerable range of problems from the outset. Yet, this does not mean that a coherent legal response cannot or should not be sought. To borrow an observation from MacCormick, made in the context of privacy yet nonetheless relevant:

> The [Younger] committee, having rightly noted that there are many rival versions of such a right [of privacy], all vying for legislative or judicial adoption, concluded that the right was indefinable and thus not a fit topic for legislation in and of itself. This is a good case of deriving false conclusions from true premises. That there are disputes between rival conceptions of such a right is actually a reason for seeking to give it definite import by intelligent legislation based on some coherent conception of the right, not a reason for rejecting it as indefinable.[8]

This analysis aims to assess the practice and theory of publicity to draw out, if possible, a coherent conception of the right of publicity, and thereafter to assess the justifications, if any, that can be made in favour of legal regulation of such a right.

II. Tracing the Development of Publicity Practice

It is helpful to start by considering briefly the development of the practice of exploitation of publicity.[9] A number of factors combined in the United Kingdom

---

[4] *Douglas v Hello!* [2006] QB 125; *Campbell v MGN* [2004] 2 AC 457.

[5] *Douglas v Hello!* [2006] QB 125.

[6] *Irvine v Talksport Ltd* [2003] 2 All ER 881.

[7] As in the US, for example: *Haelan Laboratories v Topps Chewing Gum Inc* 202 F 2d 866 (2nd Cir 1953).

[8] N MacCormick, 'General Legal Concepts', in *Stair Memorial Encyclopaedia Reissue* (Edinburgh, The Law Society of Scotland/LexisNexis, 2008) para 94, footnote omitted.

[9] Other writers who have considered this include M Madow, 'Private Ownership of Public Image: Popular Culture and Publicity Rights' (1993) 81 *Cal L Rev* 125, 156–58; H Beverley-Smith, *The Commercial Appropriation of Personality* (Cambridge, CUP, 2002) 3–4; GM Armstrong, 'The Reification of Celebrity: Persona as Property' (1990–1991) 51 *La L Rev* 443, 452; O Goodenough, 'Retheorising Privacy and Publicity' [1997] IPQ 37, 38–39; VM de Grandpre, 'Understanding the Market for Celebrity: An Economic Analysis of the Right of Publicity' (2001–2002) 12 *Fordham Intell Prop Media and Ent LJ* 73, 82; and M Richardson and L Hitchens, 'Celebrity Privacy and Benefits of Simple History' in A Kenyon and M Richardson (eds), *New Dimensions in Privacy Law* (Cambridge, CUP, 2006) 256 and 266–67. The following summary is drawn from all these sources.

in the late eighteenth and early nineteenth centuries[10] to create the first mass markets and mass marketing. At least five relevant developments can be identified:

(i) the ability to mass-produce goods, and
(ii) a newly-emerging middle class with disposable income to buy them, together with
(iii) the coming of the railways which provided increased and improved communications, thereby assisting
(iv) the growth of an increasingly national press, all of which combined to create
(v) the need for, and importance of, advertising.

Goods could be produced in sufficient quantities in Edinburgh to be distributed for sale not merely in the immediate vicinity but throughout the whole of the United Kingdom, and the railways which enabled rapid transportation of those goods also carried the national newspapers which could advertise those same goods.

Personal endorsement becomes an added boon to businesses attempting to market a product throughout the country, when the supplier's local reputation can no longer be relied upon to do the job. Moreover, '[a]s mass market products become functionally indistinguishable, manufacturers must increasingly sell them by symbolically associating them with the aura of celebrity – which may be the quickest way to establish a share of the market.'[11]

Evidence of personal endorsements can be detected in 'Champagne Charlie', a persona George Leybourne maintained not only in Victorian music halls but also offstage, under a contractual obligation to do so,[12] and in a number of cases emerging from the courts throughout the nineteenth century. These included *Byron v Johnston*[13]—use of the poet Byron's name on a publication of poems (allegedly) written by another; *Wilkie v McCulloch*[14]—use of the name of a designer of ploughs on a plough made by another; *Clark v Freeman*[15]—use of the name of a leading physician on pills dispensed by an unconnected party; and *Williams v Hodge*[16]—use of the name of another leading physician on a surgical implement manufactured by a third party.[17] The key element in the cases cited is

---

[10] For an excellent (if controversial) survey of the development of Western society through the Industrial Revolution, see E Hobsbawm, *The Age of Revolution 1789–1848* (London, Abacus, 1977), *The Age of Capital 1848–1875* (London, Abacus, 1997) and *The Age of Empire 1875–1914* (London, Abacus, 1994).

[11] Coombe, 'Author/izing the Celebrity' (1991–92) 368.

[12] J Flanders, *Consuming Passions: Leisure and Pleasure in Victorian Britain* (London, Harper Perennial, 2006) 377.

[13] *Byron v Johnston* (1816) 2 Mer 29.

[14] *Wilkie v McCulloch* 1822–1824 2S (SC) 413.

[15] *Clark v Freeman* (1848) 11 Beav 112.

[16] *Williams v Hodge* (1887) 4 TLR 175.

[17] Although misrepresentative or fraudulent use of, for example, an artist's name has a longer history than this, see www.artcult.fr/EN/_Forgeries/Fiche/art-0–1011646.htm?lang=EN.

the use of a famous name to *promote* goods. Even the testimony of unknown individuals had a value to manufacturers of goods, as can be seen in the nineteenth century advertisement in Appendix 1. These examples of personal endorsements reveal the changing face of marketing and promotion of goods and services, and indicate the start of a practice that has expanded ever since. One particularly important development was the increased acceptance over time of such practices, overturning earlier notions that exploitation of an individual in commerce was degrading or socially unacceptable.[18]

Press advertising also evolved during this period, with the development of photography and by continuing improvements in technology. The increased role of the press during this period, both in printing advertising and in catering to the interests of the reading public, is discussed by Warren and Brandeis in their seminal article on privacy, published in 1890.[19] Their analysis of the indignities suffered by individuals when the press intrudes upon their lives is credited with creating a right of privacy in the United States.[20] Warren and Brandeis's description of the average contents of the daily papers in 1890 destroys any notion that the celebrity gossip we see and hear daily is a modern development:

> Gossip is no longer the resource of the idle and of the vicious, but has become a trade, which is pursued with industry as well as effrontery. To satisfy a prurient taste the details of sexual relations are spread broadcast in the columns of the daily papers. To occupy the indolent, column upon column is filled with idle gossip, which can only be procured by intrusion upon the domestic circle.[21]

Over 100 years later, celebrity appearances in gossip columns—both printed and online—are pursued with ever more industry and effrontery. Nor is this an exclusively American problem: the United Kingdom's daily press could easily be described in similar terms.[22] However, although the United States and the United Kingdom have a largely shared experience of advertising culture and fascination with celebrity gossip, there is a marked divergence between the legal analyses and responses of the two countries. A right to privacy developed in the United States within a matter of years following the publication of the Warren and Brandeis

---

[18]   Westfall and Landau, 'Publicity Rights as Property Rights' (2005–06) 78, fn 26; Armstrong, 'The Reification of Celebrity' (1990–91) 459.

[19]   SD Warren and LD Brandeis, 'The Right to Privacy' (1890–1891) 4 *Harv L Rev* 193.

[20]   Nimmer states their article is 'the most famous and certainly the most influential law review article ever written' and refers to Roscoe Pound's claim that it added a chapter to US law: MB Nimmer, 'The right of publicity' (1954) 19 *Law & Contemp Problems* 203, 203. For a rather less flattering appraisal of Warren and Brandeis's contribution to the literature, see D Bedingfield, 'Privacy or Publicity? The Enduring Confusion Surrounding the American Tort of Invasion of Privacy' (1992) 55 *MLR* 111. DL Zimmerman assesses the contribution of Warren and Brandeis to American scholarship in 'Requiem for a Heavyweight: A Farewell to Warren and Brandeis's Privacy tort' (1982–1983) 68 *Cornell L Rev* 291.

[21]   Warren and Brandeis, 'The Right to Privacy' (1890–91) 196.

[22]   Examples abound in recent English litigation, and will be considered in chapter four.

article[23] and this right led in turn, 50 years later, to the emergence of a right of publicity based on property in *Haelan Laboratories v Topps Chewing Gum Inc.*[24]

In contrast, a privacy law in the United Kingdom only emerged in the twenty-first century, as a result of the Human Rights Act 1998, while the appropriate legal response to publicity situations remains largely uncertain. This position exposes three distinct groups to legal uncertainty: the individuals, usually celebrities, who are willing to market their image and identity; the parties who are willing to pay to use this (celebrity) image; and the third parties who are prepared to take a chance on unauthorised use but cannot be sure of the legal risks involved.[25] This is highly unsatisfactory from a legal perspective, albeit the very fact of non-regulation may also be regarded as empowering by some in the commercial world.

III. The Scope of this Project

Legal writing on publicity has tended to fall into one of two camps. In one, the focus falls on the commercial practice of publicity, and less attention is paid to the legal and theoretical bases and justifications of the right. Authors in this tradition tend to seek the most pragmatic and readily-available solution for this valuable and pervasive practice. In the other camp, theoretical analyses tend to focus on the doctrinal legal basis of publicity rights, while overlooking the commercial reality which is driving the practice forward.

Both theory and practice are of equal importance, since any right of publicity should operate not in the abstract but with reference to the practice that informs it. However, this examination will be predominantly carried out in an a-jurisdictional context, rather than in the confines of a specific legal system—although reference will be made to a range of Common law and Civilian systems,[26] particularly the two in the United Kingdom with which I am most

---

[23] The failed attempt in *Roberson v Rochester Folding Box Co* 171 NY 538 (1902), led to a 1903 statute in New York to remedy the problem, while the Supreme Court of Georgia recognised a common law right in their 1905 decision in *Pavesich v New England Life Insurance Co* 50 SE 68 (1905): see William Prosser, 'Privacy' (1960) 48 *Cal L Rev* 383, 384–89; Beverley-Smith, *The Commercial Appropriation of Personality* (2002) 146; Armstrong (n 9) 443 and 453–57; and Nimmer, 'The Right of Publicity' (1954).

[24] *Haelan Laboratories v Topps Chewing Gum Inc* 202 F 2d 866 (2nd Cir 1953). As Nimmer pointed out, 'although the concept of privacy which Brandeis and Warren evolved fulfilled the demands of Beacon Street in 1890, it may seriously be doubted that the application of this concept satisfactorily meets the needs of Broadway and Hollywood in 1954.' Nimmer, (n 20)203. (Beacon Street is a prominent thoroughfare in Boston.)

[25] For example, there is a high probability that Talksport would not have predicted the outcome of Irvine's action against them: *Irvine v Talksport Ltd* [2003] 2 All ER 881.

[26] Adopting a convention used by Reid, for example, I shall use initial capitals for 'Civilian' and 'Common' law when referring to the Romanistic-European and Anglo-American legal traditions respectively. When used in lower case, civil law can be taken to indicate private law, while common

familiar, the mixed system of Scots law and the English Common law. My intention is to analyse the practice of publicity exploitation and the justifications that can be advanced to support a legal right regarding this shared practice. A better understanding of both practice and justifications is necessary for a better understanding of the shape of any legal right. As well as setting out these aims, it is equally important to emphasise what this work is *not* about. Thus, it does not seek to review or critique the existing legal responses in a particular jurisdiction.[27] Nor does it aim to provide a sociological review of the meaning of 'celebrity' or the role of celebrity culture in modern society,[28] or to assess the socio-legal practice of brand management and merchandising in relation to celebrities.[29] Instead, it seeks to review the principles and practice relevant to future legal development in this field.

The three primary aims of this study therefore are:

(i) to provide a review of the practice of publicity, grounded in evidence of commercial practice;
(ii) to assess the justifications which support and counter a legal right to regulate this practice; and
(iii) to analyse how these justifications should shape a right of publicity—its limitations and exceptions.

This work will be divided into three parts to reflect these three aims. Part I, comprising chapters two, three and four, will explore the existing understanding of publicity rights in theory and in practice, to attempt to delineate the subject matter of publicity. It starts with a review of the publicity rights literature in Western jurisdictions (chapter two), before turning to examine the practice of publicity, including a review of some typical contracts for exploitation of publicity (chapter three). Chapter four examines the relevance of privacy rights to publicity, concluding that publicity is not and should not be treated as a sub-set of privacy. In Part II, we turn to justifying image and publicity rights—not an easy task. After setting the scene for this (chapter five), three justifications are advanced in favour of legal protection (chapter six) and competing interests are identified and examined (chapter seven). Together, these three chapters allow us to determine certain key legal features of any right of publicity, as shown in chapter eight. Part III examines the consequences for publicity of the justifications reviewed in Part II. This impacts on a right of publicity by addressing

---

law indicates those non-statutory rules of law. See E Reid, 'Protection for Rights of Personality in Scots Law: a Comparative Evaluation' (2007) EJCL 11.4, para 1.1, fn 8.

[27] See for example the works of Hazel Carty and Hew Beverley-Smith as regards English law, Niall Whitty as regards Scots law, or JT McCarthy and Michael Madow as regards the US response (all cited in the bibliography).

[28] See for example the works of Rosemary Coombe or Graeme Turner (as cited in the bibliography).

[29] This will be referred to as appropriate—see for example Andy Milligan's insider account of brand management for David Beckham, *Brand it Like Beckham* (London, Cyan, 2004).

questions such as what limits must be applied to such a right; what permitted uses are appropriate; and what remedies should be available (chapters nine, 10 and 11 respectively). Chapter 12 draws these findings together.

Part I

Understanding Publicity: Theory and Practice

2

The Theory of Image and Publicity Rights

I. The Legal Landscape

THE SOCIAL PRACTICE of publicity exploitation and the subsequent legal recognition of publicity rights have generated a vast literature. Articles and case commentaries abound in the Western world, from jurisdictions as far apart as Finland and New Zealand, California and Italy. Despite, or perhaps because of, the quantity of literature in this area, it is very difficult to draw together a comprehensive review of the theory and practice in this area, and the jurisprudence remains 'disturbingly unsettled'.[1] The purpose of this chapter is to identify the key theoretical approaches to publicity rights through an analysis of publicity rights across Western jurisdictions.

Whereas established fields of law, such as contract, benefit from a common terminology and understanding which enables analysis and development of the law to take place in a transnational and comparative framework,[2] when one turns to publicity there is seemingly little common ground, despite the wealth of literature, academic commentary and case law. For some, publicity is the 'commercialisation of popularity'[3] or the right to control commercial use of identity,[4] while for others it is media exploitation of privacy.[5] Case law reveals a wide range of publicity-type circumstances, from the publication, without consent, of an innocent photograph of a young girl taken without her consent,[6] to the interference

---

[1] JV Muhonen, 'Right of Publicity in Finland' [1997] *Ent LR* 103, 103. Matters have not changed markedly since 1997, at least in the UK.

[2] Although Common law systems prefer the promissory analysis of contract while Civilian jurisdictions typically favour mutuality and agreement, these are nevertheless distinctions that can be understood and discussed in any jurisdiction.

[3] J Klink, '50 Years of Publicity in the US and the Never-Ending Hassle in Europe' (2003) *IPQ* 363, 364.

[4] McCarthy, *The Rights of Publicity and Privacy*, 2nd edn (United States, West Group, 2001) para 1:3.

[5] J Morgan, 'Privacy, Confidence and Horizontal Effect: "Hello" Trouble' (2003) 62 *CLJ* 444.

[6] *Aubry v Les Editions Vice-Versa* (1998) 1 *SCR* 591.

with a commercial licence for use of a baseball player's image, arising from the defendant's use of the player's image with his consent.[7] The opinions, terminology and conclusions resulting from the practice of publicity are far from harmonious.

Nevertheless, it is possible to construct three broad interpretative categories in which to site the academic and judicial material. These categories attempt to recognise that authors are not necessarily tackling exactly the same thing under the umbrella terms of 'image rights' or 'publicity rights'. While it may be desirable to rationalise their approaches, it is not possible to do so within a single scheme. Unlike previous analyses, these categories should not be seen as mapping directly on to different jurisdictions. Instead, they reflect higher-level, theoretical understandings which can be illustrated by material from a range of Civilian and Common law jurisdictions.

With the caveat that any reductionist approach risks over-simplification, and with the acknowledgment that there will always be overlaps, three approaches or categories of publicity rights can be identified as follows:

(a) the 'publicity as property' approach;
(b) publicity as a subset of personality rights; and
(c) appropriation of personality.

II. The 'Publicity as Property' Approach

The emphasis in the 'publicity as property' approach is very much on commercial exploitation of identity *as a whole* and on the commercial interests at stake in exploitation of popularity. The three key unifying factors in this category are (i) the treatment of the commercial value in identity as a property right; (ii) the centrality of commercial use; and (iii) a tendency to define in wide terms the 'asset' being exploited, typically 'identity', rather than narrower notions of name or image. The commentators whose work fits into this broad canon are primarily American, and certainly Common lawyers.

This approach can be regarded as the culmination of legal developments since the early 1950s, stemming from two critical events at that time: the judgment of Frank J in *Haelan Laboratories v Topps Chewing Gum*[8] in 1953 and the seminal article by Nimmer on 'The Right of Publicity',[9] published a year later.[10]

In 1954, Nimmer recognised that

---

[7] *Haelan Laboratories v Topps Chewing Gum Inc* (1953) 202 F. 2d 866.

[8] *Haelan Laboratories* (1953) 202 F.2d 866.

[9] MB Nimmer, 'The Right of Publicity' (1954) 19 *Law & Contemp Probs* 203. The importance of Nimmer's contribution should not be underestimated. Grady says '[h]is great contribution was to provide the first reliable glosses of a new and unruly body of case precedent and thereby provide a solid foundation for the whole field'. MF Grady, 'A Positive Economic Theory of the Right of Publicity' (1994) 1 *UCLA Ent L Rev* 97, 109.

[10] See McCarthy, *The Rights of Publicity and Privacy* (2001) paras 1:26–1:27.

although the well known personality does not wish to hide his light under a bushel of privacy, neither does he wish to have his name, photograph, and likeness reproduced and publicized without his consent or without remuneration to him.[11]

Where the only legal rights available to the well-known personality look to privacy interests, the celebrity is unlikely to achieve the legal protection he or she seeks. Nimmer examined the doctrines of privacy, unfair competition and contract, and concluded that they were all inadequate to protect this publicity interest.[12] Instead, he argued that the right of publicity 'must be largely determined by two considerations: first, the economic reality of pecuniary values inherent in publicity and, second, the inadequacy of traditional legal theories in protecting such publicity values'.[13]

Comprehensive legal protection for such values had been granted in a judgment of the 'highly respected Second Circuit'[14] the year before, *Haelan Laboratories*.[15] The influence of this case has been strongly felt ever since, with the words of Frank J echoing through much academic work in this area:

> We think that, in addition to and independent of the right of privacy (which in New York derives from statute), a man has a right in the publicity value of his photograph... Whether it be labelled a 'property' right is immaterial; for here, as often elsewhere, the tag 'property' simply symbolizes the fact that courts enforce a claim which has a pecuniary worth.[16]

In the decades since *Haelan*, the right of publicity has 'matured and taken on its own distinctive identity as an altogether separate legal category'.[17] By 2001, McCarthy was able to state that 'the right of publicity is simply this: it is the inherent right of every human being to control the commercial use of his or her identity'.[18] This wide concept of 'identity', whereby 'certain celebrity identities can be appropriated as effectively or even more effectively via other means'[19] and not merely their name and image, is an inherent part of this approach to publicity. Westfall and Landau suggest that the 'vague principle initially underlying the right... as expressed in *Haelan*'[20] has meant that there have been no obvious parameters to the right to guide (or limit) judicial or legislative development,[21] resulting in protection being extended to ever-wider elements of identity.

---

[11]   Nimmer, 'The Right of Publicity' (1954) 204.
[12]   ibid 204, 210 and 214.
[13]   ibid 215.
[14]   ibid 222.
[15]   *Haelan Laboratories* (1953) 202 F.2d 866.
[16]   ibid 868 (Frank CJ).
[17]   JT McCarthy, 'Public Personas and Private Property: The Commercialization of Human Identity' (1989) 79 *TMR* 681, 685.
[18]   McCarthy (n 4) para 1:3.
[19]   D Westfall and D Landau, 'Publicity Rights as Property Rights' (2005–06) 23 *Cardozo Arts and Ent LJ* 71 94.
[20]   ibid 93.
[21]   ibid 93–96.

Those who adopt this wide approach to publicity regard it as a 'commercial and business right'[22] which should be treated as a kind of intellectual property right and, preferably, a property right.[23] Academic writing in this category is rich in the language of property and commodification,[24] while legislation also reflects this approach. In those American states that have passed legislation to regulate publicity rights, a number of them have explicitly stated that publicity is a property right.[25]

Coombe has stated that 'personality rights' (in her terminology) extend:

> to encompass the tort of appropriation of personality as it has developed at common law, the proprietary right of publicity that has developed in American law, and rights to prevent the appropriation of, *inter alia*, names and likenesses that have been enacted in provincial and state statutes as well as federal trademark legislation.[26]

Coombe relies not only on legislation and case law to inform her understanding, but also on urban legend and popular perceptions of publicity,[27] and this is typical of the Common law approach in its breadth and practical scope. One distinction that is highlighted by Coombe is the difference between the 'right of publicity' per se and appropriation of personality. This distinction is reflected in the American Law Institute's Restatements: the Restatement of Torts deals with appropriation of personality (see section IV below), while the Restatement of Unfair Competition deals with the publicity right currently under review, focusing on commercial use and trade values.[28]

One consequence of the emphasis on commercial use and proprietary interests is reflected in the attributes of the publicity right. In the words of McCarthy, '[a]s property, the right of publicity can be licensed and can be devised in a will to

---

[22]   McCarthy, 'Public Personas and Private Property' (1989) 687.

[23]   ibid 687; also JT McCarthy, 'The Human Persona as Commercial Property: the Right of Publicity' (1995) 19 *Colum-VLA JL & Arts* 129, 134. See also Armstrong, who stated in 1990 that persona was not only treated as a property right, but that it *was* the subject of property rights: '[c]elebrity persona has become a heritable, alienable "thing" from which the owner may arbitrarily exclude others. In other words, it has become property'. GM Armstrong, 'The Reification of Celebrity: Persona as Property' (1990–1991) 51 *La L Rev* 443, 444.

[24]   As well as McCarthy, see generally: Armstrong, 'The Reification of Celebrity' (1990–91)"; O Goodenough, 'The Price of Fame: The Development of the Right of Publicity in the United States: Part 1 and Part 2' [1992] *EIPR* 55 and [1992] *EIPR* 90; Westfall and Landau, 'Publicity Rights as Property Rights' (2005–06); M Madow, 'Private Ownership of Public Image: Popular Culture and Publicity Rights' (1993) 81 *Cal L Rev* 125; and DL Zimmerman, 'Who put the Right in the Right of Publicity?' (1998–1999) 9 *DePaul-LCA J Art & Ent L* 35.

[25]   See for example Illinois's Right of Publicity Act 765 ILCS 1075/15; Indiana's Publicity law IC 32–36.16; Kentucky Statute 391.170(1); Oklahoma Statute tit 12, para 1448B; Washington Chapter 63.60 RCW Personality Rights, section 030(1). For more detail, see McCarthy (n 4), ch 6, pt II.

[26]   RJ Coombe, 'Author/izing the Celebrity: Publicity Rights, Postmodern Politics, and Unauthorized Genders' (1991–92) 10 *Cardozo Arts & Ent LJ* 365, 365, fn 2.

[27]   See for example RJ Coombe, *The Cultural Life of Intellectual Properties: Authorship Appropriation, and the Law* (Durham and London, Duke University Press, 1998), particularly ch 2; Coombe, 'Author/izing the Celebrity' (1991–92).

[28]   American Law Institute's Restatement of the Law, Unfair Competition, 3d, ch 4, paras 46–49.

continue after death'.[29] The duration, alienability and descendibility of the right, together with remedies for breach, are all influenced by this property focus. This is referred to as the 'property syllogism' by Westfall and Landau, who argue that the recognition of the transferability of publicity imbued it with property status, with the result that other attributes of property ownership then followed as a matter of course.[30] These elements are now accepted features of the right: for example, most states in the United States provide for a statutory publicity right which includes a certain post mortem duration, rather than terminating the right on death, thus allowing protection and exploitation following the death of the individual.[31] Similarly, remedies are available not just for the injured celebrity, but for any authorised licensees—a recognition of the proprietary nature of the publicity right.[32] Klink is very much in favour of 'the construction of the publicity right as a property right [which] ensures more effectively the compatibility with business needs by allowing the right to be assigned per se or to be licensed'.[33]

It would be a mistake, however, to claim that this is an entirely homogenous category. There are undoubtedly divisions between certain authors on certain points. To take one example, although both McCarthy and Goodenough are agreed on the core elements of this broad right of publicity, centred on protection through property rights for the commercial exploitation of identity, McCarthy claims that publicity rights are distinguishable from the four Restatement rights of privacy,[34] while Goodenough believes that 'the separation between rights of privacy and publicity is largely accidental and artificial'.[35] Further, not all those who discuss publicity in terms of property favour this approach to legal protection, Madow being a key example.[36]

One factor which this approach typically lacks, and which is more prominent in Civilian jurisdictions, is an element of protection for the dignitarian or

---

[29] McCarthy (n 17) 687. See also Nimmer, (n 9) 216; HR Gordon, 'A Right of Property in Name, Likeness, Personality and History' (1960–1961) 55 *Northwestern University Law Review* 553.

[30] Westfall and Landau (n 19) 74 and 83 *et seq.*

[31] McCarthy notes that most states which recognise a post mortem right do so with reference to copyright law as to the term of this right (McCarthy (n 17) 694). See also Klink, who discusses and approves of these measures in California: Klink, '50 Years of Publicity in the US' (2003) 387. Goodenough takes a more sceptical view in his discussion of descendibility of publicity right in the US: Goodenough, 'The Price of Fame: Part 2' (1992) 90–91. Post mortem protection is discussed in more detail in chapter 11.

[32] *Haelan Laboratories* 202 F 2d 866.

[33] Klink (n 3) 385.

[34] McCarthy (n 17) 684.

[35] O Goodenough, 'Re-theorising Privacy and Publicity' [1997] *IPQ* 37 69. In discussing the development of rights in the US, Vaver suggests a middle ground: acknowledgment that the right of publicity 'was catapulted into the law on the strings of commercial appropriation' of privacy, but that they were separated by the court in *Haelan Laboratories*. See D Vaver, 'What's Mine is not Yours: Commercial Appropriation of Personality under the Privacy Acts of British Columbia, Manitoba and Saskatchewan' (1981) 15 *U Brit Colum L Rev* 241, 258–59.

[36] Madow, 'Private Ownership of Public Image' (1993).

personality-based interests.[37] One American writer who advanced quasi-personality rights here is Kwall. She suggests that 'a careful look at right of publicity litigation reveals that many decisions actually are more concerned with redressing rights of integrity over the images of the celebrity',[38] and argues that this implicit concern must be made explicit. Her solution is to advance a role for moral rights, in the manner of such rights in copyright works, by protecting the 'damage to the human spirit'[39] which can arise. The importance of her work is that it straddles one of the central distinctions between the broad publicity as property approach, which focuses primarily on the economic interests, and the Civilian 'rights of personality approach', considered in the next section, which places much greater emphasis on dignitarian considerations. Despite Kwall's attempt to reconcile the two, there remains a gap between protection for commercial and dignitarian interests in most jurisdictions. This tension plays a key role in shaping the right and the debate in this area, as will be seen throughout this examination.

III. Publicity as a Subset of Personality Rights

This approach is most closely associated with Civilian jurisdictions, which treat personality rights as 'a separate category of rights, distinguishable from real, personal and immaterial property rights'.[40] Personality rights are therefore very different from the notion of 'personality' in Common law jurisdictions. They are non-patrimonial and highly personal. They are intimately connected with the individual, and 'recognize a person as a physical and spiritual-moral being and guarantee his enjoyment of his own sense of existence'.[41] Thus, personality rights in this context are fundamental rights belonging to each individual. Personality is a 'convenient portmanteau term'[42] used to refer to, amongst others, 'the rights to life, physical integrity, bodily freedom, reputation, dignity, privacy, identity (including name and image) and feelings'.[43] As Reiter observes, these are the 'various attributes of personality that the modern world has erected on this premodern [ie Romanistic] foundation'.[44] The importance of these long-standing

---

[37] McCarthy, for example, is very clear that publicity is a commercial right: McCarthy (n 4) para 1:3.

[38] RR Kwall, 'Preserving Personality and Reputational Interests of Constructed Personas through Moral Rights: a Blueprint for the Twenty-First Century' (2001) *U Ill L Rev* 151, 158.

[39] ibid 152.

[40] J Neethling, 'Personality Rights: a Comparative Overview' (2005) XXXVIII CILSA 210 535.

[41] ibid 530, footnotes omitted.

[42] E Reid, 'Protection for Rights of Personality in Scots Law: A Comparative Evaluation' (2007) EJCL 11.4, para 1.1.

[43] Neethling, 'Personality Rights' (2005) 530.

[44] EH Reiter, 'Personality and Patrimony: Comparative Perspectives on the Right to One's Image' (2001–2002) 76 *Tulane L Rev* 673, 680.

personality rights in Civilian jurisdictions should not be underestimated: German law, for example, places the right to dignity at the very heart of its constitutionally protected personality rights.[45] Civilian personality rights have been delineated on a pan-jurisdictional basis by Neethling,[46] while a comparative review of French and German rights (together with Common law jurisdictions) is provided by Beverley-Smith et al.[47] More generally, insight can be drawn from the SCRIPT personality rights database.[48]

It is possible to identify common themes that arise from the treatment of publicity rights as a subset of personality rights. The first of these is the emphasis on dignitarian rights. Concepts such as human dignity and privacy are central to any legal protection for the individual's personality rights. Consequently, the *commercial* significance of infringement may be marginalised. In German law, for example, claims for damages for breach of personality rights require either evidence of a loss or the calculation of a hypothetical reasonable licence fee.[49] This latter measure would compensate damage to the claimant's commercial interests—yet it may not be available where it can be shown that the claimant would never have been prepared to license the use complained of, as in the case of 'the professor of ecclesiastical law, who had been alleged to propagate the ginseng root as a sexual stimulant, [and who] could not recover substantial damages but only a solatium'.[50] Because the court held he would never have been prepared to license his image for this use, there was no basis upon which to award him a reasonable licence fee.[51] The end result is that in many cases only *solatium* will be available, and thus arguably 'the courts deny adequate compensation in the most serious cases of personality right infringement'.[52]

A further consequence of the focus on dignitarian interests in this approach is greater controversy about the right continuing post mortem.[53] Personality rights are typically non-transferable, do not prescribe and cannot be transferred on

---

[45] Neethling (n 40) 563: 'German doctrine thereby accords all human rights the same status (apart from human dignity, which is regarded as the most fundamental value)' and this is protected by the German Constitution of 1949.

[46] Neethling provides an excellent summary of personality rights in Neethling (n 40).

[47] H Beverley-Smith, O Ansgar and A Lucas-Schloetter, *Privacy, Property and Personality*, (Cambridge, Cambridge University Press, 2005).

[48] Available at: http://personalityrightsdatabase.com/index.php?title=Main_Page. See also Charlotte Waelde and Niall Whitty, 'A Rights of Personality Database' in Niall Whitty and Reinhard Zimmermann (eds), *Rights of Personality in Scots Law, a Comparative Perspective*, (Dundee, Dundee University Press, 2009).

[49] Also referred to as the notional licence fee, this is calculated according to the hypothetical sum that the pursuer and defender would have agreed upon for the defender's otherwise unauthorised use. It will be discussed in more detail in Chapter 11.

[50] Beverley-Smith et al, *Privacy, Property and Personality* (2005) 143.

[51] A similar conclusion was reached in the first of the 'Caroline' cases, raised by Princess Caroline in Germany: since she would never have consented to the publication of the fictional interview in question, her claim for disgorgement of profits failed: BGHZ 128 – *Caroline von Monaco I*, as discussed by Beverley-Smith et al (n 47) 103.

[52] ibid 143.

[53] Waelde and Whitty, 'A Rights of Personality Database' (2009) para 11.4.3(b) and 11.4.3(e).

death: they are inherent to the individual and cannot be separated from the individual. In comparison, the broad 'publicity as property' approach does accommodate post mortem protection, since the commercial value is capable of surviving death. (Elvis Presley and Marilyn Monroe provide two clear examples of this.) Difficulties arise because of the tension between the dignitarian and commercial interests, such that post mortem protection may be more readily recognised to enable surviving relatives to protect *their* dignitarian interests in the deceased's name or image,[54] but not necessarily the commercial interest in it.[55]

Although Civilian jurisdictions as a whole treat publicity within the framework of personality rights, the specific treatment of publicity and personality rights in each jurisdiction varies. One possible reason for this is the tension that results from protecting a partially commercial, economic interest within a dignitarian framework of extra-patrimonial interests. Reiter notes that 'while the attributes of human personality, like name, reputation, image, voice, and privacy, have traditionally been seen as extrapatrimonial rights without monetary value, today these rights are being increasingly patrimonialized and brought into commerce'.[56] Consequently, the courts and commentators have had to reconcile two opposing interests, with the result that a 'patrimonialized extra-patrimonial right' emerges.[57] Accommodating the divergence between dignitarian rights and commercial interests has produced various responses in Civilian jurisdictions, often categorised as either 'monistic' or 'dualistic'.[58]

The dualistic model[59] requires two different rights, one (positive) patrimonial and one (negative) extra-patrimonial, to protect the interests in exploitation and protection of publicity. As Logeais observes, in the context of the debate in France:

> [the] general analysis is to consider that the right to the image is a 'Janus' right displaying a negative extra-patrimonial aspect which is in fact absorbed by personality rights (mainly the rights to privacy and dignity), and a 'positive' patrimonial aspect, the right to capitalise on the use of one's image.[60]

The distinction made in French law is between the right *to* one's image, which is an 'inherent part of the person', and the right *over* one's image, which is 'a

---

[54] For example, the right not to have a deceased father or mother misrepresented in the media.
[55] See chapter nine; also Beverley-Smith et al (n 47) 124 and 200–05; Neethling (n 40) 544–45.
[56] Reiter, 'Personality and Patrimony' (2001–02) 673.
[57] ibid 673.
[58] For a broad summary of these differences, see Niall Whitty, 'Overview of Rights of Personality in Scots Law' in Niall Whitty and Reinhard Zimmermann (eds), *Rights of Personality in Scots Law, a Comparative Perspective* (Dundee, Dundee University Press, 2009) para 3.4.9.
[59] See, for example, Beverley-Smith et al (n 47) 11; Neethling (n 40) 543; and Whitty, who notes that the American approach can also be regarded as dualistic, Whitty, 'Overview of Rights of Personality in Scots Law' (2009) para 3.4.9 (also para 11.4.2).
[60] E Logeais, 'The French Right to One's Image: a Legal Lure?' [1994] *Ent LR* 163, 165.

commodity to be exploited'.[61] The consequence of this is that 'a general personality right does not fit into French law'.[62] Instead, protection is achieved through
dual rights protecting material and subjective interests respectively.[63]

The alternative monistic approach is favoured, for example, in Germany.[64]
Here, one right, such as the general personality right,[65] protects both the
economic and dignitarian interests in publicity. This was specifically addressed by
the *Bundesgerichtshof* in the *Marlene Dietrich* case,[66] brought by her daughter
against a producer who had sold various items of 'Marlene' merchandising. In
reaching its decision, the Court 'stressed the two aspects of the personality right
which protected not only ideal, but also economic interests'.[67] Consequently,
unauthorised use of name, image or reputation could give rise to a claim for
damages or unjust enrichment,[68] as well as claims for *solatium*.

Despite the difference between monistic and dualistic responses to publicity in
Civilian jurisdictions, it is nonetheless possible to group together these responses
to publicity, derived from the over-arching doctrine of personality rights—a
doctrine which is 'firmly established'[69] in Civilian jurisdictions.

IV. Appropriation of Personality

A. Appropriation of Personality

Arguably the most influential and popular approach taken by English academics
is the 'appropriation of personality' classification. At the outset, it needs to be
appreciated that 'personality' in this context means the identifying elements of an
individual, typically their name, likeness and voice. It is thus akin to the
colloquial notion of someone's personality being their character, and must be
distinguished from the very different meaning accorded to 'personality rights' in
the Civilian approach discussed above.

---

[61] Both quotations from Reiter (n 44) 684–85. Reiter also equates the extrapatrimonial right to a
negative right, and the patrimonial and commercial right to a positive right (685). See also Logeais,
'The French Right to One's Image' (1994) 165.

[62] Beverley-Smith et al (n 47) 153.

[63] ibid 154–57; also Logeais (n 60) 165.

[64] Neethling (n 40) 543. See also Beverley-Smith et al (n 47) ch 4; Klink (n 3) 380; Waelde and
Whitty (n 48) para 11.4.2.

[65] This was developed by the judiciary through case law, emanating from the constitutional right
to dignity. German law also recognises a number of specific statutory rights which protect aspects of
personality, such as the right to one's name (§12 BGB) and to one's image (§22 KUG). See Neethling
(n 40) 530, 539–40. Beverley-Smith et al (n 47) 105–24—they also note that the general personality
right can act as an interstitial right where the specific rights fail (110).

[66] BGH, 1 December 1999, *BGHZ 143, Marlene Dietrich*.

[67] Beverley-Smith et al (n 47) 104.

[68] ibid.

[69] Neethling (n 40) 530.

The three features common to this approach are (i) the understanding of personality as the identifying elements of the individual; (ii) the notion of (mis)appropriation, typically for commercial uses, of personality; and (iii) a recognition that a number of discrete actions, typically torts, are the most appropriate, or at least the most practicable, home for publicity actions, rather than a single property or personality right. Further, the focus on appropriation gives rise to an implicit, yet common, understanding that the use made of personality be *unauthorised*, rather than authorised. There is thus a risk that *authorised* exploitation, by or on behalf of the individual, remains unaddressed by this analysis, since the focus is primarily on seeking remedies for infringement.[70]

Perhaps the origins of this approach can be traced to Prosser's 1960 article 'Privacy',[71] wherein he attempted to synthesise American judicial decisions and writing, starting from Warren and Brandeis' 1890 article on 'The Right to Privacy'.[72] While it would not necessarily be accurate to regard Warren and Brandeis' article as the foundation of this category, since its interest was most certainly with the 'right to be let alone', the evolution of publicity practice was such that, 70 years later, Prosser could no longer ignore the commercial practice in 'selling' privacy. Accordingly, when he formulated his tort of privacy, the four limbs he identified covered a range of invasions, concluding with the fourth: 'Appropriation, for the defendant's advantage, of the plaintiff's name or likeness.'[73]

This four-part tort protecting privacy was incorporated into the American Restatement of Torts, 2d, where the second limb reads: 'The right of privacy is invaded by... (b) the appropriation of the other's name or likeness as stated in para 652C.'[74] It is this limb which forms the starting point for this category of publicity protection.[75]

A clear lineage of writers in this canon can be traced from Prosser onwards, across jurisdictions. Vaver provides an analysis of the incorporation of this tort in privacy statutes in three Canadian provinces,[76] while Frazer's[77] and Beverley-Smith's[78] contributions form the starting point for any study of publicity rights in English law. Quotations from Vaver, Frazer and Beverley-Smith illustrate their

---

[70] See for example the approach taken by H Beverley-Smith, *The Commercial Appropriation of Personality* (Cambridge, Cambridge University Press, 2002).

[71] William Prosser, 'Privacy' (1960) 48 *Cal L Rev* 383.

[72] Warren and Brandeis, 'The Right to Privacy' (1890–1891) 4 *Harv L Rev* 193.

[73] William Prosser, 'Privacy' (1960) 48 *Cal L Rev* 383, 389. See also McCarthy (n 4) paras 1:19–1:24.

[74] American Law Institute's Restatement of the Law, Torts, 2d, para 652A.

[75] Contrast the commercial emphasis of the right of publicity protected by the American Law Institute's Restatement of the Law, Unfair Competition, 3d, which focuses on the appropriation of trade values, rather than personality.

[76] Vaver, 'What's Mine is Not Yours' (1981).

[77] T Frazer, 'Appropriation of Personality – a New Tort?' (1983) 99 *LQR* 281.

[78] Beverley-Smith, *The Commercial Appropriation of Personality* (2002).

common approach, and echo Prosser's earlier formulation. Thus, Vaver's 1981 article addresses the issue of the 'commercial appropriation of personality' and the question of 'how far an individual may control use of his personality (his name, likeness and voice) for commercial purposes, especially advertising'.[79] Frazer set out to 'examine the extent to which the law has developed, or ought to develop, to take account of one particular form of commercial practice – the use, without consent, of the name, likeness or voice of another'.[80] Beverley-Smith opens his analysis with a succinct definition:

> The essence of the problem of appropriation of personality may be put very simply: if one person (A) uses in advertising or merchandising the name, voice or likeness of another person (B) without his or her consent, to what extent will that person (B) have a remedy to prevent such an unauthorised exploitation?[81]

Interestingly, Beverley-Smith's definition appears at first sight to be narrower than the others, being limited to advertising and merchandising uses, but this is not in fact the case. His analysis discloses a wider range of publicity activities, including unauthorised media use, such as that in the *Douglas v Hello!* litigation.[82] Thus, Beverley-Smith's focus is, as the title of his monograph suggests, on the (unauthorised) commercial appropriation of personality.[83]

As already noted, the appropriation of personality approach does not rely on a single legal doctrine to protect personality. This is due in no small measure to the fact that 'unlike both the Continental European and American approaches, the English common law has traditionally been mistrustful of generalised rights'.[84] Instead, a pragmatic approach to litigation has seen a range of doctrines employed in the English courts, including passing off,[85] registered trade mark protection,[86] and privacy actions.[87] These actions are used to protect various

---

[79] Vaver (n 35) 241.

[80] Frazer, 'Appropriation of Personality' (1983) 281.

[81] Beverley-Smith (n 70) 3.

[82] Although his work predates the substantive judgments in this case, the Court of Appeal ruling on the injunction in this case is cited on 16 pages of his text, according to the case list.

[83] This terminology reflects that of Prosser, Vaver and Frazer, as discussed in the preceding paragraphs, and is repeated and rephrased in countless other articles. See, for example, S Boyd and R Jay, 'Image Rights and the Effect of the Data Protection Act 1998' [2004] *Ent LR* 159; S Bains, 'Personality Rights: Should the UK Grant Celebrities a Proprietary Right in their Personality? Parts 1, 2 and 3' [2007] *Ent LR* 16, 205 and 237; H Carty, 'Advertising, Publicity Rights and English Law' [2004] *IPQ* 209; J Hull, 'The Merchandising of Real and Fictional Characters: an Analysis of some Recent Developments' [1991] *Ent LR* 124; G Scanlan and A McGee, 'Phantom Intellectual Property Rights' [2000] *IPQ* 264; and Robinson, 'How Image Conscious is English law?' [2004] *Ent LR* 151.

[84] Carty, 'Personality Rights and English Law' in Niall Whitty and Reinhard Zimmermann (eds), *Rights of Personality in Scots Law, a Comparative Perspective* (Dundee, Dundee University Press, 2009) para 7.1.

[85] *Irvine v Talksport Ltd* [2003] 2 All ER 881.

[86] *Jane Austen Trade Mark* [2000] RPC 879, *Elvis Presley Trade Marks* [1997] RPC 543, on appeal, [1999] RPC 567; see also H Carty, 'Advertising, Publicity Rights and English Law' (2004), 210–11.

[87] *Douglas v Hello!* [2006] QB 125.

aspects of the individual's personality where this has been 'misappropriated'.[88] 'Personality' is broadly seen as the individual's name, likeness and voice.

However, a number of problems with this category can be identified. In the first place, the use of the term 'appropriation' suggests a taking of *property*, yet the use of 'property' in this context in English law is more likely to be metaphorical than indicative of the rights in question. For example, in *Douglas v Hello!*, it was stated that English law 'does not depend on treating confidential information as property, although it is often referred to, loosely or metaphorically, in those terms'.[89] The Second Restatement in the United States does state that the right so created is 'in the nature of a property right',[90] but clearly this does not mean that the right *is* one of property.[91]

Secondly, if the wrong done is *appropriation*, the focus is on the taker, rather than the 'victim' or individual in question. This seems to envisage only unauthorised use of the individual's personality by other parties. Does this mean that there is no right for the individual to exploit his or her own publicity value? A definition which centres round the 'appropriation' of personality potentially (although not necessarily[92]) excludes an individual's own exploitation of his or her personality from its scope. This is perhaps not surprising in Common law jurisdictions, since these systems typically draw their rules from the outcomes of decided cases and focus very much on remedies rather than rights. Accordingly, the right of self-exploitation is less of a concern for writers in this category than are the remedies for individuals where there has been unauthorised (or wrongful) use.

Despite these potential hurdles, the appropriation of personality category offers the most comprehensive review of what could be termed 'publicity rights' in English law to date.

B. Character Merchandising

A subset of the appropriation of personality category can be detected in a series of cases in England in the 1970s, 1980s and 1990s. These dealt with the practice of

---

[88] And Carty notes that the language of misappropriation is 'creeping into' the actions for passing off and breach of confidence: Carty (n 83) 242.

[89] *Douglas v Hello! (No 3)* [2008] 1 AC 1 [276] (Lord Walker).

[90] American Law Institute's Restatement of the Law Second, Torts Volume 3, para 652C(a), 381. This can be used to refute further McCarthy's point, although it is possible that the commercial benefit of this could be taken to accrue only to exclusive licensees.

[91] There is a question mark over whether or not 'personality' can be the subject of property rights, and this will be discussed in subsequent chapters (see for example chapter eight).

[92] It could be argued that authorised use is unobjectionable, and does not need to be addressed, although silence on the point is not entirely satisfactory. The rights and remedies, if any, of exclusive licensees also remain uncertain in this situation.

'character merchandising', but are now gradually becoming, by virtue of decisions such as *Irvine v Talksport*,[93] subsumed within the broader classification of 'appropriation of personality'—not least because of the shared reliance on tort law in both categories.

Case law in England in the 1970s onwards started to reflect the commercial practices of 'character' merchandising,[94] with actions being raised to recover for infringements under the tort of passing off[95] and, later, breach of registered trade mark rights.[96] Writers in the 1980s and 1990s reacted to these cases, and the plethora of articles and case notes generated in these two decades reflect this development and the reaction to it.[97] In particular, academics observed the changing commercial practice of merchandising and advertising goods using celebrities, and, equally importantly, society's changing understanding of it. There was therefore a drive to interpret and perhaps influence the legal recognition and analysis of the changing marketplace. This understanding of merchandising is thus united round the idea of the promotion of goods or services through the use of the name or image of a 'character', with or without that character's endorsement.

Since 1991, academics and practitioners have had the advantage of one of the most important English judgments in this area, the decision of the Vice Chancellor in the passing off action *Mirage Studios v Counter-Feat Clothing Company Ltd*.[98] In this case, the Vice Chancellor accepted that use of cartoon characters on clothing could infringe the rights of the copyright holder, not necessarily by

---

[93] *Irvine v Talksport* [2003] 2 All ER 881.

[94] Although this examination proceeds on the basis that merchandising featuring individuals can be distinguished from merchandising which uses fictional characters and/or actors who have a very strong association with a particular character (such as Paul Hogan/Crocodile Dundee and Telly Savalas/Kojak), this distinction has not always been clear or explicit. The literature and case law referred to reflects both practices, albeit the focus in this section will be on merchandising use of an individual rather than use of a fictional character. Whether publicity rights extend to fictional characters will be addressed in chapter eight.

[95] *Lyngstad v Anabas* [1977] FSR 62; *Wombles Ltd v Wombles Skips Ltd* [1975] FSR 488; *Taverner Rutledge v Trexapalm Clothing* [1977] RPC 275 (featuring a fictional character portrayed by an actor); *Mirage Studios v Counter-Feat Clothing* [1991] FSR 145.

[96] One of the earliest English trade mark cases was the *Holly Hobbie* decision, *Re American Greetings Corporation's Application* [1984] 1 All ER 426, which involved use of a fictional character. Later cases involved real, but deceased, persons: *Elvis Presley Trade Marks* [1997] RPC 543 and, on appeal, [1999] RPC 567; *Jane Austen Trade Mark* [2000] RPC 879. See also G Black (published as G Davies), 'The Cult of Celebrity and Trade Marks: the Next Instalment' (2004) 1:2 *SCRIPT-ed* 230.

[97] See for example, SCG Burley, 'Passing Off and Character Merchandising: Should England Lean towards Australia?' [1991] *EIPR 227*; J Holyoak, 'United Kingdom Character Rights and Merchandising Rights Today' 1993 *JBL* 444; J Hennigan, 'Altered Image Rights' [2003] *Ent LR* 161; G Scanlan, 'Personality, Endorsement and Everything: the Modern Law of Passing Off and the Myth of the Personality Right' [2003] *EIPR 563*; P Jaffey, 'Merchandising and the Law of Trade Marks' [1998] *IPQ* 240; H Porter, 'Character Merchandising: Does English Law Recognise a Property Right in Name and Likeness?' [1999] *Ent LR* 180; J Hull, 'The Merchandising of Real and Fictional Characters: an Analysis of some Recent Developments' [1991] *Ent LR* 124; SM Maniatis and M Chong, 'The Teenage Mutant Hero Turtles Case' [1991] *EIPR* 253; M Lewis and M Elmslie, 'Passing Off and Image Marketing in the UK' [1992] *EIPR* 270.

[98] *Mirage Studios v Counter-Feat Clothing Company Ltd* [1991] FSR 145 (Ch).

infringement of copyright (a point which was not decided), but through the tort of passing off. The importance of this decision stems from its effective reversal of two earlier passing off cases where a remedy was refused for the use of an individual's image in merchandising.[99] This was achieved, in part, through the Vice Chancellor's recognition of the fact that '[c]haracter merchandising is an industry which has grown in sophistication over the comparatively recent past',[100] together with society's increasing awareness of that industry.[101]

Such was the prevalence of merchandising in the latter part of the twentieth century that the 1995 Congress of the International Association for the Protection of Intellectual Property (AIPPI) recognised the role of merchandising as:

> the use, amongst others, of names or images of characters, real or fictional persons, events, groups and entities of the most varied kind, literary and artistic works, their titles and other distinctive elements, for the promotion or sale of products and services.[102]

As Ruijsenaars observes, the AIPPI's rather wide description 'could have been more precise, [but] problems arise from the diversity of the subject-matter of merchandising, as the large variety of merchandising symbols makes it difficult to issue general statements concerning all merchandisable elements'.[103] This is particularly the case when the merchandising symbol is an individual's image.

One point of terminology which arises here is the difference between 'character merchandising' and 'image' or 'personality' merchandising.[104] In general, 'character merchandising' can be seen as the use of fictional characters, whereas 'image' or 'personality' merchandising is the use of real individuals on goods.[105]

---

[99] *McCulloch v Lewis A May Ltd* (1948) 65 RPC 58 and *Lyngstad v Anabas Products* [1977] FSR 62.
[100] *Mirage Studios v Counter-Feat Clothing Company Ltd* [1991] FSR 145 (Ch) 148.
[101] Walton J referred to the commercial practice of merchandising in *Wombles Ltd v Wombles Skips Ltd* [1975] FSR 488 and *Tavener Rutledge Ltd v Trexapalm Ltd* [1975] FSR 479, and the House of Lords did likewise in *In Re American Greeting Corporation's Application* [1984] 1 WLR 189, indicating a growing awareness of merchandising through the 1970s and 1980s. It was not until *Mirage Studios* in 1991, however, that this recognition appeared to have an explicit impact on the application of the law. The importance of changing social practice was also commented upon by G Scanlan, 'Personality, Endorsement and Everything' [2003] *EIPR* 563, 568; SM Maniatis and S Chong, 'The Teenage Mutant Hero Turtles Case' [1991] *EIPR* 253, 257; and H Porter, 'Character Merchandising: Does English Law Recognise a Property Right in Name and Likeness?' [1999] *Ent LR* 180, 180. Porter, however, also draws attention to the views expressed by Laddie J in *Elvis Presley Trade Marks* [1997] RPC 543, to the effect that members of the public do not care who has manufactured the goods they buy, in contrast with the Vice-Chancellor's belief, in *Mirage Studios* [1991] FSR 145 (Ch) 159, that the public would not buy goods which they knew to be counterfeit. Nonetheless, Hull suggests that '[p]laintiffs who are not assiduous in gathering such evidence [of public confusion] may find courts veering back to the *McCulloch v May* line of case law, but there is now some realistic hope that the cycle of negative decisions built around *McCulloch's* case may finally have been broken'. J Hull, 'The Merchandising of Real and Fictional Characters: an Analysis of Some Recent Developments' [1991] *Ent LR* 124, 129.
[102] AIPPI Resolution 'Legal Aspects of Merchandising' (Q129) (Montreal, June 1995), para 1.2.
[103] HE Ruijsenaars, 'Legal Aspects of Merchandising: the AIPPI Resolution' [1996] *EIPR* 330, 330.
[104] A distinction alluded to, but not resolved, by the AIPPI resolution: see para 1.3.
[105] H MacQueen, C Waelde and G Laurie, *Contemporary Intellectual Property* (Oxford, Oxford University Press, 2007), para 17.30.

Although this distinction is not universally made, it is a helpful one and will be observed below where either term is used. Since the focus of this examination is on the use of individuals, rather than fictional characters, the term 'merchandising' will be used when referring to image or personality merchandising, in contrast to character merchandising which will signify the use of fictional characters.

V. A Fourth Way: Privacy and Publicity

It is possible to conceive of publicity not as a category in its own right, but as the flip-side or parasite of another right: privacy. Since 2000 there has been a flourishing of academic and judicial activity in relation to privacy which will be more closely examined in chapter four. In brief, this approach stems from breach of confidence and the article 8 right to privacy under the European Convention on Human Rights[106] (ECHR), as implemented in the Human Rights Act 1998. The privacy protection offered by article 8 of the ECHR has been heavily influenced by Civilian concepts of personality, as discussed in section III above, but now plays an increasingly important role in Scottish and English jurisprudence.[107] There is recognition of the close links between privacy and publicity in much of the American jurisprudence: Halpern refers to the right of publicity 'emerg[ing] from its privacy moorings', before which it was 'simply, and erroneously, considered the "appropriation branch" of the right of privacy'.[108]

With the increasing prominence of privacy rights in the United Kingdom, comes the secondary use of privacy in relation to publicity. This is especially prevalent where there is intrusive media use of personal information: '[t]he gravamen of invasion by the media is non-consensual dissemination of information about individuals'.[109] This invasion of privacy can be viewed as unwanted 'publicity', not least because in some cases the individual in question has willingly sought the publication of the very same facts where such publication is done in a controlled, and lucrative, manner. While the media intrusion may result in a claim for breach of privacy, the exploitation is, on one interpretation, really a form of publicity.[110]

---

[106] Convention for the Protection of Human Rights and Fundamental Freedoms, Rome, 4.XI.1950.

[107] This is despite fears that the concept of personality 'might be thought to be Continental psychobabble', Jones and Wilson, 'Photographs, Privacy and Public Places' (2007) 358.

[108] SW Halpern, 'Trafficking in Trademarks: Setting Boundaries for the Uneasy Relationship Between "Property" Rights and Trademark and Publicity Rights' (2009) 58 *DePaul L Rev* 1013–45 at 1039.

[109] Morgan (n 5) 445.

[110] Max Clifford has recently stated that, for media stars, protection is now the biggest priority, whereas it used to be promotion. (Interview given to BBC News 24 following the announcement of

This was the situation in *Douglas v Hello!*,[111] where the claimants recovered for invasion of their privacy, yet most commentators are agreed that if we 'ask what is *Douglas v Hello* really about?, common sense tells us that it is actually about commercial exploitation of image'.[112] Although the eventual remedy was found in article 8 of the ECHR and breach of confidence,[113] the 'dispute is arguably not about privacy at all. It is about the way in which celebrities and others in the public eye are entitled to make money by publishing aspects of their private lives'.[114] Thus, although *Douglas* was argued as a privacy case, it is frequently classed as an example of publicity exploitation.

If the appropriation of personality category in section IV reflects the second limb of the American privacy tort in the 2d Restatement, this category can more readily be equated to the third limb: 'unreasonable publicity given to the other's private life'.[115] This category also has closer links with the category of (Civilian) personality rights discussed in section III, raising issues of privacy, identity and information.

Data protection law has also contributed in this field, both in case law[116] and in academic commentaries. For example, Boyd and Jay argue that use of an individual's digital image without the individual's consent will constitute unfair processing contrary to data protection principles.[117] However, the Data Protection Act 1998 regulates the processing of 'personal data' rather than protecting economic or personal interests in them, and this focus limits the applicability of data protection in the broader field of privacy protection.[118]

The common themes in this canon are media publication, whether authorised or not, and the troublesome border between the concepts of privacy and publicity. Although there has been an explosion of privacy litigation in the

---

Prince William's and Kate Middleton's engagement, 17 November 2010.) Thus, privacy can be a critical right not only for privacy interests but also in seeking to enjoy publicity.

[111] *Douglas v Hello!* [2006] QB 125.

[112] Michalos, 'Image Rights and Privacy' [2005].

[113] The role of breach of confidence since 1990 will be considered in detail in chapter four.

[114] N Gardner and K Brimstead, 'Confidential Information – Damages' [2005] *EIPR* N190, N191.

[115] American Law Institute, The Restatement of the Law of Torts, 2d, para 652A.

[116] Successful claims for breach of data protection law were made in *Campbell v MGN* [2004] 2 AC 457 and *Douglas v Hello!* [2006] QB 125.

[117] S Boyd and R Jay, 'Image Rights and the Effect of the Data Protection Act 1998' [2004] *Ent LR* 159, 162. This is supported by the use of data protection as one of the heads of claim in some of the leading cases, such as *Campbell v MGN Ltd* [2004] 2 AC 457, *Douglas v Hello!* [2006] QB 125 and *Murray v Big Pictures (UK) Ltd* [2008] EWCA Civ 446.

[118] Recent cases which have considered the definition of 'personal data' include *Common Services Agency v Scottish Information Commissioner* [2008] 1 WLR 1550 and *Durant v Financial Services Authority* [2003] EWCA Civ 1746. There is, however, tension between the approach to 'personal data' in the UK and in the rest of the EU. This was one factor behind the 2007 report of the Article 29 Working Party on the meaning of the term: The Article 29 Working Party Opinion 4/2007 on the concept of personal data (20 June 2007). See further Rosemary Jay, *Data Protection Law and Practice*, 3rd edn (London, Sweet & Maxwell, 2007); G Black, 'Data Protection' in *Stair Memorial Encyclopaedia Reissue* (London, LexisNexis, forthcoming 2010).

United Kingdom since the Human Rights Act 1998 came into force,[119] the exact nature of the privacy right, and its relationship with publicity, remains uncertain. Nevertheless, the existence of a right to respect for one's private life, together with the doctrine of breach of confidence offers a pragmatic solution for an individual who wishes to protect the exploitation of his or her image or reputation. Its suitability will be further assessed in chapter four.

VI. Cross-Overs and Conclusions

The three approaches discussed above show that 'publicity' is capable of a wide range of interpretations. It can mean an economic right to be exploited through a wide-ranging property right, or a dignitarian right to be protected through the rights of personality, or an 'asset' to be protected from misappropriation and for which a remedy in tort may be found. The fourth way suggests that it may not even be appropriate to classify it as a distinct right, but instead should be regarded as an offshoot of the prior right to privacy.

While the above categories can certainly be defended as identifiable trends in Western legal thinking, the reality is less clear-cut. Particularly in the Common law tradition, academics are prepared to cross categories. Thus, while Vaver is clearly engaged in the analysis of three statutory torts in Canada regulating publicity through the 'appropriation of personality' category, he is also prepared to acknowledge the relevance of property to publicity rights, since 'many modern definitions of property focus upon the existence of a right of exclusive enjoyment rather than upon whether the object of the right is tangible or intangible'.[120] In cases like this, the boundaries between categories may become blurred, albeit not altogether erased.

One writer whose work neatly illustrates two problems with these classifications is Carty. In the first place, her work demonstrates the ongoing evolution of academic thinking in this area. Her 2004 article on 'Advertising, Publicity Rights and English Law'[121] placed emphasis on the merchandising and advertising uses of the individual within the wider category of appropriation of personality, while by 2007 her focus marked a shift towards the broader 'The Common Law and the Quest for the IP Effect'.[122] In publicity terms, this is the idea that 'the celebrity industry (including "licensees") seek commodification of the celebrity image',[123] which comes close to (while emphatically not endorsing) the broad publicity as

---

[119] For example, *CC v AB* [2006] EWHC 3083 (QB); *McKennitt v Ash* [2008] QB 73; *A v B&C* [2002] 2 All ER 545; *X v BBC* 2005 SLT 796; *Campbell v MGN* [2004] 2 AC 457; *Mosley v News Group Newspapers Ltd* [2008] EWHC 1777 (QB); *Murray v Big Pictures* [2008] EWCA Civ 446.

[120] Vaver (n 35) 260.

[121] Carty (n 83).

[122] H Carty, 'The Common Law and the Quest for the IP Effect' [2007] *IPQ* 237.

[123] ibid 240.

property approach. This observation highlights the constant evolution and shifting of parameters that occurs in publicity rights.

A second challenge offered by Carty's analysis is her insight into the role of the celebrity *as the product itself*.[124] This interpretation is shared by Colston and Middleton who argue that '[i]mage… comprises both a powerful marketing tool and creates a new product'.[125] This idea overlays a number of categories, most critically 'publicity as property', which treats the image or identity as the subject of property rights, and merchandising, which looks to the value in using image as a marketing tool. It is therefore a more nuanced interpretation, as it draws out the differing functions performed by an individual's image in different circumstances. In addition to her contribution to the debate in this area, which will be drawn upon in the chapters to follow, Carty provides a valuable reminder that the suggested categories are not exhaustive, nor are they definitive. There is no easy comparative classification of publicity rights.

Perhaps the key differences between the approaches can be summarised as:

(i) economic interests versus dignitarian interests;
(ii) property protection versus tort law; and
(iii) exploitation by self versus exploitation (or 'appropriation') by others.

These differences form the tensions which underlie and shape any analysis of publicity. They can, to some extent, be mapped on to the split between Civilian and Common law analyses of publicity rights: whereas Civilian systems predominantly protect dignitarian interests through personality or quasi-delictual rights, Common law systems focus primarily on the economic interests at stake, through property law or through torts which evolved in the context of market practices, such as passing off and breach of confidence. As Reiter has observed, 'the classificatory angst that traditionally occupies civilians affected neither Prosser nor Judge Frank. For them, it was enough to note that the right has value, without worrying overly about its nature.'[126]

While each classification offers an insight into publicity rights, the comparison between the three reveals that none is perfect. The benefits offered by one approach are offset by imperfections. As will be seen time and again, the Common law approach to the subject tends to focus on the need for remedies[127] and finds that remedy in the existing structure of actions and remedies, if necessary adapting them to meet the circumstances of the particular case.[128] This is the case whether the primary action is one of publicity or one grounded in tort

---

[124] Carty (n 83) 210.
[125] C Colston and K Middleton, *Modern Intellectual Property Law*, 2nd edn (London, Cavendish, 2005) 631.
[126] Reiter (n 44) 716.
[127] The primacy of seeking a remedy is clear from the opening sentence of Beverley-Smith's authoritative analysis: Beverley-Smith (n 70) 3.
[128] See, for example, R Buxton, 'How the Common Law Gets Made: *Hedley Byrne* and other Cautionary Tales' (2009) 125 *LQR* 60.

law. In contrast to this pragmatic commercial approach, Civilian systems respond to publicity claims with a principled scheme of extra-patrimonial rights, but one which can struggle to accommodate the patrimonial elements. The emphasis on dignitarian and moral interests inherent in an individual's personhood risks marginalising economic concerns. Thus, not one of the three conceptual categories can offer an entirely coherent account of publicity rights.

Since each has its weaknesses as well as its strengths, the question to be asked is whether there is an alternative analysis which addresses some of these flaws while retaining the benefits? For this, it is helpful to return to first principles: what can the practice of publicity tell us about the necessary characteristics of the legal right?

3

The Exploitation of Image and Publicity

I. Introduction

AS CHAPTER TWO sought to show, 'publicity' is capable of a wide range of interpretations. Part of the problem with devising any coherent legal response to publicity is the lack of a single agreed definition or understanding of publicity in practice, coupled with the absence of common terminology. What is 'publicity' or 'personality'? Does 'publicity' involve a property right over the individual's identity or a personality right to protection of dignitarian interests? The principal aim of this chapter is to develop a more nuanced account of the social practice of publicity. Allied to this, a further aim is to use this account in order to devise a framework and terminology to shape the analysis of publicity rights in future chapters.

Any publicity exploitation gives rise to two fundamental questions: what is being exploited and what form does the exploitation take? It is essential to appreciate that these are two separate aspects and require separate consideration. No contract can be drafted, no court can determine a case, and no writer can examine the right of publicity without having some idea of what is the subject matter of the contract, action or examination and to what use this subject matter has been put.[1]

For example, the very fact that the claimants in two leading English 'publicity' cases—*Irvine v Talksport*[2] and *Douglas v Hello!*[3]—used different types of action to achieve their ends, indicates some degree of difference between the two situations. To what extent are these both publicity actions? What was the reason for suing for passing off in *Irvine* and for breach of confidence in *Douglas*? These

---

[1] These questions are arguably central to the structure of many legal rights. Establishing the what and the how allows us to distinguish between copyright and patents, for example, or between employment and agency.

[2] *Irvine v Talksport Ltd* [2003] 2 All ER 881.

[3] *Douglas v Hello!* in the Court of Appeal [2006] QB 125; and in the House of Lords [2008] 1 AC 1.

divergent legal claims suggest that there is a correlation between the legal action used in English law and the *use* made of the individual's image or identity, and this correlation will be explored in more detail when considering the manner of the exploitation. The *subject matter* of the exploitation is also important. For example, has the individual's name been used, or is it the individual's image, or both, or something else altogether? What role is played by other, less tangible elements, such as reputation or 'glamour'?[4]

This chapter therefore seeks to construct a framework in which to analyse publicity cases. Without this framework, it is too easy to confuse arguments relating to one element with those relating to another and this, in turn, gives rise to confusion and artificial disagreement. One such example can be found in *Douglas v Hello!*.[5] Whereas Lord Walker stated that the Douglases' claims 'come close to claims to a "character right" protecting a celebrity's name and image such as has consistently been rejected in English law',[6] Lord Nicholls observed that '[n]or did Hello's publication of pictures of this event constitute "character merchandising"'.[7] Regardless of the correct analysis, this reveals a divergence of classification at the very highest levels. A second example of this (potential) confusion can be taken from Holyoak's discussion of *Kaye v Robertson*,[8] in which unauthorised photographs taken of the claimant in hospital were published in a national newspaper. While most commentators today would class this as an invasion of privacy, in 1993 Holyoak noted that '*Kaye* is an important decision in the evolution of recognition by the law of the practice of character merchandising'.[9] However, whether the publication of photographs of an ill actor can indeed be seen as the same activity as the application of images of ABBA to pillowcases,[10] requires further analysis.

Separating out the strands of subject matter and use allows a much clearer insight to be gained and also enables us to distinguish, with greater precision and confidence, between activities such as character merchandising and media publication. Once the subject matter and use have been identified, they can be used to provide a much more structured description of publicity in practice. This leads to a considerably more accurate definition of publicity for legal purposes. Thus, the construction of a dual framework assists our understanding of publicity exploitation with reference to two key elements of the practice: *what* is being exploited and to what *use* it is being put.

---

[4] In the words of Hazel Carty, 'Personality Rights and English Law' in Niall Whitty and Reinhard Zimmermann (eds), *Rights of Personality in Scots Law, a Comparative Perspective*, (Dundee, Dundee University Press, 2009) para 7.2.6.

[5] *Douglas v Hello!* [2008] 1 AC 1.

[6] ibid para 285.

[7] ibid para 253.

[8] *Kaye v Robertson* [1991] FSR 62.

[9] J Holyoak, 'United Kingdom Character Rights and Merchandising Rights Today' [1993] *JBL* 444, 455.

[10] In *Lyngstad v Anabas Products Ltd* [1977] FSR 62.

II. The Dual Classification Part 1: The Use Approach

A. Examining Publicity Uses

This approach focuses on the different uses that can be made of the subject matter. (The subject matter will be considered in section III. A. below and involves the individual's identifying elements.)

Colston and Middleton deploy the uses of publicity as a framework for their review of image rights, based on a tripartite structure. The three uses that they identify are:

— 'merchandising of memorabilia using "character" as a decorative device [whether real or fictional];
— endorsement of products [by the well-known];
— individuals exploiting their image for the purposes of celebrity.'[11]

This classificatory scheme can also be detected in the work of other writers in two of the three publicity rights approaches identified in chapter two.[12] Like Colston and Middleton, Madow identifies three comparable categories of publicity, being 'intense demand for information about the lives and doings of celebrities'; 'a large and increasingly lucrative market for merchandise'; and enhancement of 'the marketability of a wide array of collateral products and services'.[13]

Another American academic, Goodenough, observes that:

> While the ways of turning humanity's innate fascination with personal identity to account are probably bounded only by humanity's ingenuity, five principal modes of use can be fruitfully isolated as encompassing most of the current activity in the market-place of the persona: (i) informational use; (ii) creative use; (iii) advertising use; (iv) icon use; and (v) performance use.[14]

These five uses can be fleshed out in greater detail.[15] The informational use is news reporting where, importantly, the reported story is factual. This can be contrasted with the creative use, which is similar to informational use but where there is no longer a concern that the information is accurate. Fictionalised accounts of individuals would therefore be covered by the second category. The third use, advertising, is where an individual is used to help sell products or

---

[11] C Colston and K Middleton, *Modern Intellectual Property Law*, 2nd edn (London, Cavendish, 2005) 632.

[12] These are publicity as property and appropriation of personality. The Civilian personality rights approach focuses primarily on the subject matter, and will be considered in section III. A. below.

[13] M Madow, 'Private Ownership of Public Image: Popular Culture and Publicity Rights' (1993) 81 *Cal L Rev* 125, 129.

[14] O Goodenough, 'Re-Theorising Privacy and Publicity' [1997] *IPQ* 37 41.

[15] ibid 41–42.

services 'which are not themselves elements of the personality in question'.[16] This can be either through endorsement, where the individual is seen to use the product his or herself, or simply through drawing attention to the item. Icon use is where 'the thing of value being used is the persona itself', either through 'pure representations', such as posters and figurines, or through 'utilitarian items', where functional products are decorated with the image of the individual, such as t-shirts,[17] lunch boxes, etc. The final category is the performance use, which arises where an actor performs in character or a singer or athlete performs in his or her own right. Legal concerns may arise where the performance is recorded and can then be replayed or transmitted, with or without the consent of the performer.[18]

As well as providing a detailed description of the uses of personal identity, Goodenough also sets out a convincing argument for rejecting profit and commerce as a central factor in publicity use.[19] Although commercial use is widespread and drives much publicity exploitation, it is 'less helpful' as a defining trait since '[s]uch terms always need careful qualification and explanations... All of these uses can be, and in the relentlessly for-profit world of America generally are, carried on as commercial activities, for the purposes of trade'.[20] Accordingly, the notion of 'commercial exploitation' of image and identity is not of great assistance as a defining factor of publicity, since it is capable of covering all publicity-type uses. Publicity use may often be commercial, but it need not be.

Carty identifies a 'complex framework'[21] of image use, which consists of four different fact situations. These are:

(i) the 'allegiance' use of a celebrity, through the production of celebrity souvenirs or memorabilia such as t-shirts and posters;
(ii) the 'informational advertising use' of celebrity, which is effectively endorsement where the celebrity is used to provide a guarantee of the product or service concerned;
(iii) the 'enhancement advertising use' of celebrity, where the consumer's attention is caught by the use of the celebrity, potentially including parody; and
(iv) the 'biographical information use' of celebrity, which is 'attention-grabbing

---

[16]   ibid 41.

[17]   Vaver draws attention to the significance of t-shirts and their communicative qualities, but observing that t-shirts 'may have become the modern counterpart of the olden-day pamphlets': D Vaver, 'What's Mine is not Yours: Commercial Appropriation of Personality under the Privacy Acts of British Columbia, Manitoba and Saskatchewan' (1981) 15 *U Brit Colum L Rev* 241 307. This is supported by the South African case of *Laugh it Off v South African Breweries* 2006 (1) SA 144, which involved the use of t-shirts to parody leading commercial brands.

[18]   This recording and unpermitted broadcast of a performance was the focus of the dispute in *Zacchini v Scripps-Howard Broadcasting Company* (1977) 433 US 562.

[19]   Commercial use is particularly prevalent in the 'publicity as property' approach: see chapter two, section II.

[20]   Goodenough, 'Re-theorising Privacy and Publicity' (1997) 42 and 62; also D Zimmerman, 'Who Put the Right in the Right of Publicity?' (1998–1999) 9 *DePaul-LCA J Art & Ent L* 35, 61–62 and 67–68.

[21]   H Carty, 'Advertising, Publicity Rights and English Law' [2004] *IPQ* 209, 216.

by media features about the celebrity himself' and which 'lies somewhere between all three of the above uses as such [media] features are both selling the celebrity and selling themselves at the same time'.[22]

Carty believes these four different publicity rights should be treated differently in law and only the 'information advertising use' is worthy of legal protection.[23]

Beverley-Smith also addresses three types of use of persona. Although his initial definition focuses on the use of personality for merchandising and advertising purposes,[24] his subsequent review does include reference to a third category of use, being the privacy interests arising from media publication of information, in cases such as *Douglas v Hello!*.[25]

When these different analyses of publicity uses are compared directly, it can be seen that they all identify much the same uses, albeit using different terminology:

Good-enough	Colston and Middleton	Madow	Carty	Beverley-Smith
Informa-tional	Exploitation of image.	Intense demand for information.	Biographical information use.	Privacy interests.
Creative	*Not so relevant, but 'exploita-tion of image' where it arises.*	–	*Not so relevant, but 'biographical information use', where it arises.*	–
Advertising	Endorsement (*by the well-known*).	Enhancement of marketability of a product or service.	Two rights: (i) informational advertising use; and (ii) enhancement advertising use.	Advertising
Icon use	Merchandising	A lucrative mar-ket for mer-chandise.	Allegiance use	Merchandising
Performance	–	–	–	–

The table emphasises the coherence between the categories used or referred to by most writers and, critically, it underlines the terminological differences. All envisage Goodenough's information, advertising and icon uses, yet apply a range of different labels to these uses. For example, Goodenough's 'icon use' is variously known as 'allegiance use', 'merchandise' use, and 'merchandising'.

---

[22] ibid 216–17.

[23] ibid 258. In a later article Carty discusses areas of commercial development which are pushing for the 'IP effect'. The first of these areas is 'the celebrity industry (including "licensees") [who] seek commodification of the celebrity image' (H Carty, 'The Common Law and the Quest for the IP Effect' [2007] *IPQ* 237, 240). This is a broader over-arching category which accommodates her four earlier categories. The analysis here will proceed on the basis of her four uses.

[24] H Beverley-Smith, *The Commercial Appropriation of Personality* (Cambridge, Cambridge University Press, 2002) 3.

[25] ibid 210–11.

The one exception is Goodenough's final category of performance use (covering use of recordings of performances by actors, singers or athletes), which is not evident in the other accounts. McCarthy concludes that this type of use is not directly relevant to publicity, while noting that 'many people have been misled into thinking that the right of publicity involves something else: something called "performance values". That is, the unpermitted appropriation or imitation of an entertainer's performance or performance style.'[26] He attributes this confusion to the US Supreme Court case of *Zacchini v Scripps-Howard Broadcasting Company*,[27] where the plaintiff's performance (being fired out of a cannon) was broadcast by a television station as a news feature, and this use was held to breach his right of publicity. McCarthy, however, argues that cases such as this constitute a 'very, very small slice of the right of publicity'.[28] Further, 'performance use' is most likely to be protected by copyright, which will subsist in the words, music, script, sound recording and/or performance as appropriate.[29] Performance use will therefore be excluded from the scope of this examination.

With the performance use excluded, it can be seen from the above table that the majority approach provides a tripartite classification, which enables a meaningful distinction to be drawn between the uses without unnecessary fragmentation. This tripartite framework will be adopted, to recognise the division of publicity into (i) information or image exploitation, through news reporting; (ii) endorsement or enhancement of advertising; and (iii) merchandising or allegiance use.

B. The Tripartite Classification of Uses

These three uses can be outlined as follows:

1. **An individual agrees to allow an entity (frequently a newspaper or a magazine) access to a particular area of his or her life, typically for a fee.** Examples can readily be given, whereby an individual 'sells' photographs of his or her wedding day to a gossip magazine[30] or where a participant in a

---

[26] T McCarthy, 'Public Personas and Private Property: The Commercialization of Human Identity' (1989) 79 *TMR* 681, 689.

[27] *Zacchini v Scripps-Howard Broadcasting Company* (1977) 433 US 562.

[28] McCarthy, 'Public Personas and Private Property' (1989) 690; also T McCarthy, 'The Human Persona as Commercial Property: the Right of Publicity' (1995) 19 *Colum-VLA JL & Arts* 129, 133. Zimmerman takes this further, claiming that *Zacchini* 'bears very little relationship' to the typical publicity cases: Zimmerman, 'Who Put the Right in the Right of Publicity?' (1981–99) 45.

[29] Copyright, Designs and Patents Act 1988 (henceforth CDPA 1988) s 1, supplemented by ss 3 and 5 and s 180.

[30] Examples from the last decade include David and Victoria Beckham (to OK! in 1999 for £1 million); Michael Douglas and Catherine Zeta-Jones (to OK! in 2000 for £1 million); Jordan and Peter Andre (to OK! in 2005 for £2 million); Ashley Cole and Cheryl Tweedy (to OK! in 2006 for £1 million); Wayne Rooney and Coleen McLoughlin (to OK! in 2008 for £2.5 million), and Jade Goody and Jack Tweed (to OK! in 2009 for £700,000). Since official details of such arrangements are not published, definitive authority is hard to produce: all details taken from BBC online or Wikipedia.

high-profile current event 'tells all' to a newspaper in a (typically exclusive) deal.[31] Tabloid newspapers rely on a ready supply of gossip or scandal about 'celebrities': one need only inspect the news-stand in any newsagent, stationer or bookseller to appreciate that such celebrity tales are weekly events. This supply and demand for gossip and information can be thought of as an individual's 'media information' use-right. It relies on the name and image of the individual, together with some element of information about them. Any third party user, whether authorised or not, can be referred to as a 'publisher'.

2. **An individual agrees to endorse, support or promote a particular product or service.** In these cases, the individual 'tells the relevant public that he approves of the product or service or is happy to be associated with it. In effect he adds his name as an encouragement to members of the relevant public to buy or use the service or product.'[32] Note however that this use of name and image frequently comprises more than the provision of services such as modelling or attending a photo shoot: the supplier wishing to benefit from this support will usually have chosen a specific individual not for his or her modelling abilities (or not exclusively so), but for the added value provided by the individual's public status or reputation. Celebrity status or reputation therefore apparently has a role to play in most cases of this use.

What is critical in this use is that the individual advertises or endorses the products or services *of another party*: it is not a self-promotion, nor is the individual the product his or herself. This essential distinction has already been referred to in chapter two, section VI, where Carty and Colston and Middleton recognise the difference between the individual's image which 'comprises both a powerful marketing tool and creates a new product'.[33] The advertising and endorsement use employs the individual as a marketing tool and not as a new product. It is therefore fundamental that the individual is used in conjunction with another party's goods or services.

There may be a link between the individual's fame and the goods or services he is promoting. This is the case, for example, with Jamie Oliver (chef) and Sainsbury's (food) or with David Beckham (footballer) and Adidas (sports clothing and footwear). This can be referred to as a 'tools of

---

[31] Examples are numerous: one interesting recent example is the first couple in the UK to be diagnosed with swine flu in 2009 and who attracted criticism from a Member of the Scottish Parliament for selling their story. The publicist Max Clifford makes a living from brokering such deals. In relation to the swine flu couple, whom he represented, Clifford reportedly said: 'If it's your story, and the media are going to make money from your story, why shouldn't you make money from your story?' ('Couple Criticised for Flu Story' *BBC News Online* (1 May 2009) www.news.bbc.co.uk/1/hi/scotland/8028857.stm.

[32] *Irvine v Talksport Ltd* [2002] 1 WLR 2355 [9] (Laddie J).

[33] Colston and Middleton, *Modern Intellectual Property Law* (2005) 631; also Carty, 'Advertising, Publicity Rights and English Law' (2004) 210.

the trade' endorsement.[34] Alternatively, the supplier may favour a 'non-tools endorsement',[35] and simply wish to enjoy some 'reflected glory' from the particular reputation or popularity of the individual in question, without there being a link between the activities of the individual and the product or service to be promoted. Thus, David Beckham's star status was valuable to Pepsi without him being involved in the soft drinks industry.[36] Beverley-Smith et al also identify a third type of advertisement, where the individual is chosen solely for the purpose of 'grabbing the attention' of the public,[37] and there is no suggestion of endorsement of the product by the individual. Carty refers to these three classes of celebrity promotion, but groups both tools and non-tools endorsement together as one category, called 'information advertising use', and treats the third non-endorsement use separately as the 'enhancement advertising use' category.[38]

The variety of ways in which the individual's name and image can be used to endorse, support or promote a product or service leads to a dilemma over the most appropriate name for this category: 'advertising' (as favoured by Goodenough, Carty and Beverley-Smith) signifies the attention-grabbing use, but could potentially operate to exclude cases where there is endorsement; conversely 'endorsement' (as used by Colston and Middleton) is inappropriate for those cases where there is no indication of support from the individual. In both cases, however, the underlying aim is the promotion of products and services through the attachment of the name and/or image of an individual, whether this is done through using the individual to catch the public attention or to vaunt the benefits of the product. This use can therefore be thought of as the 'promotion use', while emphasising that the promotion by the individual is on behalf of a third party, referred to as the 'supplier', although where done with the consent of the individual, it may well promote the interests of both parties.[39]

3. **An individual agrees to produce or authorise production of goods which carry his or her name and/or image.** Common examples of these 'mere image carriers', as the Trade Marks Registry has termed them,[40] include posters, calendars, t-shirts and mugs. Here, the goods are not being bought solely because the purchaser wishes a new mug, nor are they being sold as trade marked items in the sense that the purchaser is specifically keen to buy

---

[34] H Beverley-Smith et al, *Privacy, Property and Personality* (Cambridge, Cambridge University Press, 2005) 2.

[35] ibid.

[36] In 2004, Beckham's deal with Pepsi was apparently worth £3 million: A Milligan, *Brand it Like Beckham* (London, Cyan, 2004) 120.

[37] Beverley-Smith et al, *Privacy, Property and Personality* (2005) 2.

[38] Carty (n 21) 216–17.

[39] This element of mutual benefit will be apparent time and again throughout this investigation.

[40] G Black (published as G Davies), 'The Cult of Celebrity and Trade Marks: the Next Instalment' (2004) 1:2 *SCRIPT-ed* 230.

a mug from a certain manufacturer as identified by its trade mark. Instead, they are seen as 'badges of loyalty';[41] souvenirs or indicia of support for, or interest in, the individual who features on the product. An example of merchandising was given in (the non-merchandising case of) *Irvine v Talksport*, where reference was made to 'the sale of memorabilia relating to the late Diana, Princess of Wales. A porcelain plate bearing her image could hardly be thought of as being endorsed by her, but the enhanced sales which may be achieved by virtue of the presence of the image is a form of merchandising.'[42]

In these cases the individual effectively becomes the product:[43] when the consumer buys the David Beckham calendar or the Elvis Presley mug, they are 'buying' David Beckham or Elvis Presley. The significant distinction between the promotion use outlined above and the merchandising use is the difference already alluded to, between, respectively, image as a marketing tool and as the product itself. In merchandising, the individual arguably becomes the product.[44]

Merchandising may involve products which are either a 'pure representation' (for example, posters) or a 'utilitarian' item (for example, t-shirts or calendars), as per Goodenough's classification above. In some cases there may be a perception of endorsement by the individual involved, but this is not necessary: all that is required is that the product bears the image of the individual which renders it attractive to its target audience.[45] Whether authorised or not, the practice of production of mementoes is typically known as merchandising: where this practice is exploited, it will be referred to as the 'merchandising use' and a third party exploiter (whether authorised or not) who produces goods bearing the image of the individual will be the 'merchandiser'.

Together, the media information, promotion and merchandising uses can be seen as the most commonly cited (and evidenced) types of publicity activity. It is important to stress that the list cannot be treated as exhaustive, but should remain open. A rigid classification would risk stagnation and hamper development of the law, particularly as regards future evolution of commercial or social practices. However, the above three categories appear broad enough to cover 'humanity's ingenuity' to date.

One important qualification to all use types is that there must be 'public' use: where the use of the image or identity is exclusively private, there will be no

---

[41]   As used in *Arsenal v Reed* [2003] 3 All ER 865. See also Zimmerman (n 20) 63.
[42]   *Irvine v Talksport* [2002] 1 WLR 2355 [9] (Laddie J).
[43]   See the distinction made above between the individual as a marketing tool and as the product itself: text and reference at n 33.
[44]   Colston and Middleton (n 11) 632.
[45]   *Irvine v Talksport* [2002] 1 WLR 2355 [9].

element of publicity.[46] The requirement for public use is implicit in each of the three uses discussed above: none of these publicity uses could be achieved by keeping the relevant publication, promotion or merchandise private. This is not something which is explored by other writers[47] and no court has had to consider the nature of the use in these terms, yet it stands to reason that an action for infringement of 'publicity rights' can only lie where the use made involves some element of communication to the public.[48] However, this requirement for public use does not equate to commercial or for-profit use since a charity, for example, could make use of an individual's persona to promote its cause without directly raising income or making a profit. The rejection of 'commercial use' as a defining criterion in section II. A above therefore still stands.

While the concept of 'public' use may be difficult to pin down, it is not impossible. The Data Protection Act 1998 provides that the 'special purposes' exemption (regarding journalistic literary or artistic material) only applies where there is publication of the work. Section 32(6) states that, for the purposes of that Act, 'publish' means to make available to the public or any section of the public. This is not limited to hard copy publications and could therefore encompass online publication or dissemination. It is suggested that a similar qualification should be applied to publicity use, so that only where the use in question is made available to the public or any section of the public will it constitute publicity use.

C. The Paradigm Publicity Use Cases

It is possible to identify a leading case in English law which is illustrative of each of these three uses and which can be used as a convenient point of reference for future discussion. This section provides a brief summary of the paradigm publicity cases, without (at this stage) passing comment on the merits or otherwise of the legal actions.

Douglas v Hello! typifies the media information use. In this case, a paparazzo photographer gained access to the Douglases' wedding, which was held in private in the Plaza Hotel in New York in November 2000. The paparazzo managed to obtain a number of unauthorised photographs of Catherine Zeta Jones and Michael Douglas at their wedding, which he sold to Hello! magazine. Hello!'s publication of these photographs caused distress to the Douglases[49] and

---

[46] Private use may of course breach a different legal right, in which case it can be prevented by way of that right.

[47] One exception is Halpern who notes that '[b]y its nature, the right of publicity implicates speech' —this of course reflects on publicity use itself and also its impact on the freedom of speech of others: SW Halpern, 'The Right of Publicity: Maturation of an Independent Right Protecting the Associative Value of Personality' (1995) 46 *Hastings LJ* 853, at 867.

[48] This can be contrasted with privacy actions, where the invasion itself may be actionable even absent dissemination, as will be seen in chapter four.

[49] They were left 'devastated and shocked' according to their evidence at trial: *Douglas v Hello!* [2003] EWHC 786 (Ch) [82]–[84] (Lindsay J).

destroyed the exclusivity of the deal which the Douglases had concluded with OK!, a rival magazine to Hello!. The Douglases' successful action against Hello! was based upon the action of breach of confidence, as supplemented by the article 8 right of privacy. The Court of Appeal's decision in favour of the Douglases was handed down in 2005,[50] while the House of Lords' ruling in favour of OK!, as exclusive licensee of the official wedding photographs, was delivered in 2007.[51]

The eventual award to the Douglases at first instance (and confirmed on appeal), comprised three elements:

(i) £3,750 each for distress;
(ii) £7,000 in respect of 'additional costs incurred by reason of their having to bring forward preparation, approval and provision of the authorised photographs so as to enable them to appear in OK! issue 241 as part of the Claimants' mitigation exercise';[52] and
(iii) £50 each for breach of their data protection rights.[53] (OK! was awarded £1,033,156 by Lindsay J—this was overturned by the Court of Appeal, but was reinstated on appeal to the House of Lords.)[54]

In respect of the promotion use, the leading case is *Irvine v Talksport*.[55] This case arose from the unauthorised use by Talksport of a photograph of Eddie Irvine, the Formula 1 racing driver, to promote its radio station. The manner in which the (legally obtained) image of Irvine had been doctored by Talksport suggested that Irvine was endorsing Talksport radio. Irvine's successful claim against Talksport for this use relied on the tort of passing off, alleging misrepresentation and confusion resulting in loss to Irvine. The Court of Appeal affirmed the High Court's judgment in 2003, and increased the award of damages to Irvine from £2,000 to £25,000.[56] It is critical to note that the image at the heart of the dispute had been doctored. Whether Irvine's claim would have been successful had the legally obtained image been left undoctored remains uncertain—and this fact operates as a substantial limit on the applicability of the case in future promotion use cases.[57]

The merchandising use can be illustrated by two cases. The first involved the unauthorised use of the images of real persons, when members of ABBA sued a company for applying their images and the band name to pillowcases. *Lyngstad v*

---

[50] *Douglas v Hello!* [2006] QB 125.
[51] *Douglas v Hello!* [2008] 1 AC 1.
[52] *Douglas v Hello!* [2003] EWHC 2629 (Ch) [57] (Lindsay J).
[53] ibid.
[54] *Douglas v Hello!* [2003] EWHC 2629 (Ch); overturned [2006] QB 125; reinstated [2008] 1 AC 1.
[55] *Irvine v Talksport Ltd* [2002] 1 WLR 2355, on appeal [2003] 2 All ER 881.
[56] *Irvine v Talksport Ltd* [2003] 2 All ER 881.
[57] The use of passing off as a vehicle for enabling recovery has been questioned by a number of commentators, including Carty (n 21) 238–43; Beverley-Smith, *The Commercial Appropriation of Personality* (2002); and Beverley-Smith et al (n 34) 23.

Anabas[58] was, like *Irvine*, argued on the grounds of passing off. Unlike *Irvine*, however, the band's action was unsuccessful in the High Court, in part because precedent was against the plaintiffs since an action for passing off had been dismissed in a similar situation in 1948, *McCulloch v Lewis A May Ltd*.[59] Nonetheless, *Lyngstad* remains the leading English case in relation to merchandising of real individuals which does not rely on registered trade mark protection.[60]

However, a 1991 decision of the High Court regarding the unauthorised use of fictional characters indicates increasing judicial awareness of the changing social and commercial practice of merchandising,[61] and suggests that there is no guarantee that *Lyngstad* would be followed today.[62] In *Mirage Studios v Counter-Feat Clothing Company Ltd*,[63] the defendant applied imitations of the plaintiff's cartoon characters, the Teenage Mutant Ninja Turtles, to a range of clothing. The Vice Chancellor accepted that this could constitute passing off, particularly given the evidence of public confusion in this case. The scope of the Vice Chancellor's judgment therefore suggests that a similar result could be reached in respect of individuals in merchandising cases, contrary to the decision of the High Court in *Lyngstad*. Further support can be drawn from Laddie J's opinion in *Irvine*, where he gave the example of a porcelain plate bearing the image of Diana, Princess of Wales, as an example of merchandising, as distinct from endorsement.[64] Taken together, these cases can be used to illustrate the category of merchandising use and provide some insight into the changing perception of merchandising practices.

Throughout this study, these cases will be used to provide a reference point for each of the three uses identified here. One feature of these cases which is worthy of note is that they all involved unsought and unauthorised use of the claimants' names, images and identities. It is therefore helpful to examine authorised and unauthorised use in greater detail.

---

[58] *Lyngstad v Anabas Products Ltd* [1977] FSR 62.

[59] *McCulloch v Lewis A May* (1948) 65 RPC 58.

[60] English cases such as *Jane Austen Trade Mark* [2000] RPC 879 and *Elvis Presley Trade Marks* [1999] RPC 567 have focused on trade-marked names.

[61] Walton J referred to the commercial practice of merchandising in *Wombles Ltd v Wombles Skips Ltd* [1975] FSR 488 and *Tavener Rutledge Ltd v Trexapalm Ltd* [1975] FSR 479, and the House of Lords did likewise in *In Re American Greeting Corporation's Application* [1984] 1 WLR 189, indicating a growing awareness of merchandising through the 1970s and 1980s, but it was not until *Mirage Studios v Counter-Feat Clothing Company Ltd* that this had an explicit impact on the development of the law. See also the discussion of this case in chapter two, section IV. B.

[62] Although Laddie J made a clear distinction between the false endorsement practice in *Irvine* and the merchandising practice: *Irvine v Talksport Ltd* [2002] 1 WLR 2355 [44].

[63] *Mirage Studios v Counter-Feat Clothing Company Ltd* [1991] FSR 145. See also chapter two, section IV.

[64] *Irvine v Talksport* [2002] 1 WLR 2355 [9] (Laddie J).

D. Authorised and Unauthorised Use

The distinction between authorised and unauthorised use depends on the circumstances of the exploitation, rather than on the use made or the subject matter of that use. Essentially, it is the difference between the Douglases' contract with OK! for authorised publication of their wedding photographs and their litigation against Hello! for unauthorised publication.

Despite the practice of authorised exploitation (which will be explored in detail in section IV below), the judicial and academic focus has been very much on the unauthorised exploitation. This is perhaps not surprising, since all litigation in the United Kingdom to date has arisen from this unauthorised use. Yet the commercial value of publicity lies in negotiated deals for authorised exploitation. Whereas the Douglases were awarded less than £15,000 from Hello! by the High Court, the value of their contract with OK! was £1 million. From press evidence as to the fees paid for other celebrity weddings in the United Kingdom, it would seem that £1 million was the standard rate for such publication deals in the decade 1998–2008, with some couples even managing to negotiate fees in excess of that.[65] Similarly, it has been suggested that of David Beckham's weekly earnings of £90,000 at Manchester United, £20,000 was attributable to the Club's use of his 'image rights'.[66] If true, this means that Beckham was earning more than £1 million per year for his image rights alone, from his club alone. The unauthorised use of persona may hit the headlines and occupy court time, but it is the authorised and controlled exploitation which is the focus of commercial practice.

A closer look at the concept of rights, however, reveals a small but important difference between authorised and unauthorised use of persona. MacCormick considers the 'right' to do something and the 'power' to do it.[67] Whereas *rights*, whether active or passive,[68] can be seen as 'positions of benefit or advantage secured to persons by law'[69] which 'make[s] it appropriate for a relevant constraint to fall on another person',[70] *powers* are a different type of legal concept:

> The empowering aspect of law can be envisaged as involving a legally conferred capability to alter the legal situations or relationships of legal persons. Powers in law in their simplest form are powers to vary in some way what it is right or wrong to do.[71]

---

[65] See n 30.

[66] Colston and Middleton (n 11) 631.

[67] N MacCormick, *Institutions of Law: An Essay in Legal Theory* (Oxford, Oxford University Press, 2007) chs 7 and 9.

[68] MacCormick explores the notion of active and passive rights in some details (ibid 120 *et seq*). Note that his use of active and passive in relation to rights does not equate to my notion of the positive authorised use and the negative unauthorised use: this division is better characterised by rights and powers as will be discussed immediately below. Instead, an active right is the right of a right-holder to do, or not do, as he chooses, in respect of that right. ibid 124–25.

[69] ibid 120.

[70] ibid 120.

[71] ibid 155.

This distinction between legal rights and powers can be applied in the context of exploitation of image. If the law were to prohibit unauthorised use, an individual would have a passive *right* not to have his or her image and identity exploited without consent. As part of this, the individual would also have an *active* right of choice as to whether to enforce this right or not: 'it is normally a matter of free choice whether or not to exercise any... remedial rights in case of breach'.[72] On the other hand, where the law chooses to recognise the ability to exploit in person, that is authorised use. This is not a right, strictly speaking. Instead, authorised use is a *power* of the individual: the individual is enabled, if the individual so chooses, to contract for use or exploitation of his or her image, thereby transforming the otherwise wrongful action of the party into authorised, permitted use. It should be noted, however, that the individual does not have a *right* to do so, as no individual can demand that his or her image be used to promote products, for example.[73] All the individual can do is contract for its exploitation where the opportunity arises.[74] For this reason, it is preferable to talk of a right *of* publicity, rather than a right *to* publicity.[75]

It is worth noting that the existence of a right does not equate to the obligation to exercise that right. MacCormick notes, in the context of privacy, that there is

> nothing wrong with conferring or recognising human rights to things which not everyone (even not many people) wants; for, of course, to have a right is, normally, to have the option whether one exercises it or not. Those who don't want privacy are in no way inconvenienced by being given a right to it.[76]

This applies equally for all permissive rights: there should be no compulsion to exercise a right of publicity if one were to be granted.

Any analysis of publicity rights should therefore take account of the difference between attempting to prevent or recover for unauthorised use of persona (the negative right) and attempting to control the use of persona (the positive power). A balanced review of publicity requires consideration of both elements.

---

[72] ibid 120; also 129.

[73] This analysis finds support from JE Penner, *The Idea of Property in Law* (Oxford, Clarendon, 1997) 91.

[74] Problems, of course, arise for those who cannot consent, by virtue of lack of capacity, for example. This is not unique to publicity, and applies in many areas of law. It is not suggested that people who lack the ability to consent should be denied a publicity right, especially the right to prevent exploitation: rather the exercise of any right would need to be made on their behalf by, for example, a power of attorney or guardian.

[75] This can be contrasted with fundamental human rights such as the right to life.

[76] N MacCormick, *Legal Right and Social Democracy* (Oxford, Clarendon Press, 1982, reprinted 1986) 178.

III.   The Dual Classification Part 2: The Subject Matter Approach

A.   Identifying the Subject Matter

Whereas the use approach provides a way to distinguish between the *methods* for exploiting individuals for publicity purposes, it does not categorise *what* is being exploited. One benefit of considering what is being exploited is that it helps to distinguish publicity from other rights that can be enjoyed by individuals. For example, where an individual enters into a contract for the provision of services in return for a regular salary, we can identify this as a contract of employment. Similarly, where there is exploitation of an individual's painting, this is a matter for a copyright licence. Alternatively, where there is exploitation of a brand, such as Coca-Cola, we can distinguish this from the promotion use identified above, because the subject matter is a registered trade mark, rather than an individual. The subject matter of the exploitation in each case allows it to be distinguished from other types of exploitation.

We therefore need to identify what is being exploited in publicity cases, whether there is media information, promotion or merchandising use of an individual. All of the conceptual approaches to publicity rights identified in chapter two can be drawn upon here.

McCarthy, for example, writing in the publicity as property approach, asks (and answers) the question:

> What aspects of human identity does the right of publicity protect? It protects anything by which a certain human being can be identified. This covers everything: personal names, nicknames, stage and pen names, pictures, and persona in a role or characterization. It can also include physical objects which identify a person… And the Bette Midler decision reaffirms that a person can be identified by voice.[77]

He notes that 'persona' is preferable as the collective term used to describe the elements of human identity exploited, since 'the traditional phrase "name and likeness" was inadequate to describe the many aspects of a person which can identify him or her.'[78]

Also writing in this tradition, Coombe gives a similarly broad definition of 'celebrity image' which develops the theme of identifying the individual by referring to the individual's recognition value. Publicity therefore affects 'not only or exclusively a celebrity's visual likeness but rather all elements of the

---

[77]   McCarthy (n 26) 689.

[78]   T McCarthy, *The Rights of Publicity and Privacy*, 2nd edn (United States, West Group, 2001) para 4:45. See also D Westfall and D Landau, 'Publicity Rights as Property Rights' (2005–2006) 23 *Cardozo Arts and Ent LJ* 71, 91 and 93–96 where they reflect on the expansive range of indicia, and the causes of this; see also chapter two, section II.

complex constellation of visual, verbal, and aural signs that circulate in society and constitute the celebrity's recognition value'.[79]

The all-embracing notion of what is covered by a right of publicity in the United States is reflected in much of the state legislation which provides for a right of publicity or commercial exploitation of identity. To take two examples,[80] the Indiana right of publicity is defined as a property interest in name, voice, signature, photograph, image, likeness, distinctive appearance, gestures, or mannerisms.[81] The State of Washington creates a property right over the name, voice, signature, photograph or likeness of the individual[82] and then defines each of these individual terms (except 'voice') in some detail.[83] The broad right of property in the United States therefore extends over a broad concept of persona.

The Civilian personality rights approach refers to 'appropriation of a person's identity (name or likeness)'.[84] Although this does not expand in any detail on the concept of 'identity', it is helpful to cross-reference this with the (separate) notion of the right to identity.[85] Here, identity is defined as a person's 'uniqueness which individualizes him as a particular person and this distinguishes him from others... Identity is manifested in various indicia by which a person can be recognized, such as his name, image, voice, fingerprints, handwriting, etc.'.[86] The two key elements which can be taken from this approach are first, an understanding of identity as a factor which distinguishes the individual from every other individual[87] and second, an extensive, yet non-exhaustive, list of the sort of factors which serve to distinguish the individual.

This definition of 'identity' finds support from another writer in the Civilian tradition, Logeais, who notes that 'fame is best conveyed through the name or picture which are inherent to the person'.[88] However, while she is prepared to accept personal attributes of the individual as part of the individual's identity, she does not agree with the annexation of external objects to represent that individual.[89] Thus, she disputes the outcome of an Italian case which protected the

---

[79]   R Coombe, *The Cultural Life of Intellectual Properties: Authorship Appropriation, and the Law* (Durham and London, Duke University Press, 1998) 89, fn 5.

[80]   For others, see the Florida Regulation of Trade, Commerce, Investments and Solicitations ch 540 s 08; the Illinois Right of Publicity Act (765 ILCS 1075); the New York Civil Rights statute art 5: Right of Privacy; Kentucky Acts 1984, 391.170; Massachusetts General Lawpt III, title I, ch 214, s 3A; the Nevada Right of Publicity, NRS 597.770 – 597.810; Oklahoma Stat tit 12, paras 1448–49; and Rhode Island Title 9 ch 9–1 s 28.

[81]   Indiana's Publicity law, in the Indiana Code Title 32 (Property) art 36 (Publicity) at ch 1 ss 1–7

[82]   The Revised Code of Washington (RCW) title 63 (Personal Property) ch 60 (Personality Rights) s 010.

[83]   ibid s 020(4) – (9).

[84]   J Neethling, 'Personality Rights' in Jan M Smits (ed), *Elgar Encyclopaedia of Comparative Law* (Cheltenham, Edward Elgar, 2006) 543.

[85]   The right to identity is infringed where identity is used 'in a way which cannot be reconciled with his true identity', per Neethling, 'Personality Rights' (2006) 540.

[86]   ibid 540.

[87]   The potential problems posed by identical twins are not considered.

[88]   E Logeais, 'The French Right to One's Image: a Legal Lure?' [1994] *Ent LR* 163, 169.

[89]   ibid.

'most distinctive elements of [the plaintiff's] personality: a woollen cap and a pair of small round glasses'.[90] In contrast, an Italian commentator on this case notes (with apparent approval) that the plaintiff 'had worn and still wore these accessories constantly and not occasionally, just to mark his personal identity, enriching it with *something peculiar* to be used as a recall of his features'.[91] A similar outcome can be found in a Canadian case where a line drawing of an unidentifiable water skier was held to infringe the plaintiff's exclusive right to market his personality. Although the line drawing did not identify any individual, the drawing showed a water skier in a distinctive pose and was very similar to a photographic image used by the plaintiff. It was therefore sufficient to give rise to the infringement.[92]

Vaver lends support to this wider interpretation, by noting that ' "[l]ikeness" cannot mean merely a person's unadorned or nude appearance; a person's characteristic dress may be as much a part of his personality as his face'.[93] Consequently, even where the individual cannot be identified in person but only from surrounding factors, such as the individual's clothes or accessories, there is sufficient identification to constitute use of the individual's image.[94] Vaver in fact returns to the idea of identification and recognition, which is present in both the Civilian and American interpretations of identity.[95] He extends the scope of protection to any aspect of the individual which can identify the individual in the minds of the public:

> Betty Grable's legs were at least as valuable an asset to her as her face, and at least as recognizable by the crowds who flocked to see her movies... There should be no a priori exclusion even of a person's big toe if such has become sufficiently known as constituting part of his likeness.[96]

Recognisability and identification are therefore central aspects of exploitation of the individual. This leads to the possibility that the exploitation in fact relies on *reputation*: the fact that the individual can be recognised and identified by the public at large requires that individual to have a public status, or reputation. Support for the importance of reputation can also be derived from the fact that most of the claimants are famous. This notion of recognisability, deriving from reputation, will be considered in the following section.

---

[90] As discussed by S Martuccelli, 'An Up-and-Coming Right – the Right of Publicity: its Birth in Italy and its Consideration in the United States' [1993] *Ent LR* 109, 109.

[91] ibid 110, emphasis in the original.

[92] *Athans v Canadian Adventure Camps Ltd* (1977) 17 OR (2d) 425. Whether the legal basis for the judgment is sound is another matter: see criticism of it by Beverley-Smith (n 24)121–22.

[93] Vaver, 'What's Mine is not Yours' (1981) 274.

[94] ibid.

[95] As per the quotations above. See also Reiter, for example, who refers to the celebrity's 'recognition factor' which is 'both marketable and valuable': E Reiter, 'Personality and Patrimony: Comparative Perspectives on the Right to One's Image' (2001–2002) 76 *Tulane L Rev* 673, 726.

[96] Vaver (n 17) 274.

Evidence of the elements of the individual that are exploited in publicity practice can also be taken from case law.[97] In three of the paradigm cases identified above,[98] the defendants had made use of (i) image and photographs, containing personal information about the subjects, in the case of *Douglas*; (ii) image, without name, in *Irvine*; and (iii) image and band name (ABBA) in *Lyngstad*. Turning to other cases, we can see a broad similarity in the subject matter in question. In Scotland, the name of an inventor of a new type of plough was used in advertising for ploughs designed and manufactured by the defender, and the Court allowed the pursuer's claim for interdict to stop this use.[99] In England, a claim for unauthorised use of the nick-name of a popular children's broadcaster, 'Uncle Mac', was rejected, because there was no common field of activity between the parties (radio broadcasting compared with breakfast cereals).[100] American cases cover the same indicia featured in the above cases—name, image, reputation—but have also introduced some more exotic indicia. Plaintiffs in the United States have raised actions for use of a catchphrase,[101] sound-alikes,[102] and even a robotic look-alike.[103]

In addition to these elements of image and indicia, there is evidence from publicity practice and from case law which indicates that in some cases, private information has also been used and exploited. This is most obviously the case in the media information use. The photographs of the Douglases' wedding, for example, were important not just because they contained the image of the Douglases, but also because they conveyed information about the wedding: what the bride and groom wore, the flowers, the venue, and so on.

The picture that emerges is of the use of photographs and images, names and nick-names, sound-alikes and look-alikes. In some cases, these images and indicia will convey otherwise private, personal information. Typically, the key element appears to be use of image, followed by name. However, all these cases are linked by an underlying value. The focus on image and indicia and information is very much a physicalist approach: it considers *what* was physically used or exploited in the media information, promotion and merchandising uses. It is possible, and indeed necessary, to take a different approach, which asks *why* the image of one person is worth £1 million while the image of another is worth nothing? What

---

[97] Whether every claim for unauthorised use has succeeded is not necessarily relevant at this stage, because all that is sought to be discerned here is a greater understanding of the subject matter of the exploitation.

[98] The fourth, *Mirage Studios v Counter-Feat Clothing* [1991] FSR 145 involved fictional characters.

[99] *Wilkie v McCulloch* 1822–1824 2S (SC) 413. Interdict granted and upheld by the First Division, on the grounds that 'although he [Wilkie] had not the exclusive privilege of making and vending these improved ploughs, yet he was entitled, at common law, to prevent any one from impressing his name on those which were not made by him, or under his authority'. (at 414.)

[100] *McCulloch v Lewis A May* (1948) 65 RPC 58.

[101] *Carson v Here's Johnny Portable Toilets Inc* 698 F 2d 831.

[102] *Midler v Ford Motor Company* 849 F 2d. 460 (9th Cir 1988).

[103] *White v Samsung Electronic America Inc* 971 F.2d 1395 (9th Cir 1992).

effects this value transformation? The following section will explore the underlying value which is arguably the unifying element in the majority of instances of publicity exploitation.

B. The Underlying Element: Reputation

There is plenty of evidence that the identity of, and personal information about, individuals is valuable. However, it is arguable that image, indicia and information are important because they can be *identified* with a particular individual. Out of the many women who gave birth to twins in February 2008, only one was allegedly offered $6 million by People Magazine for the first pictures of the twins.[104] It can therefore be suggested that it is not the photograph of twins which is worth $6 million to People Magazine, but the fact that the mother of the twins in this instance was Jennifer Lopez. Her celebrity status is what endowed the baby photographs with their interest to the media and the public, and which generated a price tag far beyond the typical media response (or lack thereof). Lord Nicholls referred to this idea in his opinion in *Douglas v Hello!*: 'The identity of this couple made their wedding an eminently newsworthy event.'[105] Presumably other couples were married in New York on the weekend of 18 November 2000, but only Michael Douglas and Catherine Zeta Jones licensed use of their wedding photographs for £1 million.

In addition to these examples of media information use, the importance of identity, and recognisability, can also be seen in the promotion and merchandising fields. The reason that David Beckham was used by Police to promote sunglasses in preference to using a model is because the (majority of the) public recognise David Beckham and associate his fame and success with the product in question:

> We identify with and buy into celebrities for the same reasons we buy into brands. They add colour and excitement to our life. They provide a promise or a reassurance of a particular experience. We admire what they do, how they look or what they represent. They offer a shared frame of reference that enables us to bond with other people.[106]

The colour and excitement and the shared frame of reference come not solely from image or indicia or information, but from the underlying reputation and fame: the 'celebrity aura is a potent force'.[107] This is not the case with less- or non-famous individuals. As Holyoak notes, 'the world is not crying out for Jon

---

[104] http://news.bbc.co.uk/1/hi/entertainment/7272956.stm.
[105] *Douglas v Hello!* [2008] 1 AC 1 [253] (Lord Nicholls).
[106] Milligan, *Brand it Like Beckham* (2004) 31. This echoes the message which is drawn out time and again in the works of Madow and Coombe, amongst others: Madow, 'Private Ownership of Public Image' (1993); Coombe, *The Cultural Life of Intellectual Properties* (1998) ch 2.
[107] Coombe (n 79) 92. Coombe defines 'celebrity image' as those elements which constitute the celebrity's 'recognition value' ibid 89 fn 5.

Holyoak sweatshirts now nor, it seems likely, in the future'.[108] Absent a reputation which makes Holyoak readily identifiable by the wider public, there is little demand for use of his image.

The underlying element which apparently creates the value and the attractiveness of a celebrity image is the recognisability of the individual, and this stems from the individual's reputation.[109] On this analysis, Beckham's reputation becomes the core element which attracted Police or Pepsi, just as Lopez's reputation attracts People magazine and its chequebook. The role played by reputation, or celebrity, popularity, fame, notoriety, glamour or goodwill, in publicity exploitation thus requires further examination: to what extent is reputation essential to the exploitation, or is it simply one factor of many?

Given that the cases discussed in section II. C. above all involved celebrities, it is reasonable to speculate that this fame has been the primary attraction for any third party exploiter. If so, then the subject of the use and exploitation could be the individual's reputation rather than, or in addition to, the individual's image or indicia or personal information.

Support for this arises from reliance by claimants in England upon passing off to recover for unauthorised publicity exploitation. Passing off is founded upon the reputation and goodwill of the claimant: Irvine's case against Talksport succeeded because, in the words of Laddie J, 'Mr Irvine has a property right in his goodwill which he can protect from unlicensed appropriation consisting of a false claim or suggestion of endorsement of a third party's goods or business'.[110] Irvine's recovery was thus not based upon unauthorised use of his image alone. In fact, Irvine only objected to the doctored image of him which created a false impression of endorsement: no action was pursued against Talksport for its use of the other (unaltered) image of him on the winner's podium. Rather, an essential element of Irvine's claim was to demonstrate that he had goodwill in himself, which had been exploited through use of a falsified image.[111]

It is possible, however, to question the weight that can be attached to this example. A central factor in such litigation is likely to be the claimant's need to fit his *commercial or personal* grievance within an existing *legal* cause of action. Irvine's case relied on establishing that he had reputation and goodwill which he controlled and exploited in a series of other deals. But this emphasis on reputation and goodwill would have been driven by the requirements of the tort of passing off and can therefore be seen as a tactical and expedient approach. Passing off requires the claimant to prove the existence and appropriation of the

---

[108] Holyoak, 'United Kingdom Character Rights' [1993], 456.

[109] At this stage it is sufficient to note that it is recognisability which is important, rather than whether the reputation or association is good or bad.

[110] *Irvine v Talksport Ltd* [2002] 1 WLR 2355 [75] (Laddie J).

[111] The centrality of the doctored image in this case reflects Carty's point that passing off 'remains a tort of misrepresentation, not misappropriation *per se*'. Carty (n 4), para 7.2.3. It was the lack of misrepresentation that defeated a claim for unauthorised use of image by the Spice Girls, in *Panini SpA v Halliwell*, discussed by Carty (n 4) para 7.2.4.

claimant's goodwill, rather than 'image': Irvine's case focused on goodwill rather than image. Arguably, the importance of goodwill in this case tells us no more than that a claimant needs to demonstrate goodwill to prove a claim of passing off.

Further, under this analysis, image or indicia are important because of the relationship between physical identity and intangible reputation. It does not make sense to exploit 'reputation' in the abstract. Like goodwill, reputation is intangible, and must be represented in some tangible form. If I wish to take advantage of David Beckham's reputation, I *must* use some tangible representation of it, such as his name, signature or image. The image or identity exploited in each case can be seen as the physical manifestation of the reputation.

Logeais explores this point in her review of French case law. She recognises that 'the image is protected because it is the closest reflection or personification of the person's fame achieved either because of artistic or professional skill or holding of positions entailing public exposure'.[112] She expresses uncertainty, however, as to whether image is protected in order to protect the underlying fame or to recognise the 'efforts or personal or professional achievements which resulted in fame'.[113] However, since fame does not always result from personal or professional achievements ('accidental' heroes being one example), yet the French right still exists, it is perhaps the fame which is the underlying protected interest. In any event, the method of achieving this protection is through the individual's image or identity, which is the tangible representation of the underlying fame. Image and reputation are therefore inter-dependent and mutually reinforcing.

The majority of examples of exploitation have featured celebrities with a reputation to exploit, and will presumably continue to do so. Reputation is undoubtedly the magical ingredient which attracts the attention, and the fees, in the first place. Accordingly, reputation can be seen as the underlying element which is exploited through use of the individual's image or other indicia, together in some cases with personal information about the individual. This is the case even where the reputation is negative.[114] One curious development arose from the use of Woody Allen's image by American Apparel on advertising posters, without consent. When Allen sued for $10 million in damages, American Apparel responded by saying he had no reputation left to damage and that 'Woody Allen overestimates the value of his image… corporate America's desire to have Woody

---

[112] Logeais, 'The French Right to One's Image' (1994) 168.

[113] ibid.

[114] One example is the advertisement that Ryanair chose to run, featuring a picture of Major Charles Ingram, who was found guilty of conspiring to cheat the television programme on 'Who Wants to be a Millionaire?'. Despite his notoriety at the time, Ryanair used this to its advantage in its advertisement. A slightly different example of the marketability of negative press is provided by Kate Moss, whose reputation was tarnished when photographs of her using cocaine appeared in the press, and she subsequently lost a number of high profile modelling contracts. Since then, however, her career has revived, with significant deals with Topshop, for example: http://news.bbc.co.uk/1/hi/business/5363414.stm. Whether Tiger Woods' marketability will experience a similar revival in the wake of the revelations in 2009–10 about his personal life remains to be seen.

Allen endorse their product is not what he may believe it is'[115]—a defence which seems somewhat at odds with their desire to use his image to promote their goods in the first place. At any rate, while there is a clear difference between a positive reputation and a negative or tarnished one, both may operate to bring the individual (and, of course, the goods or services in question) to the public's attention.

Yet there are, as ever, exceptions. A number of cases, primarily from North America, suggest that it is not always reputation which is the underlying attraction. These cases involved unknown individuals who were used to advertise products, as in *Roberson v Rochester Folding Box Co*[116] and *Pavesich v New England Life Insurance Co*,[117] or simply pictured in a magazine, as in *Aubry v Editions Vice-Versa*.[118] Only the image was exploited, without name or reputation, presumably because, as non-famous individuals, use of name would be meaningless, and there was no evidence of a pre-existing reputation. A distinction can therefore be drawn between cases which use an individual's image or indicia, together with the benefit of reputation and those cases which simply rely on the indicia, typically image rather than name. Despite this lack of fame or notoriety, the claimants in two of these cases were successful, while the claimant in *Roberson* lost by a majority decision of 4–3 and was probably the inspiration for the privacy legislation which was enacted shortly thereafter, and which 'aimed quite directly at the facts of the *Roberson* case'.[119] As Goodenough notes, '[o]therwise anonymous people can provide images of value to wrap around products and services to draw attention and good associations to them'.[120]

However, the successful actions were based on privacy in *Pavesich*,[121] and on the constitutionally-protected human right of privacy in one's image in *Aubry*.[122] This suggests that unauthorised exploitation of an individual's image can be prevented without the need to show an established reputation in some jurisdictions. Where such protection is afforded, however, it typically arises from privacy, rather than a publicity rights action.

Without an underlying reputation or public status, the use of the private individual is arguably no different from use of a model. Madow recognises this where he argues that

---

[115] See www.out-law.com/page-9961.
[116] *Roberson v Rochester Folding Box Co* 171 NY 538 (1902).
[117] *Pavesich v New England Life Insurance Co* 50 SE 68 (1905).
[118] *Aubry v Editions Vice-Versa* (1998) 78 CPR (3d) 289.
[119] O Goodenough, 'The Price of Fame: The Development of the Right of Publicity in the United States: Part 1' [1992] *EIPR* 55, 58.
[120] Goodenough (n 14) 41. An example of such an advertisement is included in Appendix 1.
[121] *Pavesich* 50 SE 68 (1905).
[122] *Aubry* (1998) 1 SCR 591. See also Beverley-Smith (n 24) 225; Beverley-Smith et al (n 34) 51–52; and Goodenough, 'The Price of Fame, Part 1' (1992) 57–58.

it is only because star images are sources and bearers of *meaning* that they have the power to 'sell' commodities with which they are associated. Their economic value… derives from their *semiotic* power – their power to carry and provoke meanings.[123]

Individuals without a public reputation, such as agency models, are not able to provide additional meaning to a promotion use, for example. Thus, where Roberson and Pavesich were used to advertise flour and insurance, the companies in question were not attempting to trade on their reputation or recognisability in the public mind: all that was being exploited was the image of the individual, without any sub-text. In this way, Roberson and Pavesich were effectively non-professional models, whose images were used without their consent. Further support for this analysis comes from Reiter, who refers to a case where

> a young man was unknowingly photographed during a gathering in a public park and the image was used to advertise beer. The plaintiff claimed substantial sums for moral prejudice and unjust enrichment, because the brewery profited through the use of his image. The court granted modest awards for the violations to his privacy and reputation, but on the unjust enrichment claim, awarded only the small amount the brewery would have had to pay to procure a similar photo from an image bank.[124]

The quantification of the commercial element for this non-famous claimant was based on a quasi-modelling fee, not on the value of his 'identity' to the brewery.

The problem with this analysis, which places the emphasis on the exploitation of fame and reputation, rather than image and indicia, is that it would risk precluding non-famous individuals from the scope of any available legal remedy enjoyed by their famous counterparts. Whereas all individuals have an image and indicia, only the well-known have a 'reputation'. Accordingly, private individuals would have to rely primarily on privacy-based remedies to seek redress for the unsought public exposure they have endured.

Yet it is not clear why famous people should enjoy an additional legal right which is denied to the majority. Although it would appear that most cases involve famous people, this is not a reason for excluding the majority of the population from such protection. Further, reputation is a variable commodity: some may have 'more' than others. Fame is not an all or nothing factor, but rather one which varies along a spectrum—and, with it, the fees that can be sought for exploitation. It is something that everyone can attempt to cultivate, and to different degrees. If fame or reputation is central to publicity, we are faced with a definitional problem in delineating 'fame', as regards both the necessary quantity and quality. These observations make it difficult to determine, without more,

---

[123] Madow (n 13) 185. Madow uses this to argue against a right of publicity, since the value is created by public awareness, not by the celebrity, and the celebrity does not 'deserve' the value in his or her image. Madow's arguments against justifications for a publicity right will be considered in detail in chapter five.

[124] Reiter, 'Personality and Patrimony' (2001–2002) 701.

whether a publicity right should arise only for celebrities or for all individuals. This point will be considered in greater detail in chapter eight.

Regardless of the ideological arguments for and against reputation as an essential element in any legal right, it certainly appears to play a pivotal role in publicity practice. Indeed, reputation and exploitation are bound up in a symbiotic relationship, whereby the publicity exploitation feeds and develops the reputation which is then increasingly valuable and desirable for future exploitation. Image, indicia and information can be seen as the physical manifestation of the individual's fame—or notoriety. Since reputation cannot be exploited without some physical representation, image, indicia and information[125] still have an important role to play.

IV. Analysis of Contracts for Publicity Exploitation

Whereas the above review has drawn on case law and literature to produce a clearer understanding of use and subject matter, there is a third source of insight to publicity exploitation. Commercial contracts between the individual and the publisher, promoter or merchandiser for exploitation of the individual's identity can provide a valuable understanding of the interests of both parties. What is particularly helpful here is that the focus shifts from unauthorised to authorised use. In contrast to case law, which typically arises from use made without the consent of the individual in question, commercial contracts for exploitation involve authorised use of the individual's identity.

One obstacle to the study of such contracts is that they are usually a private matter between the contracting parties. However, it is possible to derive some details of these contracts from other sources. First, law reports of those cases involving *unauthorised* exploitation often reveal valuable details of *authorised* contracts because, all too often, unauthorised use will be made against a background of controlled, authorised exploitation. Thus in *Douglas v Hello!*, details were discussed in court of the contract between the Douglases and OK! for authorised exploitation.[126] Similarly, in *Irvine v Talksport*, the focus was on Talksport's unauthorised use, but the High Court and the Court of Appeal set out in some detail contracts between Irvine and other parties, including the F1 team for which he raced, Ferrari, for exploitation of his image and indicia.[127] A second source of information is a *pro forma* 'Personality Rights Agreement' prepared by a Scottish commercial law firm, for use by sports clubs and their players. Third,

---

[125] Albeit information appears to play a more prevalent role in the media information use than it does in relation to promotion or merchandising.

[126] The most detailed discussion of the contract was in the Court of Appeal's decision: the House of Lords referred to the contract but not with such thoroughness.

[127] *Irvine v Talksport* [2002] 2 All ER 414 in the High Court and [2003] 2 All ER 881 in the Court of Appeal.

evidence of such authorised deals can be drawn from the work of other academics in this area and from the media.

Turning first to the details that can be derived from *Douglas v Hello!*, the discussion by the Court of Appeal of the contract between the Douglases and OK! was extensive. Clause 2 of that contract apparently stipulated that OK! was to have the exclusive right to publish the 'Photographs' for a period of nine months following the wedding.[128] Clause 6 defined the 'Photographs' as colour photographs taken by a photographer at the Douglases' wedding and clause 7 ensured that only pictures approved by the Douglases would be published by OK!.[129] The photographs were not the only subject of the contract, as clauses 4 and 5 authorised OK! to use, for the nine-month period, the names, voices, signatures, photographs or likenesses of the Douglases *in connection with the wedding for advertising purposes.*[130] The contract repeatedly refers to the subject matter being the wedding photographs and restricts the grant of other elements of image and indicia to use in connection with the wedding. The focus of this relationship was clearly the event of the Douglases' wedding, rather than the Douglases per se.

The second source is the *pro forma* 'Personality Rights Agreement' which takes the form of a licence to the Club from the contracting player (by way of the company incorporated to manage the player's intellectual property rights, as defined). It is envisaged in the *pro forma* that the player will also have a separate service agreement with the Club for the player's sporting services, but this remains unseen. The subject matter of the licence is very widely defined to cover (i) the player's name, likeness and image; (ii) photographs, recording, film, video footage and graphical images of the player; and (iii) any other information or images relating to the player, together with any intellectual property rights that exist in each of these categories. It is not immediately obvious from this definition whether the subject matter is connected to a particular event, as with the Douglases' wedding, or a particular product, as with some of Irvine's promotion deals. The focus of the agreement can in fact be discerned from the scope of the licence granted to the Club rather than the definition of the subject matter. This licence is exclusive and perpetual in relation to the player's Club activities and the player's provision of services to the Club, such as appearing in team kit. In relation to any non-Club activities, the licence is non-exclusive and of limited duration.

While the subject matter to be exploited by OK! and the Club are similar—name, image and photographs—the scope of the two agreements is radically different. OK! benefited from an exclusive deal in relation only to the wedding photographs, and to material necessary to promote these photographs. This deal expired after nine months. The Club, however, is granted what amounts almost to

---

[128]   *Douglas v Hello!*, [2006] QB 125 [5].
[129]   ibid [6] and [7].
[130]   ibid [131].

an assignation: a perpetual, exclusive licence, which survives termination of the contract, in relation to images of the player in the team kit or the player performing duties under the service agreement.[131] This means that the player has no right to control the use of his or her image when the player is wearing the team kit or playing for the Club. As the term of this licence is stated to be perpetual, a calendar produced by the Club in future decades, featuring notable players from the Club's history, could feature a photograph of the player in the team kit, entirely at the option of the Club, with no reference to the (potentially now elderly or deceased) player or the player's surviving family. In other matters, outwith the parameters of the player's sporting career, the Club benefits from a non-exclusive licence which terminates when the player's service agreement terminates. Evidence from *Irvine v Talksport* suggests that Irvine's agreement with Ferrari was on broadly similar terms to the Club *pro forma*. For example, Laddie J's judgment refers to Irvine's contract with Ferrari which stipulated that Irvine 'could not appear in the distinctive Ferrari red clothing in an endorsement save where that endorsement was through and on behalf of Ferrari'.[132] Even when not wearing his racing colours, Irvine stated that 'I would always obtain the consent of the team I drove for in respect of any such endorsements or sponsorships.'[133] These restrictions mirror those imposed on the player by the Club *pro forma*.

The impression given by the Club *pro forma* and the brief insight we have into Irvine's relationship with Ferrari is of a highly restrictive and controlling sporting body and a player or driver who has little bargaining power. This marks a powerful contrast to the terms of the Douglases' deal with OK!, which allowed the Douglases to have full control over the photographs and text published, and even to refuse to provide any wedding photographs at all. Evidence from the Court of Appeal judgment in *Irvine v Talksport* does, however, suggest that these ongoing obligations are not as restrictive in practice as they might appear on paper: Irvine had a number of independent, non-Ferrari related promotion deals in 1999, worth at least £323,000.[134] Even if the contract with Ferrari was restrictive, it did not appear to preclude the addition of a considerable sum to his income through other deals. In fact, it is arguably thanks to this relationship with Ferrari, and his skill as a racing driver, that Irvine was able to attract additional promotion deals at all. As with most publicity deals, both parties stand to benefit from the arrangement.

Little is revealed of Irvine's other authorised promotion deals, but the Court of Appeal judgment does give some indication of what was provided by Irvine for his fee in each case. For example, his deal with Hilfiger, worth £125,000 in fees and free products, permitted 'images of Mr Irvine to be used in advertising the

---

[131] It is, however, still only a licence: a perpetual and exclusive licence may be a powerful grant to the Club, but it does not equate to a full assignation.

[132] *Irvine v Talksport* [2002] 1 WLR 2355 [75].

[133] ibid [49].

[134] *Irvine v Talksport* [2003] 2 All ER 881 [53]–[58].

product and for him to make personal appearances'.[135] For a mere £25,000, plus £63,000 of free products, Irvine agreed to 'supply an image for promotional purposes and to wear the product', the Bieffe racing helmets. In addition, a fee of £75,000 bought Valleverde footwear 'an image of Mr Irvine to be used for print advertising, a personal appearance at a promotion, and an appearance in a television commercial in Italy'.[136] The focus in these brand-specific deals is on the use of Irvine's image, together with an element of personal endorsement to promote the product.

All the contracts reviewed appear to include provision for much the same subject matter: elements of identity—name, likeness and image—together with information, photographs, footage or personal appearances. It is difficult to isolate one factor in any contract which operated as the key focus of the deal. This is in contrast to the paradigm cases of unauthorised exploitation discussed in section II. C. above, where the focus was very often on one element—name or image, for example. Thus, in *Irvine v Talksport*, as noted, the use of a (doctored) photograph of Eddie Irvine was the subject of the action: there was no use of his name or any personal information or signature, for example. So too with *Douglas v Hello!* where Hello!'s unauthorised exploitation was of specific wedding photographs containing personal information, in contrast with the extensive subject matter granted to OK!, which included the names, voices, signatures, photographs or likenesses of the Douglases, as well as their wedding photographs.

Part of the reason for the extensive grants made under these authorised deals, compared with the apparently more restricted scope of image used in unauthorised exploitation, may arise from the legal and commercial uncertainty surrounding this area of commercial practice. This leads to two related conclusions. As regards the agreements for authorised use, a cautious solicitor is likely to draft the terms of the licence as widely as possible, reflecting the fact that it is not certain how one successfully licenses name, image and reputation. Interestingly, despite the conclusion in section III. B. above regarding the importance of reputation in most cases of commercial exploitation, none of the licences considered here was explicitly for use of reputation. This does not mean that reputation is *not* the underlying right that the parties are keen to exploit, but it does indicate that commercial practitioners do not wish to attempt to define it or explicitly trade in it. It is difficult to know how much significance to attach to its absence, but it is certainly worth noting. It is probably not possible to determine precisely the subject matter as being *either* reputation *or* image/indicia/information, and there is certainly no reason to think that parties would limit their licence to one or the other, even if this were possible. It is therefore not entirely surprising that contracts for authorised exploitation are drafted in such wide terms. Further, it is

---

[135] ibid [55].
[136] ibid [57].

difficult to determine how reputation could be licensed without making reference to the tangible elements representative of that reputation, such as name and image.

The second conclusion to be drawn relates to the much narrower scope of the subject matter in cases of unauthorised exploitation. Here, uncertainty over litigation for unauthorised use suggests that claimants are likely to frame their claim more narrowly, in terms of existing actions, rather than casting the net too widely, thereby risking an unfocused and irrelevant claim. Thus, the Douglases' claim against Hello! relied on breach of confidence and accordingly focused on use of the Douglases' 'information' in the wedding photographs, rather than use of reputation and goodwill or a more general claim for use of 'image'. Since information is the constituent element of the action for breach of confidence, this is hardly surprising. Accordingly, as noted in section III. B. above, the more limited focus in litigation can be seen primarily as a tactical consideration, in fitting the facts of the case into the most appropriate cause of action.

This review demonstrates that contracts for authorised exploitation of image and indicia are too complex to be easily categorised by subject matter: it is not possible to pigeonhole them as contracts for use of name *or* image *or* information *or* reputation. Instead, the key difference between these deals arises from the use made of the subject matter. This is the primary difference between the media information deal struck by OK! for the (exclusive) right to publish the Douglases' wedding photographs and the promotion right sought by Hilfiger and others to use Irvine to endorse their goods. Further, the focus of these agreements can be distinguished, especially when the longer-term contracts between sportsman and club are considered. The Irvine/Ferrari deal and the Club *pro forma* contract revolve around an ongoing long-term relationship and involve a level of detail and control that is not required, or necessary, or even possible, in the one-off deals. In contrast, the one-off deals (such as Douglas/OK!, Irvine/Valleverde and Irvine/Bieffe) are fixed-term agreements providing the benefit of the individual to be exploited in relation to a specific event (a wedding) or a specific brand or product (Valleverde footwear, Bieffe helmets).

The complexities and uncertainties discussed above, regarding the subject matter, have been confirmed by this review of contracts for exploitation. It is not possible to reduce publicity practice to the use of one element of the individual. Instead, information, such as wedding photographs, together with name and image and indicia (perhaps including racing colours) are all important elements. Further, underlying all these constituent parts is the intangible, yet ever-present, reputation of the famous individual in question. The one distinction that can be drawn more clearly is the *use* to be made of the individual, using the tripartite classification of media information, promotion and merchandising uses.

V. Conclusion

This chapter has sought to build upon the analysis of legal responses to publicity in chapter two by assessing the practice of publicity in a commercial setting. The primary objectives of this chapter arose from the need to understand more clearly what the social and commercial practice of publicity is and how this affects the legal response to it. Chapters two and three are therefore intended to work together to provide a foundation for the rest of the work.

This review of practice relied upon evidence from case law, contracts and commentaries to develop a more structured understanding of the practical reality of exploitation of 'publicity'. From this, it has been possible to construct a coherent framework of publicity uses and to gain an understanding of the subject matter of these uses. The three uses are:

Media information use:	The use of an individual's persona in the media, usually by way of an 'exclusive' story.
Promotion use:	The use of an individual's persona to advertise or endorse or otherwise promote the goods or services of another party.
Merchandising use:	The use of an individual's persona on goods, where the individual effectively becomes the product his or herself, whether as a pure representation (such as a poster) or a utilitarian item (such as a t-shirt).[137]

They can be represented by the three English cases of *Douglas v Hello!*, *Irvine v Talksport*, and *Lyngstad v Anabas* respectively.

Together, the three uses can be thought of as the core of publicity practice. Any publicity right should therefore be capable of addressing the exploitation, whether authorised or not, of these three uses. A further defined term is therefore **'publicity'**, meaning the use of persona by making available to the public or any section of the public through the media information, promotion or merchandising uses, as defined above.

The subject matter is more complex. It can be thought of as the individual's persona, which can be broken down into the narrower elements of image, indicia and information. However, these can also be regarded as the physical manifestation of the underlying 'asset' which is being exploited: reputation. Without reputation, fame and public status, it is arguable that much of the publicity practice would not exist. The relevant defined terms for subject matter are:

---

[137] As per the distinction at section II. A. above.

Image:	The individual's image in any format from which the individual can be identified, such as a photograph, drawing, computer generated image, some other graphical representation, or look-alike.
Indicia:	Any element of the individual which can be used to identify the individual, whether (i) an inherent part of that individual, including but not limited to name, nickname, image and voice, including sound-alikes, or (ii) an adopted act or phrase or costume.
Information:	Personal information regarding the individual which can be divulged or not, at the individual's choosing, but which is otherwise not in the public domain (such as wedding photographs).
Reputation:	The public reputation of the individual, whether negative or positive.

Together, these elements can be thought of as an individual's **persona**—and 'persona' will be used as a defined term in the remainder of this work to refer to the individual's image, indicia, information and reputation (individually and collectively). Image is of course a fundamental part of persona, but terminology such as 'image rights' obscures the fact that exploitation will often stretch further than image, to encompass other indicia, information and reputation. Thus, the terminology of publicity rights and persona, as defined, is to be preferred.

A further distinction can be made as regards authorised and unauthorised exploitation. The use classes and the subject matter are neutral, in the sense that they are present in both authorised and unauthorised exploitation. There is no legal wrong involved in publicity use per se: instead the focus turns to whether the use is authorised or unauthorised. The media information use can just as easily be exploited by the individual through an authorised deal as it can by the unauthorised publication of the image and information by another party. So too with the promotion and merchandising uses. Cases such as *Douglas v Hello!* demonstrate this very neatly, with a contract for authorised use between the Douglases and OK! sitting alongside the litigation against Hello! for unauthorised use. The authorised use can be regarded as a *positive power* of the individual to control and exploit, while the individual's legal right to prevent or claim for unauthorised use can be thought of as a *negative right*. The positive/negative distinction is therefore a critical one to make. Together, the use classification and the positive/negative classification provide a clearer framework in which to locate this study.

4

Privacy as a Basis for Protecting Publicity Rights

I. Introduction

THE CLOSE RELATIONSHIP between privacy and publicity has already been highlighted in previous chapters, most notably chapter two. While accepting that they are 'distinct in some respects', Waelde and Whitty assert that privacy and publicity are 'fundamentally two sides of the same coin, namely, the right to prevent and to control the dissemination of one's image'.[1] Cornish and Llewellyn have suggested, less flatteringly, that publicity is privacy's 'underbelly',[2] its key trait being the exploitation, by waiver or licence, of personal information and identity (ie persona) which could otherwise be kept private, at the option of the individual. While 'all but the most unremittingly secretive can be induced to reveal home truths at some price'[3], it is also true that commercial organisations are prepared to exploit these same home truths and to pay the price to do so. For the right fee, privacy can give way to publicity.

Nonetheless, it was noted in chapter two that where the only legal rights available to the well-known personality look to his or her privacy interests, the personality is unlikely to achieve the legal protection he or she seeks.[4] In jurisdictions where publicity rights exist as independent rights, those rights often started out as privacy rights.[5] Although this indicates the closeness between the

---

[1] C Waelde and N Whitty, 'A Rights of Personality Database' in N Whitty and R Zimmermann (eds), *Rights of Personality in Scots Law: A Comparative Perspective* (Dundee, Dundee University Press, 2009) para 11.4.5; *contra* H Carty, 'Advertising, Publicity Rights and English law' [2004] *IPQ* 209, 212–15.

[2] Cornish and Llewelyn, *Intellectual Property: Patents, Copyright, Trade Marks and Allied Rights*, 6th edn (London, Sweet & Maxwell, 2007) para 9–04.

[3] ibid para 9–04.

[4] See for example Nimmer, 'The Right of Publicity' (1954) 19 *Law & Contemp Probs* 203.

[5] See Madow's account of it, and his view that publicity arose from frustration with privacy rights: M Madow, 'Private Ownership of Public Image: Popular Culture and Publicity Rights' (1993) 81 *Cal L Rev* 125, 167.

two, it also suggests that publicity exploitation requires different treatment from privacy, since it has evolved into a separate right.

So, it is accurate or appropriate to categorise publicity as a subset, or the progeny, of privacy? In order to determine if publicity is a type of privacy, it is necessary to identify the core elements of privacy protection (here in a jurisdiction-specific context), and then to compare privacy with the practice of publicity identified in chapters two and three.

Privacy in the United Kingdom is a complex and evolving area.[6] The Human Rights Act 1998 has had a profound impact on jurisprudence, and there are many (many) academic commentaries on these developments.[7] It is not proposed to repeat them here, but instead to provide a brief outline of privacy in the United Kingdom to enable to a comparison between privacy and publicity.

II. The Right to Privacy in the UK

A. Introduction

Cornish and Llewelyn define privacy as 'the desire of an individual to be free of intrusion'.[8] This echoes the basis of privacy as expressed by MacCormick, who additionally notes the importance of *control* of privacy to the individual:

---

[6] It has recently been judicially noted that 'the last word' has yet to be said on privacy, at least in the context of civil liberties in the modern surveillance society: *Wood v Commissioner of Police for the Metropolis* [2009] EWCA Civ 414 [para] 100 (Collins LJ).

[7] Highlights include: A Kenyon and M Richardson (eds), *New Dimensions in Privacy Law* (Cambridge, Cambridge University Press, 2006); HL MacQueen, 'A Hitchhiker's Guide to Personality Rights in Scots Law, Mainly with Regard to Privacy' in N Whitty and R Zimmermann (eds), *Rights of Personality in Scots Law: A Comparative Perspective* (Dundee, Dundee University Press, 2009); NA Moreham, 'The Right to Respect for Private Life in the European Convention on Human Rights: a Re-Examination' [2008] *EHRLR* 44; NA Moreham, 'Privacy in Public Places' (2006) 65 *CLJ* 606; NA Moreham, 'Privacy and Horizontality: Relegating the Common Law' (2007) 123 *LQR* 373; R Mulheron, 'A Potential Framework for Privacy? A Reply to *Hello!*' (2006) 69 *MLR* 679; T Aplin, 'The Development of the Action for Breach of Confidence in a Post-HRA Era' [2007] *IPQ* 19; H Delany and C Murphy, 'Towards Common Principles Relating to the Protection of Privacy Rights? An Analysis of Recent Developments in England and France and before the European Court of Human Rights' [2007] *EHRLR* 568; G Phillipson and H Fenwick, 'Breach of Confidence as a Privacy Remedy in the Human Rights Act Era' (2000) 63 *MLR* 660; Gavin Phillipson, 'Transforming Breach of Confidence? Towards a Common Law Right of Privacy under the Human Rights Act' (2003) 66 *MLR* 726; H Fenwick and G Phillipson, *Media Freedom under the Human Rights Act* (Oxford, Oxford University Press, 2006); C Michalos, '*Douglas v Hello*: The Final Frontier' [2007] *Ent LR* 241; C Michalos, 'Image Rights and Privacy: After *Douglas v Hello!*' [2005] *EIPR* 384; J Morgan, 'Privacy, Confidence and Horizontal Effect: "Hello" Trouble' (2003) 62 *CLJ* 444. Wacks laments that the 'voluminous literature... has failed to produce a coherent or consistent meaning' of the notion of privacy: R Wacks, 'Why There Will Never be an English Common Law Privacy Tort' in A Kenyon and M Richardson (eds), *New Dimensions in Privacy Law* (Cambridge, Cambridge University Press, 2006) 175.

[8] Cornish and Llewelyn, *Intellectual Property* (2007) para 9–01.

some kind of desire for seclusion… This desire for seclusion should not be construed in all cases as a desire to exclude all other human beings from one's life or some aspect of it; rather it is a desire to have the last say on which other human beings will be brought within the circle of one's seclusion for certain purposes.[9]

While this may be the conceptual basis of privacy, it does not address how that desire is to be achieved in law.[10]

As recently as 1983, Frazer could state that, in law, the 'concept of "privacy" is so subjective that there is substantial disagreement among writers as to its nature and scope'.[11] While there is still no specific tort of privacy,[12] consequently forcing Scots and English law to protect such interests 'in a piecemeal fashion in several disparate areas',[13] it would nevertheless be fair to say that the law has moved on considerably since 1983. Privacy in the United Kingdom, although still evolving, owes its current existence to the European Convention on Human Rights (ECHR) and to the Human Rights Act 1998.[14] Article 8 of the ECHR provides that '[e]veryone has the right to respect for his private and family life, his home and his correspondence'.[15] It is this which offers individuals the right to prevent, or subsequently recover for, an invasion of their privacy. However, the scope of article 8 is far wider than the particular application of it to be considered here: the focus in the following analysis will be restricted to protecting informational privacy.[16]

---

[9] N MacCormick, *Legal Right and Social Democracy* (Oxford, Clarendon Press, 1982, reprinted 1986) 175.

[10] Moreham also draws this distinction between the theoretical desire underlying privacy and the objective standard applied in law: see Moreham, 'Privacy in Public Places' (2006) 617.

[11] T Frazer, 'Appropriation of Personality – a New Tort?' (1983) 99 *LQR* 281, 295. This level of disagreement reflects MacCormick's comment about the consequent need for achieving certainty through 'intelligent legislation': see chapter one, text at n 8.

[12] And never will be at common law, according to Wacks, in part because of the 'notorious judicial inertia in this field': R Wacks Why There Will Never be an English Common Law Privacy Tort' (2006) 155. See also *Wainwright v Home Office* [2004] 2 AC 406 [51] and [52] (Lord Hoffmann).

[13] Beverley-Smith et al, *Privacy, Property and Personality* (Cambridge, Cambridge University Press, 2005) 77. These areas include data protection, the Protection from Harassment Act 1997, defamation and breach of confidence, amongst others. See also HL MacQueen, 'A Hitchhiker's Guide to Personality Rights in Scots Law, Mainly with Regard to Privacy' (2009). Note, however, that the disparate areas may differ north and south of the border: N Whitty, 'Overview of Rights of Personality in Scots Law' in N Whitty and R Zimmermann (eds), *Rights of Personality in Scots Law, a Comparative Perspective* (Dundee, Dundee University Press, 2009) paras 3.4.5–3.4.7.

[14] This came into force in the UK on 2 October 2000: helpfully, this was just in time for the Douglases, whose wedding took place the following month (18 November 2000).

[15] Convention for the Protection of Human Rights and Fundamental Freedoms, Rome, 4.XI.1950 article 8(1).

[16] Thus, other potential privacy infringements—for example by way of strip searching or state surveillance—will not be directly relevant.

B. Breach of Confidence

The problem originally facing claimants in privacy actions was how to introduce article 8 into court in the absence of direct horizontal effect[17] or a specific action for privacy. The answer, in most cases, was to rely on the doctrine of breach of confidence. Restated by Lord Goff in the *Attorney-General v Guardian Newspapers* (No 2) (*Spycatcher*) case[18] in 1990, it has since taken some interesting turns as lawyers have made it the most likely vessel for introducing privacy concerns of this nature in court. By 2004 the House of Lords was able to state (at least in relation to English law) that in privacy cases the action for breach of confidence 'has now firmly shaken off the limited constraint of the need for an initial confidential relationship... The essence of the tort is better encapsulated now as *misuse of private information*.'[19]

This approach was also present in the Court of Appeal's 2005 decision in *Douglas v Hello!* where it stated: 'In so far as private information is concerned, we are required to adopt... the cause of action formerly described as breach of confidence.'[20]

This use of breach of confidence as the 'home' for informational privacy has caused considerable problems,[21] since information which is confidential is not necessarily private, and vice versa. Thus, confidential information is that which is secret, yet to 'confine the law of privacy to cases involving secrets of some kind would, however, be to ignore both the result in the *Hannover* case, and the fact

---

[17] Section 6 of the Human Rights Act 1998 restricts the application of the Act to 'public bodies'. A human rights claim cannot be raised directly against a private body, but human rights issues must be considered by the courts (which are public bodies) in any case brought before them. In any action against a private body, therefore, there must be a prior cause which enables the claim to reach court, where human rights issues can then be considered. For a brief review of the problems of horizontal application and privacy in England, see NA Moreham, 'Privacy and Horizontality: Relegating the Common Law' (2007) 123 *LQR* 373. An earlier and more detailed analysis in this field is Morgan, 'Privacy, Confidence and Horizontal Effect' (2003). There is no longer any doubt over the availability of the remedy in horizontal relationships, and this approach was underscored by Resolution 1165 of the Council of Europe (passed against the background of the death of the Princess of Wales in a car crash following pursuit by reporters) which emphasised that article 8 privacy rights should be enforceable against private persons, including the media. See para 12 of the Resolution, available at http://assembly.coe.int/Main.asp?link=/Documents/AdoptedText/ta98/ERES1165.htm; and HL Mac-Queen (n 7) para 12.2.1.

[18] *Attorney-General v Guardian Newspapers* (No 2) (*Spycatcher*) [1990] 1 AC 109.

[19] *Campbell v MGN* [2004] 2 AC 457 [14] (Lord Nicholls), emphasis added; also [17] where Lord Nicholls says: 'The time has come to recognise that the values enshrined in articles 8 and 10 are now part of the cause of action for breach of confidence.' See also *Murray v Big Pictures* [2008] EWCA Civ 446 [24].

[20] [2006] QB 125, para 53.

[21] Not least in relation to the scope of the action in cases of commercial confidence. See H Carty, 'An Analysis of the Modern Action for Breach of Commercial Confidence: When is Protection Merited?' [2008] *IPQ* 416.

that the privacy interest is different from the interest in preserving confidentiality'.[22] Nevertheless, since 2000, a number of individuals have relied on article 8, supported where necessary with breach of confidence, to claim against the media and other parties for invasion of their private lives, seeking either an interdict or injunction[23] or damages.[24] The European Court of Human Rights (ECtHR) has also been involved in article 8 cases, including those where the intrusion has been by way of taking or publishing personal images, such as *Peck v The United Kingdom*,[25] *von Hannover v Germany*,[26] and *Reklos v Greece*.[27]

Infringement of privacy under article 8 can now arise where the information in question is either (i) protected against an 'old-fashioned breach of confidence by way of conduct inconsistent with a pre-existing relationship',[28] as in cases such as *Spycatcher*,[29] *McKennitt v Ash*,[30] and *Mosley v News Group Newspapers Ltd*[31] or (ii) protected by virtue of its private nature, as in cases such as *Campbell v MGN*,[32] *CC v AB*,[33] and *Murray v Big Pictures*.[34] As Eady J noted in *Mosley v News Group Newspapers Ltd*, the reason the law protects information which is private even if there is no relationship of confidence is 'because the law is concerned to prevent the violation of a citizen's autonomy, dignity and self-esteem'.[35]

C. A Reasonable Expectation of Privacy

Judicial development, heavily influenced by ECtHR jurisprudence, has moved away from assessing the existence of a right of privacy based on whether or not the images or information were publicly available, and instead looks to whether the invasion was sufficiently serious and, if so, whether the individual had a

---

[22] V Jones and A Wilson, 'Photographs, Privacy and Public Places' [2007] *EIPR* 357 360. See also Michalos, '*Douglas v Hello*: The Final Frontier' (2007) 204.

[23] Actions to prevent media publication include: *CC v AB* [2006] EWHC 3083 (QB); *McKennitt v Ash* [2008] QB 73; *A v B&C* [2002] 2 All ER 545; *X v BBC* 2005 SLT 796; *Lord Browne of Madingley v Associated Newspapers Ltd* [2008] 1 QB 103; *Murray v Big Pictures* [2008] EWCA Civ 446; *LNS (John Terry) v Persons Unknown* [2010] EWHC 119 (QB).

[24] For example, *Campbell v MGN* [2004] 2 AC 457; *Mosley v News Group Newspapers Ltd* [2008] EWHC 1777 (QB).

[25] *Peck v The United Kingdom* (App no 44647/98 (28 January 2003), (2003) 36 EHRR 41.

[26] *Hannover v Germany* (App no 59320/00 (24 June 2004), (2005) 40 EHRR 1. See also *Sciacca v Italy* (App no 50774/99), (2006) 43 EHRR 20.

[27] *Reklos v Greece* (App no 1234/05) (15 April 2009), [2009] EMLR 16.

[28] *McKennitt v Ash* [2008] QB 73 [8].

[29] *Spycatcher* [1990] 1 AC 109.

[30] *McKennitt v Ash* [2008] QB 73.

[31] *Mosley v News Group Newspapers Ltd* [2008] EWHC 1777 (QB).

[32] *Campbell v MGN* [2004] 2 AC 457.

[33] *CC v AB* [2006] EWHC 3083 (QB).

[34] *Murray v Big Pictures* [2008] EWCA Civ 446.

[35] *Mosley v News Group Newspapers Ltd* [2008] EWHC 1777 (QB) [7]. See also *Wood v Commissioner of Police for the Metropolis* [2009] EWCA Civ 414 [20].

reasonable expectation of privacy.[36] As regards the severity of the intrusion, Laws LJ has argued that this is an important safeguard[37] to ensure that the article 8 right is not 'read so widely that its claims become unreal and unreasonable'.[38] Only where the invasion reaches a 'certain level of seriousness' will there be a threat to the individual's personal autonomy.[39]

In most cases, however, the focus has been on the concept of a 'reasonable expectation of privacy'. In *Peck v The United Kingdom*[40] the reproduction on television and in the press of CCTV footage of Peck carrying a knife in Brentwood was an invasion of his right to privacy.[41] The ECtHR held that Peck 'was in a public street but he was not there for the purposes of participating in a public event and he was not a public figure'.[42] The media publication of the CCTV images meant that his presence in the street 'was viewed to an extent which far exceeded any exposure to a passer-by or to security observation... and to a degree surpassing that which the applicant could possibly have foreseen'.[43] The scope of the public dissemination of these images contravened Peck's reasonable expectation of the degree of public exposure to which he would be subject. The impact of this decision can be seen in a Scottish case from 2005, *X v BBC*. Here, the Court of Session was prepared to accept that the pursuer had a stateable case in her privacy action, despite the fact that part of the information in question related to proceedings in open court.[44]

Perhaps the most important ECtHR decision on this point is *von Hannover v Germany*,[45] where photographs of Princess Caroline were taken in public, though secluded, places. Publication of these photographs, and the harassment by the paparazzi which accompanied the taking of them, constituted a breach of her article 8 right, even though the images revealed nothing of a sensitive or personal nature and had been predominantly taken in non-private spaces.

As a result of cases such as these

> [i]t is no longer possible to draw a rigid distinction between that which takes place in private and that which is capable of being witnessed in a public place by other

---

[36] For an analysis of both these points, see *Wood v Commissioner of Police for the Metropolis* [2009] EWCA Civ 414 [22]–[25] (Laws LJ). (Laws LJ delivered the dissenting judgment, but the point of disagreement with the other judges related to the application of the law to the specific facts.)

[37] He suggests it is one of three safeguards, the other two being whether there is a reasonable expectation of privacy and whether there are justifications for the invasion available to the state under article 8(2): see *Wood v Commissioner of Police for the Metropolis* [2009] EWCA Civ 414[22].

[38] ibid.

[39] ibid, with reference to Lord Bingham in *R (Gillan) v Commissioner of Police for the Metropolis* [2006] 2 AC 307, giving the example of an 'ordinary superficial search' of the person and bags at the airport.

[40] *Peck v The United Kingdom* (App no 44647/98) (28 January 2003), (2003) 35 EHRR 41.

[41] ibid.

[42] ibid [62].

[43] ibid.

[44] *X v BBC* 2005 SLT 796.

[45] *Von Hannover v Germany* (App no 59320) (24 June 2004), (2005) 40 EHRR 1.

persons… a decision excluding privacy protection simply because the claimant was in public could now be subject to challenge in Strasbourg.[46]

Recent guidance from the Press Complaints Commission echoes this conclusion, by stating that photographs should not be taken of people in private places without their consent, and it defines 'private places' as 'public or private property where there is a reasonable expectation of privacy'.[47]

Where the information in question is widely available, however, then a remedy may (but will not always) be denied on the grounds that there can be no reasonable expectation of privacy. In *Mosley*, it was held that there could be no such reasonable expectation sufficient to warrant an injunction, in respect of images which were already widely available, although this did not exclude the possibility of damages in respect of these images.[48] However, this outcome is fact-dependent, since there may well be cases where repeated publication of the private images or information may well constitute further invasions of privacy. Lord Phillips in *Douglas v Hello!* was of the view that the re-publication of images could indeed infringe the claimant's privacy:

> Insofar as a photograph does more than convey information and intrudes on privacy by enabling the viewer to focus on intimate personal detail, there will be a fresh intrusion of privacy when each additional viewer sees the photograph and even when one who has seen a previous publication of the photograph, is confronted by a fresh publication of it.[49]

Whether repeated publication will infringe an individual's reasonable expectation of privacy is therefore likely to depend on the facts of the case, particularly the extent of the previous circulation:[50] a noticeable divergence from 'pure' breach of confidence actions.[51]

Even in circumstances where the party attempting to disclose has a connection with the images or information in question, the courts have been prepared to

---

[46] Moreham (n 7) 610. See also *Hosking v Runting* [2004] NZCA 34[19].

[47] See the Press Complaints Commission's Code of Practice at article 3 and the Note thereto: www.pcc.org.uk/cop/practice.html.

[48] *Mosley v News Group Newspapers Ltd* [2008] EWHC 687 (QB). This was the (unsuccessful) action for an injunction to stop the News of the World from posting video footage of Mosley's sadomasochism (S&M) session on its website. The subsequent action by Mosley for infringement of privacy raised, amongst other issues, a different question as to loss of the right to privacy because of the extent of prior public exposure: Eady J was asked to consider the argument that 'the Claimant forfeited any expectation of privacy partly because of the numbers involved; that is to say, with so many participants [in the S&M session] it should not be regarded as private. This was coupled with reliance upon the fact that he liked to record these gatherings on video, with the consent of all those present, so as to have a "memento".' Eady J rejected this argument and upheld the claimant's privacy action, awarding damages of £60,000. *Mosley v News Group Newspapers Ltd* [2008] EWHC 1777 (QB) [109] and [236].

[49] *Douglas v Hello!* [2006] QB 125 [105]. Michalos points out that this has granted the Douglases what is in effect a permanent injunction against publication of the unauthorised images: Michalos (n 7) 245–46.

[50] See Moreham (n 7) 612 and 615–16.

[51] ibid; also Michalos (n 7).

respect the claimant's reasonable expectation of privacy and refuse the right to publish. In *CC v AB*[52] the information in dispute was highly personal, but arguably not particularly worthy of protection: the intimate relationship to be disclosed in the tabloids was adulterous. As Eady J observed, 'even an adulterous relationship may attract, at least in certain respects, a legitimate expectation of privacy'.[53] In addition, and emphasising the close links between breach of confidence and privacy in this area, the party seeking to disclose may be subject to a duty of confidentiality, even where he or she is also involved in, or part of, the information to be disclosed. Thus, in *Mosley v News Group Newspapers Ltd* a member of a sadomasochist (S&M) group was in breach of her duty of confidence to all other participants by recording and selling details of an S&M session, regardless of her wish to disclose it.[54] In the very different factual circumstances of *McKennitt v Ash*[55] there was also an 'old-fashioned breach of confidence by way of conduct inconsistent with a pre-existing relationship'.[56] Ash's claim that the information also concerned her was insufficient to overcome this obligation of confidence.[57]

A final factor is likely to be the nature of the information, with the highly personal details of Campbell's medical treatment for drug addiction and the sexual predilections of Mosley, for example, both being regarded as intimate matters which carried a high expectation of privacy. As Fenwick and Phillipson note, based on such factors of sensitivity and intimacy, the 'Article 8 interest can thus be weighted'.[58]

These cases indicate that the basis for enforcing one's article 8 privacy right is whether the individual has a reasonable expectation of privacy. This is influenced by factors such as the nature of the information, the nature of any relationship between the parties,[59] particularly whether or not a duty of confidence was

---

[52] *CC v AB* [2006] EWHC 3083 (QB).

[53] *Mosley v News Group Newspapers Ltd* [2008] EWHC 1777 (QB) [30]. In fact, the judge appeared to have considerably more sympathy for the adulterous claimant than for the defendant who sought 'revenge' and 'some financial gain' [10] and who demonstrated 'remarkable hypocrisy' [28].

[54] ibid [105]–[108]. This presumably overturns, or can be distinguished from, Ouseley J's view that prostitutes do not owe a duty of confidentiality to their clients: *Theakston v MGN Ltd* [2002] EWHC 137 (QB) [73]–[75].

[55] *McKennitt v Ash* [2008] QB 73.

[56] ibid [8].

[57] ibid [28]–[32].

[58] Fenwick and Phillipson, *Media Freedom* (2006) 779.

[59] Delany and Murphy, 'Towards Common Principles Relating to the Protection of Privacy Rights?' (2007) 580, citing *Browne v Associated Newspapers Ltd* [2008] 1 QB 103.

owed,[60] the way in which the information was obtained,[61] and the location.[62] The *Murray v Big Pictures* case also suggests that children will have a higher expectation of privacy.[63]

One element which may impact upon (albeit not necessarily negate[64]) the reasonable expectation of privacy is the prior conduct of the claimant. Where the information sought to be disclosed is intended to correct a prior lie that the claimant has propagated, the courts are likely to recognise the public interest in the publication.[65] This was the situation in *Campbell v MGN*, where the House of Lords agreed that MGN was at liberty to publish the fact that Campbell used illegal drugs, since this revelation would correct the prior misleading image created by Campbell's adoption of an anti-drugs stance. Even where there is such a justification, however, this does not entitle the publisher to disregard article 8 entirely: although the story itself was justified, the use of photographs to illustrate the *Daily Mirror's* exposé of Campbell was excessive and thus infringed her privacy.[66]

Case law over the last eight years has shown a gradual convergence of contrasting European approaches to privacy.[67] Whereas French law has traditionally afforded 'almost startlingly high levels of protection'[68] for privacy, it now gives increased recognition to the importance of the freedom of the press, influenced in part by the ECtHR. Conversely, the traditionally media-friendly approach in English law, and even the more balanced German approach to privacy, is being strengthened in favour of the private life of the individual as a result of the Strasbourg jurisprudence.[69]

---

[60]   As for example in *McKennitt v Ash* [2008] QB 73.

[61]   *Mosley v News Group Newspapers Ltd* [2008] EWHC 1777 (QB) [17] (Eady J). The covert nature of the photography in *Douglas* and *Campbell* arguably points towards the claimants' reasonable expectations of privacy. See also Moreham (n 7) 628–32.

[62]   Moreham (n 7) 621–23.

[63]   *Murray v Big Pictures* [2008] EWCA Civ 446, also *Reklos v Greece* ECtHR (App no 1234/05) (15 April 2009). Contrast the earlier decision of the New Zealand Court of Appeal in *Hosking v Runting* [2004] NZCA 34 [159], where the Court looked for evidence of a 'serious risk' to the children.

[64]   See for example the analysis by A McLean and C Mackey, 'Is there a Law of Privacy in the UK? A Consideration of Recent Legal Developments' [2007] *EIPR* 389, 393.

[65]   Gordley puts forward an interesting critique of this, suggesting that in some cases hypocrisy is preferable to the disclosure of vice: J Gordley, *Foundations of Private Law: Property, Tort, Contract, Unjust Enrichment* (Oxford, Oxford University Press, 2006) 236. This point was also made by Max Mosley in his oral evidence to the House of Commons Culture, Media and Sport Committee: 'A sensible society would not publicise the fact that a role model has done something he should not do precisely because he is a role model. It gives the wrong message to the young people.' (HC275-ii, 10 March 2009, in answer to Q145.)

[66]   Photographs may well be treated as particularly intrusive, as *Campbell* illustrates. This is echoed in *John v Associated Newspapers Ltd* [2006] EWHC 1611 (QB) [3], where the claimant only sought to restrain publication of a photograph, and not the accompanying text.

[67]   Although differences do remain. For analysis of both convergence and continuing differences see, for example, Waelde and Whitty, 'A Rights of Personality Database' (2009) para 11.8.2; Delany and Murphy (n 7).

[68]   Delany and Murphy (n 7) 569.

[69]   ibid 572–74 and 581–82.

Article 8 will therefore be engaged if there is a reasonable expectation of privacy in the images or information combined, in some cases, with a duty of confidence owed. Once article 8 is engaged, 'the next question would be how the balance should be struck as between the individual's right to privacy on the one hand and the publisher's right to publish on the other',[70] thereby taking account of the defendant's article 10 right to publish. It is thus necessary to examine the right of freedom of expression under article 10.

D. Freedom of Expression

Article 10 guarantees the right to freedom of expression, but this right is subject to 'such formalities, conditions, restrictions or penalties as are prescribed by law and are necessary in a democratic society... for the protection of the reputation or rights of others, for preventing the disclosure of information received in confidence'.[71] Thus, article 8 can operate to limit the extent of the article 10 right. Conversely, article 8 may be limited by such interference as is necessary in a democratic society, for example for the protection of the rights and freedoms of others.[72] Both rights are of equal importance, and both must recognise limitations arising from the other.[73]

This legal background can be contrasted with that in America, where the First Amendment right to free speech is typically paramount at the expense of other interests: '[t]he un-balanced American approach flows from factors peculiar to that jurisdiction, namely the absolute nature of the First Amendment, and the fact that it is not balanced by any constitutional right to *informational* privacy'.[74]

Since neither article 8 nor 10 takes priority, the courts must assess the interests at stake on each occasion, and this balancing process involves

---

[70] *Murray v Big Pictures* [2008] EWCA Civ 446 [40].
[71] Convention for the Protection of Human Rights and Fundamental Freedoms, Rome, 4.XI.1950 art 10(2).
[72] ibid art 8(2).
[73] *Campbell v MGN* [2004] 2 AC 457 [113] (Lord Hope); *In re S* [2005] 1 AC 593 [17] (Lord Steyn). For commentary on this point, see Delany and Murphy (n 7) 570; MacQueen (n 7); Fenwick and Phillipson (n 7) 691.
[74] G Phillipson and H Fenwick, 'Breach of Confidence as a Privacy Remedy in the Human Rights Act Era' (2000) 63 *MLR* 660, 686. See also *Hosking v Runting* [2004] NZCA 34 [73]. *Contra* Coombe, who fears that '[w]hen "public" speech interests come up against "private" property interests, the latter almost invariably triumph, ensuring that "the law insulates vast sectors of the social hierarchy from official scrutiny and public accountability"', R Coombe, 'Author/izing the Celebrity: Publicity Rights, Postmodern Politics, and Unauthorized Genders' (1991–1992) 10 *Cardozo Arts & Ent LJ* 365, 390, fn omitted.

what is sometimes called an 'intense focus' on the facts, that is, a sensitive, nuanced and contextually specific examination of the particular factual circumstances of each case, incorporating an evaluation and attachment of weight to *both* of the competing interests.[75]

Eady J has expressly stated that broad generalisations of the kind used in the past, such as 'public figures must expect to have less privacy', are now incompatible with this process. Such 'generalisations can never be determinative. In every case 'it all depends' (i.e. upon what is revealed by the intense focus on the individual circumstances).'[76]

When carrying out this balancing exercise, however, one of the key tests is the public interest.[77] It has been observed that 'what interests the public is not necessarily in the public interest'.[78] Instead, '[t]he judge will often have to ask whether the intrusion, or perhaps the degree of the intrusion, into the claimant's privacy was proportionate to the public interest supposedly being served by it'.[79] Whether publication is in the public interest will depend on a number of factors, the first being whether the information can be said to 'contribute to any debate of general interest to society'.[80] Eady J applied this test in *Mosley*, noting that the nature of the 'public debate' prompted by the *News of the World's* publication of the S&M story in question was unlikely to be the type of public debate envisaged by the ECtHR in *von Hannover*.[81]

The public interest may also depend upon a number of specific factors, including the disclosure of criminality,[82] the need to correct lies,[83] and the nature of the use to be made of the information in order to serve the public interest. As a general rule, political speech can expect to be afforded greater weight (and therefore be more likely to be protected against competing rights by article 10)

---

[75]   Waelde and Whitty (n 1) para 11.5, emphasis in the original. The language of 'intense focus' comes from *In re S* [2005] 1 AC 593 [17] (Lord Steyn). For an analysis of this balancing process, and the divergence between the common representation of it as 'a bout between two bruisers' and the more nuanced theoretical basis, see Wacks (n 7) 169–73.

[76]   *Mosley v News Group Newspapers Ltd* [2008] EWHC 1777 [12].

[77]   Fenwick and Phillipson assert that 'the weight of any claim under article 10 should be assessed by reference to the contribution that the publication in question makes to a debate of serious public concern', Fenwick and Phillipson (n 7) 780. See also Moreham (n 7) 627; T Aplin, 'The Development of the Action for Breach of Confidence in a Post-HRA Era' [2007] *IPQ* 19, 44–51.

[78]   *McKennitt v Ash* [2008] QB 73 [66]. See also *Mosley v News Group Newspapers Ltd* [2008] EWHC 1777 [114]; and *Douglas v Hello!* [2006] QB 125 [254], where the public interest is contrasted with 'public curiosity'.

[79]   *Mosley v News Group Newspapers Ltd* [2008] EWHC 1777 [14].

[80]   As formulated by the ECtHR in *Von Hannover v Germany* (App no 59320) (24 June 2004), (2005) 40 EHRR 1 [65], and see also [60], [63], [66] and [76].

[81]   *Mosley v News Group Newspapers Ltd* [2008] EWHC 1777 [132].

[82]   ibid paras 110–21.

[83]   *Campbell v MGN* [2004] 2 AC 457 [58] and also [117], where it was accepted that the public had an 'undoubted' right to know that Campbell had misled them as regards drug taking.

than that attaching to artistic expression or commercial expression.[84] However, even where such public interest factors are present, disclosure will not always be justified. In the words of Eady J:

> Would it justify installing a camera in someone's home, for example, in order to catch him or her smoking a spliff? Surely not. There must be some limits and, even in more serious cases, any such intrusion should be no more than is proportionate.[85]

Also, respecting privacy itself has been recognised to be in the public interest.[86]

Despite judicial and academic guidance on the nature and extent of the public interest, 'there continues to be a difference of opinion on the extent to which certain material, particularly relating to the private lives of celebrities, contributes to debate on matters of legitimate public concern'.[87] In all cases, the balancing test will come down to what is proportionate in the circumstances. However, recent decisions have tended to favour the individual's right of privacy at the expense of freedom of expression: 'despite the continuing theoretical presumption of equality as between the two articles, significant restrictions have been placed on the enjoyment of Art. 10 rights in order to protect a right to privacy'.[88]

E. Summary

Judicial protection of privacy in the United Kingdom can thus (currently) be said to arise under breach of confidence and article 8 in one of two ways, depending on whether the information is protected by a confidential relationship or whether it is allegedly private and the individual had a reasonable expectation of privacy. Once article 8 is engaged, the court will usually have to balance the pursuer's article 8 interests with the exceptions to article 8, including the defender's article 10 interests, to determine, on the facts of each case, which right should be protected.

The alliance of breach of confidence and article 8 has not only been used to protect against unwelcome dissemination of details of private lives. It has also featured successfully in one case which involved the *commercial* exploitation of an individual's private information: *Douglas v Hello!*. Here, the Douglases sought to use privacy rights to claim against Hello! for its unauthorised publication of

---

[84] ibid [117] (Lord Hope), where he makes reference to *Clayton and Tomlinson: The Law of Human Right*(Oxford, OUP, 2000). In a pre-*Campbell* article, Munro notes (and challenges) the position that '[i]n the Strasbourg case law, it appears that the necessity of a legitimate interference is more readily accepted when the instance of expression is categorised as commercial speech', Munro, 'The Value of Commercial Speech' (2003) 62 *CLJ* 134, 141. See also Fenwick and Phillipson (n 7) 689–90.

[85] *Mosley v News Group Newspapers Ltd* [2008] EWHC 1777 [112].

[86] ibid [130].

[87] Delany and Murphy (n 7) 574.

[88] ibid 570. Similarly, Fenwick and Phillipson refer to the current Strasbourg jurisprudence as revealing 'a strikingly restrictive view of the role of the press': Fenwick and Phillipson (n 7) 695.

their wedding photographs (that is, enforcing their negative right), while at the same time granting the right to OK! to publish photographs of the same event (that is, exploiting their positive power). This evidence of commercial exploitation of publicity on the one hand and an attempt to restrict publication on the other has led to the conclusion that *Douglas* is a publicity action masquerading as a privacy action.[89] It also reinforces the observations made earlier that there is often a close link between the two interests. Can privacy, as developed under article 8, operate to protect the publicity interests of individuals?

III. Publicity as a Privacy Right

A. Introduction

When the Douglases sought to recover from Hello! for publication of unauthorised photographs of their wedding, it was this emerging concept of privacy upon which they relied. In the words of the Court of Appeal:

> Applying the test propounded by the House of Lords in *Campbell v MGN*, photographs of the wedding plainly portrayed aspects of the Douglases' private life and fell within the protection of the law of confidentiality, as extended to cover private or personal information.[90]

Importantly, *Douglas* demonstrates the dual aspects of publicity, both of which must be examined against our understanding of privacy established above. In enforcing the *negative* right to prevent unauthorised use, what role does the current privacy action have to play? And can waiver of privacy constitute the *positive* power to exploit? Four areas will be considered below in order to determine whether the right of publicity identified in chapter three can be protected through the right of privacy.

---

[89] This is a popular claim: see for example J Phillips and A Firth, *Introduction to Intellectual Property Law*, 4th edn (London, Butterworths LexisNexis, 2001) para 20.21, where they claim that the role of breach of confidence in this case was 'perhaps more akin to a right of publicity than to a right of privacy'. Whitty describes use of privacy in cases such as the Douglases' as a 'mere pretence', in Whitty (2009) para 3.4.9. Carty refers to the Douglases' 'hidden agenda' in H Carty, 'The Common Law and the Quest for the IP Effect' [2007] *IPQ* 237, 253. See also R Mulheron, 'A Potential Framework for Privacy? A Reply to *Hello!*' (2006) 69 *MLR* 679, 700; Michalos, 'Image Rights and Privacy: After *Douglas v Hello*' (2005) 385; M Richardson and L Hitchens, 'Celebrity Privacy and Benefits of Simple History' in Andrew Kenyon and Megan Richardson (eds), *New Dimensions in Privacy Law* (Cambridge: Cambridge University Press, 2006) 251; and N Gardner and K Brimstead, 'Confidential Information – Damages' [2005] *EIPR* N190, N191.

[90] *Campbell v MGN* [2006] QB 125 [95].

B.   The Need for a Confidential Relationship or a Reasonable Expectation of Privacy

Whether an article 8 remedy is available depends on whether there is a reasonable expectation of privacy or a confidential relationship (express or implied). As with *Douglas*, where the claimant can demonstrate this, any unauthorised use will, on the face of it, be remediable.

When this test is applied to two of the cases advanced as paradigm publicity cases in chapter three, we see the limits of article 8 as a basis for publicity cases. In *Irvine v Talksport Ltd*,[91] the element of persona used (Irvine's image) was a publicly available photograph, which was not provided in circumstances of confidence nor was it such as to give rise to a reasonable expectation of privacy. So too with the subject matter in *Lyngstad v Anabas*, where the photographs used on the badges and pillowcases were obtained by way of copyright licence from the studios responsible.[92] Even if the claimants in these cases had tried to demonstrate a reasonable expectation of privacy in respect of the particular images used, the defendants would have been able to avail themselves of the defence that the images, and the information they contained, were already widely known. There could therefore be no privacy-based action in these instances, yet the claimants suffered a wrong which, in Irvine's case, was remediable under another tort.

An article 8 privacy action is relevant where the aim is to keep images and information out of the public domain—even if, as in *Douglas*, the claimant intends to make subsequent controlled use of that information through his or her own exploitation of it.[93] Where the publicity action arises from a fact situation in which there could be no claim for privacy,[94] then the basis for the publicity action must be sought elsewhere, as indeed happened in *Irvine* and *Lyngstad*.

Thus, privacy under article 8 is too narrow a basis for publicity rights. The publicity use identified in chapter three encompasses unauthorised dissemination of *any* images or information, whether or not they are subject to an obligation of confidence or a reasonable expectation of privacy.

C.   Private Information: Invasion versus Dissemination

The taking of the photograph, private possession of the photograph and the publication of the photograph are entirely separate. So far it is publication that has been

---

[91]   *Irvine v Talksport Ltd* [2003] 2 All ER 881.

[92]   *Lyngstad v Anabas* [1977] FSR 62, 65 (Oliver J).

[93]   *Douglas v Hello!* [2008] 1 AC 1. Here the unauthorised images were not publicly available—a (controversial) factor which played a key role in the House of Lords decision. See section III. F. below.

[94]   The alternative principle of inaccessibility under the 'traditional' doctrine of breach of confidence has been analysed by Carty, 'The Modern Action for Breach of Commercial Confidence' (2008). However, this is of limited value since, as Carty notes, the two actions have very different rationales (at 428).

enjoined but we may be moving into a world where delivery up of the original images is on the cards if the complaint is the actual act of photography.[95]

One distinction which is not always made explicit in privacy cases under article 8 is whether the infringement arises from the *invasion* or from the subsequent *dissemination* of the private elements. For example, Eady J in *Mosley* refers to the action being 'breach of confidence and/or the unauthorised *disclosure* of personal information'.[96] Although '[m]ost of the decided cases are concerned with the publication of the offending photographs... in some cases there may be anteced- ent acts which ought also to be wrongful'.[97]

This distinction undoubtedly needs to be made, since the article 8 right to private life has been used in much wider circumstances than publication of private information. Such cases have involved invasions of privacy arising from, for example, strip-searching,[98] covert surveillance,[99] or stalking.[100] Even the simple act of taking a photograph can breach an individual's privacy,[101] regard- less of whether or not the photograph is then published. These diverse ways in which privacy can be infringed, together with the cases already examined in this chapter, reflect Prosser's analysis of privacy, wherein he identified four distinct ways in which privacy can be invaded:[102]

1.   Intrusion upon the plaintiff's seclusion or solitude, or into the plaintiff's private affairs.
2.   Public disclosure of embarrassing private facts about the plaintiff.
3.   Publicity which places the plaintiff in a false light in the public eye.
4.   Appropriation, for the defendant's advantage, of the plaintiff's name and likeness.

---

[95]   Michalos (n 7) 385. Michalos's foresight has been realised: (i) in the ECtHR case of *Reklos v Greece*, where the 'key issue' was not the nature of the photographs 'but the fact that the photographer kept them without the applicants' consent'. *Reklos v Greece* (App no 1234/05) (15 April 2009) [42]; and (ii) in *Wood v Commissioner of Police for the Metropolis* [2009] EWCA Civ 414, where the article 8 infringement arose from the taking and retention of the photographs, without any intention or design to publish them.

[96]   *Mosley v News Group Newspapers Ltd* [2008] EWHC 1777 (QB) [3], emphasis added. See also, for example, the judgment of Patten J in *Murray v Big Pictures (UK) Ltd* [2007] EWHC 1908 (Ch), where he observed that such article 8 claims call upon the courts to prevent dissemination by 'imposing limitations *on the publication* of events which were visible to any member of the public who happened to be around at the time'. ([20], emphasis added.) This was followed in the Court of Appeal, which referred to the principles in cases of 'wrongful publication of private information'. *Murray v Big Pictures* [2008] EWCA Civ 446 [27].

[97]   Jones and Wilson, 'Photographs, Privacy and Public Places' (2007) 359. See also Moreham (n 7); Morgan (n 7).

[98]   *Wainwright v Home Office* [2004] 2 AC 406, albeit the Human Rights Act 1998 did not apply retrospectively in this case. Note also Lord Hoffmann's observation in this case that the courts have refused to formulate a general principle of 'invasion of privacy' ([19]).

[99]   *Martin v McGuiness* 2003 SLT 1424; *Howlett v Holding* [2006] EWHC 41 (QB).

[100]   *Ward v Scotrail* 1999 SC 255.

[101]   *Reklos v Greece* (App no 1234/05) (15 April 2009), [2009] EMLR 16; *Wood v Commissioner of Police for the Metropolis* [2009] EWCA Civ 414.

[102]   WL Prosser, 'Privacy' (1960) 48 *Cal L Rev* 383, 389.

Only the last of these can be aligned to the publicity right under investigation.

The breadth of the article 8 privacy action is in marked contrast to a publicity action which, by its nature, arises from the unauthorised *dissemination*, rather than the antecedent invasion. As noted in chapter three, it is a key element of the publicity right (and wrong) that the use must involve an element of public use. Cases such as *Wood v Commissioner of Police for the Metropolis*[103] illustrate the difference, since the wrongful retention of the photographs by the police was a breach of Wood's article 8 rights, but it is difficult to see where any *publicity* complaint could lie, unless or until the police disseminated the image publicly. Merely taking the photograph would not infringe the media information, promotion or merchandising uses—whereas it may in some cases infringe the article 8 privacy right.[104]

This distinction highlights one of the differences between privacy and publicity: while privacy can be breached by the invasion *or* the subsequent dissemination of private information, a publicity action is concerned only with the dissemination or public use of persona (whether it be name, image, or information). Privacy is effectively concerned with inward-looking actions as well as their external communication, whereas publicity's concern is external control of the persona, being what is brought to the public attention. Article 8 privacy rights are therefore in this sense much broader than the right sought by publicity (in contrast to the test of a reasonable expectation of privacy, which was concluded to be too narrow to support a publicity action). While this does not necessarily preclude privacy as the basis of a right of publicity, it does indicate that there is not a terribly close fit between the two rights.

D. Defences to Privacy Infringements

A further reason why there may be a close relationship but no close legal fit between publicity and privacy relates to possible defences. Where an action for invasion of privacy is raised, one justification for the invasion may be derived from the article 10 right to freedom of expression.[105] If publicity interests are enforced through privacy rights, then the same defences would be available in both cases. Yet it is not obvious that the defences available in privacy actions are appropriate for publicity cases. Freedom of expression, for example, may not be shown in a publicity case, where the unauthorised use is commercial speech with no value other than advertising. An action based on privacy would therefore succeed. Nonetheless, there may be good reason why the publicity use in that particular case should be permitted, and the publicity claim be denied. Thus, the

---

[103] *Wood v Commissioner of Police for the Metropolis* [2009] EWCA Civ 414.

[104] *Reklos v Greece* (App no 1234/05) (15 April 2009), [2009] EMLR 16; *Wood v Commissioner of Police for the Metropolis* [2009] EWCA Civ 414.

[105] This is a popular, if often unsuccessful, line of defence with the media: *Campbell v MGN* [2004] 2 AC 457; *Mosley v News Group Newspapers Ltd* [2008] EWHC 1777 (QB).

features of a publicity action—and its justifications—may dictate that certain defences or exceptions to the right should be recognised. Where publicity is shoehorned into a privacy framework, the opportunity for this consideration is denied, and the scope for considering limitations and defences is adversely affected. As will be seen in subsequent chapters, the limitations on publicity rights and permitted uses form an important element of the right: freedom of expression is just one of those possible defences.

E. Positive Exploitation

While the previous sections have considered problems with using privacy rights to protect the negative right of publicity, or unauthorised use, this section assesses whether or not privacy can offer a route to enable positive exploitation of persona, through consensual use. This requires analysis of the right as between the individual and the exploiter, and between the exploiter and unauthorised users.

i. Waiving the Right to Privacy

Once an individual has a right to exclude others from a sphere of his or her life, a potentially lucrative market then arises in which to *waive* the right, in return for a fee. The control of private information which results from breach of confidence/article 8 enables the individual to exploit this control as the individual chooses. Morgan observes that 'an injunction... would naturally place the protected party in a position to exploit his image commercially – by negotiating payment to release it'.[106] Such controlled waiver of privacy arguably creates the possibility of publicity in respect of any material covered by confidence and privacy. Where an individual is willing to reveal truths for a price, as in *Douglas*, there is no breach of confidence and no interference with the individual's private life, because the individual has consented to this dissemination of information: the individual has waived the right to be let alone. However, it remains to be seen whether this is sufficient to constitute a *right* of publicity.

Certainly, this interpretation of the logical consequence of privacy protection (in practical terms, at any rate) has considerable attraction for those keen to exploit any interest in their personal lives. Yet it perhaps ignores the commercial basis of such deals: 'in reality, advertisers would not pay famous people such as sports and entertainment personalities for giving up their privacy, but would pay because such persons' images already had a "recognition value"'.[107]

Can a waiver of article 8 rights constitute a positive power to exploit? Those who advocate the derivation of the right of publicity from the prior right of

---

[106] Morgan (n 7) 450. See also Whitty (n 13) para 3.4.9; C Colston and K Middleton, *Modern Intellectual Property Law*, 2nd edn (London, Cavendish, 2005) para 18.7.5.
[107] Beverley-Smith et al, *Privacy, Property and Personality* (2005) 59, fn omitted.

privacy effectively argue for a right to exploit the interest in private images or information through waiver: if 'either English or Scots law were to recognise a common law or delictual right to privacy against individuals, it would enable anyone to protect information and images concerning them, and indirectly allow a right to publicity'.[108] Although the private law right of breach of confidence *could* be waived, it is less easy to separate out the human rights aspect of this right, and the question of whether or not human rights can be waived is not an easy one to answer.

Some writers believe that '[h]uman rights, by doctrine, can – and in fact should – not be transferred, waived or inherited'[109] and certainly it is troubling to conceive of the right to life or to freedom from torture being capable of waiver: no-one is likely to advocate consent or waiver operating as a defence to murder.[110] However, it remains the case that '[t]here is no rule that rights enshrined in the ECHR may in no circumstances be waived'.[111] Indeed, a guilty plea is, on one interpretation, a waiver of the article 6 right to a fair (or, in this case, any) trial. This suggests that there are 'tiers' of human rights, such that it is possible for an individual to contract to waive his or her right to privacy under article 8, but not his or her right to life, for example. Even allowing for this distinction, it is hard not to sympathise with the view that 'human rights based concepts… are not well suited to protect comprehensively the value of popularity. They fail to secure damages and can stand in the way of essential trade requirements'.[112]

Further, waiver operates to remove the granter's right of action against the 'infringer', rather than making the use legal.[113] The third party user therefore only gains the right as against the person granting the waiver, and would have no defence against any other individual who may have an action, such as a second person featured in the private images.[114] Waiver of a privacy right may be a pragmatic response to publicity exploitation, but it is by no means straightforward.

Moreover, where a third party (such as a newspaper) has paid for the exclusive right to publish otherwise private information, what is the extent of its right against an unauthorised publisher of the same (or similar) information? The grant of a licence, which is effectively a waiver, 'only makes an action lawful

---

[108]   Colston and Middleton, *Modern Intellectual Property Law* (2005) para 18.7.5.

[109]   J Klink, '50 Years of Publicity in the US and the Never-Ending Hassle in Europe' [2003] IPQ 363.

[110]   EC Reid and J Blackie, *Personal Bar* (Edinburgh, Scottish Universities Law Institute, Thomson/W Green, 2006) para 18–10.

[111]   ibid para 18–10. See also para 5–17.

[112]   J Klink, '50 Years of Publicity in the US' (2003) 381.

[113]   For example, see *Haelan Laboratories v Topps Chewing Gum Inc* 202 F 2d 866 (2nd Cir 1953), 867, Beverley-Smith *et al* (n 13) 130–31, and A Milligan, *Brand it Like Beckham* (London, Cyan, 2004) 130.

[114]   Where the exploiter seeks to use images regarding two people, the exploiter would need to see consent of the second person (also through waiver) in order to avoid this situation.

which would otherwise have been unlawful.'[115] Personal bar is 'a doctrine which suppresses rights rather than creates them',[116] by preventing the party who granted the licence (and is thus personally barred) from enforcing his or her rights. A licence of the right to publish is effectively a waiver of article 8 and is thus a shield but not a sword.[117] While this will aid the authorised user in a direct claim with the individual, it is far less likely to help where the authorised user wishes to claim against an unauthorised party and needs a sword, rather than a shield, to do so.[118] This was effectively the situation in which OK! found itself, following the unauthorised publication of unauthorised wedding photographs by Hello!—the question for the House of Lords was whether or not the licence granted by the Douglases gave OK! an enforceable right. The grant of a waiver thus does not place the third party exploiter in an ideal position in law, although large sums will frequently have been paid for this privilege. It was in just this situation that the 2nd Division recognised a property right in *Haelan Laboratories v Topps Chewing Gum*,[119] to enable the plaintiff, as licensee, to recover from the third party infringer—a pragmatic, if problematic, solution.[120]

F. Exploiting Publicity by Licensing a Privacy Right: *Douglas v Hello!*

Douglas v Hello![121] in the House of Lords is a decision which encapsulates the considerable difficulties of attempting to found a licensable commercial interest on a waiver of the right of privacy.[122] Although the Douglases' claim in privacy was disposed of in the Court of Appeal, the dispute between the two commercial rivals—the authorised and unauthorised publishers—was appealed to the House of Lords.

In order to determine whether OK! had an enforceable right against Hello!, the Lords had to consider three issues:

[115] Michalos (n 7) at 243. Where the licence is supported by a statutory scheme, an exclusive licensee may benefit from an enforceable right, as for example with copyright under s 92 of the Copyright, Designs and Patents Act (CDPA) 1988.
[116] Reid and Blackie, *Personal Bar* (2006) para 5–21.
[117] ibid.
[118] The English concept of equitable estoppels may, however, be more effective in such situations: ibid paras 5–22–5.23.
[119] *Haelan Laboratories v Topps Chewing Gum* (1953) 202 F.2d 866.
[120] See for example the comments made by D Westfall and D Landau, 'Publicity Rights as Property Rights' (2005–2006) 23 *Cardozo Arts and Ent LJ* 71, 74 and 83 et seq; and also in chapter 2 above.
[121] *Douglas v Hello!* [2008] 1 AC 1.
[122] The Douglases' claim was disposed of by the Court of Appeal in favour of the Douglases, and Hello! chose not to appeal the outcome to the Lords. Thus, the Lords were only required to consider the rights of OK! vis-à-vis Hello!: 'this appeal is not concerned with the protection of privacy. Whatever may have been the position of the Douglases, who, as I mentioned, recovered damages for an invasion of their privacy, OK!'s claim is to protect commercial confidential information and nothing more.' *Douglas v Hello!* [2008] 1 AC 1 [118] (Lord Hoffmann).

1. whether the Douglases' wedding photographs amounted to confidential information;
2. whether OK! benefited from that confidence; and, if so, then
3. whether Hello! had infringed that confidence by publishing the unauthorised images, or whether OK! had already placed the information in the public domain by publishing authorised photographs, thereby destroying any confidentiality in those images.[123]

Lord Hoffmann, for the majority, concluded that these wedding photographs did constitute confidential information.[124] Given that the wedding photographs qualified as confidential information, the second issue to be determined was the nature of OK!'s right in the Douglases' photographs, that is to say, what right was granted to OK! under its contract with the Douglases? A significant factor for the Court appears to have been the high value of the information[125] to both contracting parties:

> The point of which one should never lose sight is that OK! had paid £1m for the benefit of the obligation of confidence imposed upon all those present at the wedding in respect of *any* photographs of the wedding. That was quite clear. Unless there is some conceptual or policy reason why they should not have the benefit of that obligation, I cannot see why they were not entitled to enforce it. And in my opinion there are no such reasons. Provided that one keeps one's eye firmly on the money and why it was paid, the case is, as Lindsay J held, quite straightforward.[126]

In the absence of any conceptual or policy reasons against protection, OK!'s interest in the confidentiality of the wedding photographs, derived from the high value contract with the Douglases, was one that the Law Lords were prepared to protect.

This conclusion leaves a number of questions unanswered. If the information had been held to be 'private' but not confidential, yet still licensed for the same fee, would their Lordships have reached the same conclusion? In either case, if the Douglases had not charged a fee at all, or if they had charged a much lesser sum, would the law still have protected OK!'s exclusive right? The commercial value of the deal might be negligible, yet the facts and subject matter would otherwise

---

[123] Although the facts were novel, their Lordships were clear that the principles to be applied were those previously established in the leading breach of confidence cases in England, *Coco v AN Clark (Engineers) Ltd* [1969] RPC 41 and *Attorney General v Guardian Newspapers Ltd (No 2)* [1990] 1 AC 109.

[124] *Douglas v Hello!* [2008] 1 AC 1 [118].

[125] Carty observes that the focus on the fee paid meant that the debate moved 'from protecting "secrecy" to protecting the value of OK's investment': in Carty (n 21) 448.

[126] *Douglas v Hello!* [2008] 1 AC 1 [117] (Lord Hoffmann), emphasis in the original. Lord Hoffmann was supported by Lord Brown: 'Having paid £1m for an exclusive right it seems to me that OK! ought to be in a position to protect that right and to look to the law for redress were a third party intentionally to destroy it.' ([325]). Lindsay J also took this approach at trial, but the Court of Appeal held that the obligation of confidence in the photographs only attached to the authorised photographs, and not the unauthorised images. [2003] 3 All ER 996 and [2006] QB 125.

remain the same. Since the value of the deal appears to form the basis in law of OK!'s enforceable right (described by Michalos as a 'jurisprudential leap'[127]), it is essential to have as much clarity about the scope and extent of this alleged right and the means of creating it—clarity which is currently lacking.

The third issue was whether Hello!'s publication breached that confidence. Baroness Hale and Lord Brown agreed with Lord Hoffmann's analysis that OK!'s publication of certain authorised images meant that *those* images were in the public domain[128] but 'no other pictures were in the public domain and they did not enter the public domain merely because they resembled other pictures which had'.[129] Noting that he could not understand Lord Nicholls' view that publication of *approved* photographs rendered publication of *unapproved* photographs acceptable,[130] Lord Hoffmann (and the majority) concluded that OK! had an enforceable right of confidence in the authorised photographs.[131] Nonetheless, the distinction between the *information* contained in the two sets of images is rather slender, and exposes the final outcome to the suspicion that what was protected was not information (as per a privacy action) but specific (valuable) images.[132]

This decision arguably makes commercial sense, by reflecting the intentions of the Douglases and OK!. There is, of course, merit in a legal system which is grounded in the reality of commercial practice: Laddie J endorsed this approach in the context of passing off (rather than privacy), where he said 'passing off is closely connected to and dependent upon what is happening in the market place... [it] responds to changes in the nature of trade'.[133] Yet this very appeal to

---

[127] Michalos (n 7) 243. In relation to the applicability of this case in Scots law, Reid observes that if 'an obligation between A and C is to be recognised in Scots law, it will require a more principled foundation than the assertion that A has paid a great deal of money to B'. E Reid, 'Protection of Personality Rights in the Modern Scots Law of Delict' in N Whitty and R Zimmermann (eds), *Rights of Personality in Scots Law, a Comparative Perspective*, (Dundee, Dundee University Press, 2009) para 4.4.2.

[128] Any unauthorised reproduction of the approved images would thereafter be a breach of copyright rather than breach of confidence.

[129] *Douglas v Hello!* [2008] 1 AC 1 [122] (Lord Hoffmann).

[130] ibid [121] (Lord Hoffmann).

[131] It is clear, however, that Lord Hoffmann was content to apply the established principles of breach of confidence in reaching this decision. For example, he considered two of the other elements of the action and acknowledged that, even if OK! had an enforceable right, it would not be breached if the information used by Hello! was obtained otherwise than in breach of confidence or if publication of the information was in the public interest (ibid [120]).

[132] Carty (n 21) 451; Whitty (n 13) para 3.4.9.

[133] *Irvine v Talksport Ltd* [2002] 1 WLR 2355 [13]–[14]. This can be seen in the context of other developments in passing off in the character merchandising cases of the 1980s and 1990s: see chapter two, section IV. B. See also the arguments typical of legal realism, which advance the view that law is 'a means to social ends and not... an end in itself; so that any part needs constantly to be examined for its purpose, and for its effect, and to be judged in the light of both and of the relation to each other'. K Llewellyn, 'Some Realism about Realism – Responding to Dean Pound' (1930–1931) 44 *Harv L Rev* 1222, 1236.

commercial reality is the weakest part of the judgment,[134] and one that was opposed by Lord Walker, who argued that 'the confidentiality of any information must depend on its nature, not on its market value'.[135] Relying on the commercial value of a deal to determine its status as a legally protected right is intellectually troublesome, and creates considerable legal uncertainty.[136] Parties who purchase a licence of private or confidential information are effectively paying for a waiver of the individual's article 8 rights: the basis of any rights against third parties remains uncertain.

IV. Conclusion

The above analysis has examined the connection between the existing right of privacy and the nature of a right of publicity. Although privacy actions are available as a rather pragmatic basis for certain publicity type actions, as in *Douglas*, the attempt to rely on privacy is unsatisfactory, on both theoretical and practical grounds. There are undoubtedly similarities between the two actions, not least as regards the desire to control public access to private image and information. Nevertheless, they are not the same, and shoe-horning publicity into privacy does not benefit either interest. Key differences lie in:

1. The need for a confidential relationship or reasonable expectation of privacy, which will not always be present in publicity situations.
2. The defences appropriate to each action.
3. The waiver of privacy rights as the basis for third party rights.

In addition to these substantive issues, there are also very serious concerns about recognising an extension to privacy rights, in the form of publicity protection, without open debate on this extension. Whitty argues that '[r]ecognising the different natures of privacy and publicity is more intellectually honest than trying to subsume the latter into the former.'[137] This sentiment is also expressed by Michalos:

> The courts need to deal with the fact that trade secrets, commercial property in images and genuinely private personal information are different animals and need different causes of action. It may be that, whilst decreed undesirable, legislation is the only way out of the mire.[138]

---

[134] And has been criticised by Michalos (n 7) and also Carty (n 21); Waelde and Whitty (n 1) para 11.4.4(e); and questioned by R Arnold, 'Confidence in Exclusives: *Douglas v Hello!* in the House of Lords' [2007] *EIPR* 339, 343.
[135] *Douglas v Hello!* [2008] 1 AC 1 [299].
[136] Other criticisms have been advanced by Carty (n 21).
[137] N Whitty (n 13) para 3.4.9.
[138] Michalos (n 7) 387. See also Wacks: 'The solution, as I have said, plainly lies in clearly drafted legislation that provides a remedy in tort for unwanted publicity.' Wacks (n 7) 183.

Legislation also brings the benefit of an open discussion: 'the creation of some form of image or publicity right needs to be expressly debated as a possible separate right, not slipped under the radar of the action for breach of confidence by the celebrity industry'.[139] Absent such a debate, privacy appears to be one course of action the celebrity industry is taking to protect publicity—where the publicity in question involves (fortuitously) the use of otherwise private or confidential images or information.

---

[139] Carty (n 21) 453—although she goes on to say that a 'public merit' basis for image rights is 'conspicuously lacking' (at 453). See also Carty, 'Advertising, Publicity Rights and English law' (2004) 215.

Part II

Justifying Publicity Rights

5

Justifying Publicity Rights: Setting the Scene

I. Introduction

T HE PREVIOUS CHAPTERS outlined the nature and function of a publicity right. However, outlining the characteristics of a right is one thing: justifying its creation or existence is another.

If a legal right of publicity is advocated, it must be justified. It is not enough simply to assert this, as 'the defence of any legal, economic or social institution should be backed up by reasons or considerations likely to sway the free understanding of the participants in social life in favour of the institution that is being defended'.[1]

Such justifications are particularly important when the matter in question is a legal right which would impose duties as well as benefits, and would be supported by the sanction of the civil law against those in breach. It has been said that when governments make decisions about intellectual property rights they should allow change 'only if a rigorous analysis clearly demonstrates that it will promote people's basic rights and economic well-being'.[2] A new right of publicity thus requires rigorous analysis, to provide the reasons and considerations in favour of such a right.

While many jurisdictions have recognised a right of publicity or a right to control the use of persona, the lack of unity in this *legal* response can be contrasted with the near uniformity of the *practice* in Western jurisdictions.[3] One

---

[1] HM Spector, 'An Outline of a Theory Justifying Intellectual and Industrial Property' [1989] *EIPR* 270, 270.

[2] The Adelphi Charter, adopted by the Royal Society for the Arts, 13 October 2005.

[3] Advertising, the media and merchandising are remarkably similar in Western jurisdictions. Moreover, most jurisdictions can name at least one high profile celebrity who has litigated (in person or through his or her estate) in the field of publicity in that country: Marlene Dietrich (Germany); Johnny Hallyday (France); Paul Hogan (Australia); Michael Douglas and Catherine Zeta Jones (England); Michael Hosking (New Zealand); George Athans (Canada). The largest selection of course comes from the US, where plaintiffs have included Vanna White, Bette Midler, Tom Waits, and Johnny Carson.

particular problem facing advocates of publicity rights is that the assorted justifications which can be advanced in favour of such a right are often open to criticism because the legal responses are so variable: a justification of a property right of publicity will be, of necessity, very different from a justification which responds to a right grounded in personality and human rights. There is a real risk, therefore, that any assessment of the justifications for protecting publicity practice is confused with an assessment of the nature of the legal right in question, regardless of the merits in protecting publicity per se.

If, however, publicity practice is removed from the confines of any one jurisdiction, and the focus is instead transferred to the shared experience of publicity in all Western jurisdictions, the quest for justifications becomes simplified: it focuses on the practice and not the legal response. Once the practice is justified in its own right, it is then possible to use those justifications to shape the legal response—or, indeed, to conclude that no legal response is justified at all. Thus, the justifications that can be advanced in favour of legal protection of publicity in general can be used to inform the nature of the right in particular.

This review of publicity practice and justifications therefore takes as its starting point our common experience of publicity in practice and the shared values and principles which underlie our legal systems,[4] in order to assess the need for legal protection for publicity and the competing interests to such a right. As these justifications are examined, the consequences for the subsequent nature of the legal right will be noted, whether in relation to the right itself, or its limits.

In assessing justifications, reference will be made to the three broad theoretical approaches to publicity outlined in chapter two. However, it is important to appreciate that writers appear to be capable of accepting or rejecting justifications for publicity rights regardless of which of these conceptual categories their work falls into. It would be wrong to conclude, for example, that those writers who discuss publicity rights in the broadest category of 'publicity as property' are united in advocating such rights, whereas those who are classed in the personality rights approach reject them. Although Madow has suggested that in the American tradition (which is broadly the 'publicity as property' approach) there is 'a solid, indeed an overwhelming consensus... that the right of publicity is a good thing',[5] there are plenty of writers in this approach who take a critical line. Madow's own analysis, for example, falls within this broad category of an all-encompassing publicity right, yet he has written a comprehensive critique of

---

[4] For example, those protected by the American Constitution and the European Convention on Human Rights (ECHR).

[5] M Madow, 'Private Ownership of Public Image: Popular Culture and Publicity Rights' (1993) 81 *Cal L Rev* 125.

publicity right justifications.[6] Writers in each category are capable of maintaining either a healthy scepticism or a pro-right conviction.

A more problematic trend seems to be the varying rigour of the arguments advanced by those in the opposing camps. As Carty notes, the pro-celebrity industry seems to think it is '"obvious" that the commercial worth of the celebrity magnet (particularly in advertising) belongs to them and that unauthorised use should be prevented by law'.[7] This assumption by pro-publicity rights writers frequently results in a brief or sketchy consideration of the justifications for such an 'obvious' right.[8] In contrast, those who claim that publicity rights are insufficiently justified[9] usually make their case against publicity in compelling detail. Existing writing therefore tends to challenge rather than support any search for justifications[10]—albeit Madow, who makes a highly persuasive case against publicity rights, observes that: '[i]t may be possible to make a coherent and convincing case for the right of publicity. But that case has yet to be made.'[11] What follows is an attempt to address these challenges.

II. Benefits and Harms: Identifying the Interests at Stake

Rights in law typically have one of two aims: to enable individuals to advance their interests as they see them, or to protect them from harm. Part of the task of justifying legal protection for persona is to consider the benefits that a right of publicity would bring to the individual, and the interests it would protect. It is therefore helpful to consider the legal and commercial interests at stake in publicity practice. What interest would be harmed by unauthorised use of persona? What interest would be protected by the grant of a publicity right?

This task becomes particularly important because, for many writers, it is the apparent lack of harm to the individual which is their primary objection to the

---

[6] ibid. Fisher identifies Madow as one of a 'small group of commentators' who 'began drawing explicitly on theories of intellectual property to criticize the right of publicity' in the 1990s: W Fisher, 'Theories of Intellectual Property' available at http://cyber.law.harvard.edu/people/tfisher/iptheory. pdf, 37.

[7] H Carty, 'The Common Law and the Quest for the IP Effect' [2007] *IPQ* 237, 240–41.

[8] Madow also recognises this point: Madow, 'Private Ownership of Public Image' (1993) 136.

[9] Including ibid, H Beverley-Smith, *The Commercial Appropriation of Personality* (Cambridge, Cambridge University Press, 2002) and H Carty, 'Advertising, Publicity Rights and English Law' [2004] *IPQ* 209.

[10] A notable exception is Westfall and Landau, who conclude that 'it is difficult to either support or criticize the existence of publicity rights all that strongly'. D Westfall and D Landau, 'Publicity Rights as Property Rights' (2005–2006) 23 *Cardozo Arts and Ent LJ* 71, 117 and 118.

[11] Madow (n 5) 135.

case for publicity rights. Carty, in particular, is a strong proponent of the need for the existence of a harm to justify the grant of any legal right. In her discussion of the broader 'IP effect'[12] she argues that:

> The IP effect would offer claimants wider protection, not intrinsically based on 'harm' or 'wrongs'. Rather, it would provide redress where the defendant has benefited from the claimant's creation or effort. So it is the prevention of unjust enrichment or misappropriation which is the nub of the IP effect.[13]

This, Carty argues, is flawed, since legal protection must respond to a harm rather than to a (harmless) transfer: it is insufficient to point to a benefit which has been transferred. Instead, it must be possible to demonstrate that there has been harm caused through the unauthorised use of persona. Consequently, 'in the absence of specific wrongs such as trade mark infringement or defamation, the use of the celebrity magnet is open to all'.[14] Carty is also quite clear that 'no wrong *per se* resulted from the unauthorised exploitation of the persona of a celebrity, however "unfair" this may appear to the celebrity industry'.[15] The need for law to respond to wrongs, protected by specific actions, rather than to assert general rights, is a much stronger tradition in Common law jurisdictions than in Civilian ones.[16] Nonetheless, identifying the legal and commercial interests which are protected by publicity rights, and which are harmed by the lack of a publicity right, should be seen as an essential element of any consideration of justifications.

Two relevant interests can be discerned from the jurisprudence and academic writing. These are (i) economic or commercial interests and (ii) dignitarian interests, which include, but are broader than, privacy interests.

A. The Dual Interests in Publicity Literature

One of the most detailed analyses of the economic and dignitarian interests comes from Beverley-Smith, whose work can be located primarily in the 'appropriation of personality' approach.[17] He acknowledges that both interests are

---

[12] That is, the idea that there is ever-increasing pressures for legal protection for intangibles, outwith the traditional categories. Publicity, she argues, is one such example. See Carty, 'The Quest for the IP Effect' (2007).

[13] ibid 239. See also Carty, 'Personality Rights and English Law' in Niall Whitty and Reinhard Zimmermann (eds), *Rights of Personality in Scots Law, a Comparative Perspective* (Dundee, Dundee University Press, 2009).

[14] Carty, 'Advertising, Publicity Rights and English law' (2004) 211.

[15] ibid 238.

[16] For example, J Gordley, *Foundations of Private Law: Property, Tort, Contract, Unjust Enrichment* (Oxford, Oxford University Press, 2006) 164; Carty, 'Personality Rights and English Law' (2009) para 7.2.1.

[17] Prosser, another writer in this category, also discusses these interests: see Prosser, 'Privacy' (1960) 48 *Cal L Rev* 383, particularly at 406.

present in personality, which is a 'hybrid' problem.[18] Beverley-Smith defines dignitary[19] interests as 'a generic term for the essentially non-pecuniary interests that a person might have in his own personality: reputation, personal privacy and freedom from mental distress'.[20] He also notes, however, that there is no single recognised definition of this term, which he believes reflects the 'fact that there is no coherent notion of human dignity as a legal value'.[21] This view is reflective of the Common law tradition, in contrast with Civilian legal systems which *would* recognise a 'coherent notion' of human dignity in law.[22]

In the case of economic interests, however, Beverley-Smith is able to give a more extensive definition, centred round the concept that 'a finite sum of money can provide complete recompense'[23] for wrongful use of personality, such that the claimant feels 'no further sense of loss, having received a sum of money which accurately reflects the value of what has been lost'.[24] The economic value of publicity is derived from the commercial value individuals have to advertisers and the media, amongst others, allowing them to grant licences or otherwise trade in their persona.[25] De Grandpre explains it rather neatly, by noting that '[f]amous people offer advertisers relationships with which they can communicate with the purchasing public'[26] and that '[i]n the market for eyeballs, people who have the ability to deliver public attention are in high demand'.[27] This creates the economic interest and, critically, should be capable of being objectively valued leaving no room for subjective values and beliefs, according to Beverley-Smith. It is this objectivity which results in full compensation for economic harms being found in a 'finite sum of money': only where there is a subjective loss (such as harm to a dignitarian interest) may this no longer be possible for the pursuer, and the interest will be compensated with an award of *solatium*.

---

[18] See for example Beverly-Smith, *The Commercial Appropriation of Personality* (2002) 322.

[19] Beverley-Smith uses slightly different terminology, referring to dignitary interests instead of dignitarian ones in ibid Part III. I shall use the term 'dignitarian' predominantly, but treat the two interchangeably.

[20] ibid 141.

[21] ibid 10. Although he accepts, at 141, that this is not the case in those jurisdictions which recognise *injuria*.

[22] See for example J Neethling, 'Personality Rights' in Jan M Smits (ed) *Elgar Encyclopaedia of Comparative Law* (Cheltenham, Edward Elgar, 2006) 530; N Whitty and R Zimmermann (eds), *Rights of Personality in Scots Law: A Comparative Perspective* (Dundee, Dundee University Press, 2009); and chapter two, section III.

[23] Beverley-Smith (n 9) 8.

[24] ibid 8.

[25] ibid 8.

[26] V De Grandpre, 'Understanding the Market for Celebrity: An Economic Analysis of the Right of Publicity' (2001–2002) 12 *Fordham Intell Prop Media and Ent LJ* 73, 95. See also J Klink, '50 Years of Publicity in the US and the Never-Ending Hassle in Europe' [2003] *IPQ* 363, 365 and R Coombe, *The Cultural Life of Intellectual Properties: Authorship Appropriation, and the Law* (Durham and London, Duke University Press, 1998) 88–92.

[27] De Grandpre, 'Understanding the Market for Celebrity' (2001–2002) 94.

An earlier review of these interests can be found in Frazer's article on 'Appropriation of Personality'.[28] Using slightly different terminology from Beverley-Smith, he concludes that

> privacy and property interests in personality may exist together or separately and should be treated accordingly, but without attracting the disadvantages of treating the two interests as the subject of different *torts*... [T]he courts [would] award damages in respect of the distress and annoyance suffered *and/or* the financial loss incurred (or reasonably expected to be incurred) by the plaintiff.[29]

These co-existent grounds for damages arise from the privacy and property interests that Frazer discusses, and can be mapped onto the dignitarian and economic interests respectively.[30]

Those writers who fall within the broad 'publicity as property' category identified in chapter two are more likely to focus on the economic interest at the expense of the dignitarian.[31] Nimmer observes that actions such as privacy are generally unsatisfactory for publicity protection because there is often no infringement of dignitarian interests in such actions.[32] Where a claimant has to rely on privacy-based actions, the claimant may struggle to find redress since the claimant has not suffered any harm to his or her dignitarian interests, yet the action is not intended to protect the claimant's economic interests, which may well have suffered harm. Thus, the following situation can arise:

> plaintiff [a famous performer] frankly admitted that the use of his name and picture by the defendant did not subject him to any ridicule or cause him any humiliation whatever. The court held there was a technical violation of the New York privacy statute but since the use of the plaintiff's name and picture was non-offensive to him, plaintiff received nominal damages in the sum of six cents. Plaintiff might well have taken the position that the use of the name and picture of a famous performer on the defendant's program was worth a great deal more to defendant than six cents.[33]

The emphasis here is undeniably on the economic interests of the plaintiff, rather than any dignitarian ones arising from loss of control or dignity. Note, however, that the absence of humiliation was specific to the facts of this case: there is no suggestion by the court that such unauthorised commercial use could *never* give rise to ridicule.[34]

---

[28] T Frazer, 'Appropriation of Personality – a New Tort?' (1983) 99 *LQR* 281.

[29] ibid 312, emphasis in the original.

[30] In Civilian terminology, Frazer appears to advocate a monistic right, which is one which protects both interests, rather than two separate rights. See chapter two, section III, particularly the discussion of the monistic right in German law.

[31] A good example here is SW Halpern, 'The Right of Publicity: Maturation of an Independent Right Protecting the Associative Value of Personality' (1995) 46 *Hastings LJ* 853, 857–60.

[32] M Nimmer, 'The Right of Publicity' (1954) 19 *Law and Contemporary Problems* 203, 204.

[33] ibid 208.

[34] Indeed, one does not have to look far to find an example of such a use: the 'Gentleman rider' case from Germany involved the use of the image of a professor of ecclesiastical law in an

In fact, both Nimmer and McCarthy can be seen to distinguish between dignitarian privacy harms and economic publicity harms. In McCarthy's analysis, 'certain unpermitted uses of a person's identity in advertising can give rise to one, or both, of these rights of privacy and publicity. But while privacy is a personal and mental right, publicity is a commercial and business right.'[35] The individual would presumably have a claim for breach of both rights, under McCarthy's analysis, but they would remain separate rights and interests.[36]

Even in the approach which focuses most strongly on the inherently personal nature of publicity, the (predominantly Civilian) personality rights category, the economic interest is now increasingly recognised in addition to the dignitarian one. In German law, for example, Beverley-Smith et al point to a long history of judicial protection for ideal interests which is now, gradually, being supplemented by recognition of the economic aspects of personality rights, albeit '[s]ome uncertainties remain'.[37] Similarly, in France, the 'traditional assertion, according to which personality rights are extrapatrimonial on the basis that the person is not a marketable commodity, seems to be giving way, however, since some attributes of the personality are increasingly being marketed'.[38] As Neethling explains, the traditional division between patrimonial and non-patrimonial interests is problematic in cases where an individual's identity 'has a market or advertising value'[39] since this use 'infringes not only his personality, but also a patrimonial interest'.[40] Where there is a patrimonial loss, Neethling states that this 'can only mean that, in such instances, apart from personality harm, a patrimonial interest connected to the personality has also been damaged'.[41] Both interests are acknowledged and are apparently of growing importance in Civilian jurisdictions, although the economic interest cannot be so easily accommodated within the scheme of dignitarian-based personality rights.[42]

The tension caused by the duality of interests is emphasised by Carty's approach, which sees the exercise of personal choice in publicity as the assertion of an economic interest, rather than a dignitarian one. Although 'dignitary interests may be encompassed within a publicity right – part of the publicity

---

advertisement for a sexual stimulant: BGHZ 26, 349, as cited in H Beverley-Smith et al, *Privacy, Property and Personality* (Cambridge University Press, Cambridge, 2005) 144 and discussed in chapter two, section III.

[35] T McCarthy, 'Public Personas and Private Property: The Commercialization of Human Identity' (1989) 79 *TMR* 681, 687.

[36] This reflects the dualistic protection favoured in France, for example. See chapter two, section III.

[37] Beverley-Smith et al, *Privacy, Property and Personality* (2005) 95. These economic uncertainties include whether substantial damages will always be available, and whether personality rights can be licensed (also at 95).

[38] ibid 154.

[39] Neethling, 'Personality Rights' (2006) 543.

[40] ibid 543.

[41] ibid 535.

[42] And Neethling suggests economic interests can be 'controversial': ibid 535.

right may indeed involve the ability to *control* commercialisation of the image rather than simply to *profit* by it'[43], she argues that these are not 'personal' dignitary interests but 'commercial' ones:

> Rather than impacting on the private space of the celebrity they impact on celebrity as brand...At the heart of such objections based on controlling dignitary interests are essentially commercial concerns: the celebrity seeks to control the use of his persona in order to maintain full impact in its further and future commercial use.[44]

Control here is not primarily a dignitarian concern, but a commercial one. However, this analysis does not necessarily undermine the underlying dichotomy. Control, even for commercial purposes, can still be seen as a dignitarian interest, allowing the individual to make his or her own life choices. My ability to choose whether to be a solicitor or an athlete is a commercial choice in that it determines how I will earn a living, yet it is also a dignitarian choice in that I can opt for the career that will offer personal rewards and fulfilment. Carty's emphasis on the commercial relevance of control in publicity is indisputable, but the dignitary element of control also remains central to the right. Arguably, her work serves to highlight just how tightly entwined these two interests are. As Beverley-Smith et al conclude, 'an ability to control the commercial exploitation may be seen both as an economic right in maintaining commercial exclusivity and as an aspect of an individual's dignity or autonomy'.[45] Control is therefore the lynchpin of both interests.

B. The Dual Interests in Publicity Practice

These dual dignitarian and economic interests can also be seen in practice. Milligan's case study of David Beckham provides an insight into the world of celebrity branding and publicity practice. By reviewing Beckham's key endorsement deals from the late 1990s to 2003, Milligan assesses what each deal offered Beckham, implicitly revealing the control and management behind each endorsement contract. Beckham appears to have decided which brands to endorse not solely on the basis of the fees offered, but also according to his image and priorities.[46] Thus, whereas Beckham's deal with Brylcreem was 'a good launch pad',[47] his subsequent deal with Pepsi was 'an ideal commercial opportunity'[48] because 'it gave him global distribution... and it sat with his mildly rebellious image'.[49] In the case of Police sunglasses, the 'deal was important in being the first

---

[43] Carty (n 9) 212, emphasis in the original.
[44] ibid 213. Also Carty, (n 13) section 7.3.
[45] Beverley-Smith et al (n 34) 3.
[46] This can be thought of as the difference between the value of the deal (£) and its added value (a good fit with his personal brand).
[47] A Milligan, *Brand it Like Beckham* (London, Cyan, 2004) 120.
[48] ibid.
[49] ibid 122.

commercial contract that didn't draw on Beckham's image as a footballer, but promoted his looks and fashion sense instead.... In terms of brand building, it was a clever move'.[50] The increasing value and scope of these deals provides an insight into the level of control and planning that underlies the commercial exploitation of a celebrity brand. This exploitation demonstrates the need for protection of dignitarian interests, through control and autonomy in managing Beckham's publicity career, as well as the obvious economic interests advanced by these deals.

Evidence in support of these dual interests can also be drawn from two of the paradigm English publicity cases, *Irvine v Talksport*[51] and *Douglas v Hello!*.[52] In *Irvine*, 'control of the use of [Irvine's] identity in giving endorsements enables him to enhance his image as a racing driver, and that in consequence he charges less for endorsing a fashionable product than an unfashionable one'.[53] Control of persona, in itself a dignitarian interest, is also a critical part of future financial gain. *Irvine* also provides us with guidance as to the longer-term implications of unauthorised use. Laddie J was prepared to accept that it 'is possible that the damage already done to Mr Irvine may be negligible in direct money terms but the potential long term damage is considerable'.[54] Thus, economic harm can be distinguished from non-economic (or dignitarian) harm, and the longer-term consequences of *both* have been judicially recognised.

The Douglases licensed exclusive publication of their wedding photographs for £1 million, apparently placing them in the commercial-interest bracket. In the House of Lords, Lord Nicholls noted that 'Mr Douglas said his name and likeness are valuable assets to him. It is important for him, for professional reasons, to protect his name and likeness and prevent unauthorised use of either.'[55] However, the action against Hello! was primarily for the emotional distress caused. Regardless of the scepticism of some commentators,[56] it is certainly the case that 'whilst the Claimants' case is now chiefly for money it was not always so and it was not by their choice that it became so'.[57] The action for financial compensation became necessary only when the Douglases' application for an injunction was refused, indicating that their priority was to prevent publication rather than to recover economic compensation for use of the images. While control was undoubtedly important for economic reasons—notably their exclusive deal with

---

[50] ibid 105.
[51] *Irvine v Talksport* [2003] 2 All ER 881.
[52] *Douglas v Hello!* [2006] QB 125.
[53] *Irvine* [2003] 2 All ER 881 [59].
[54] *Irvine v Talksport* [2002] 1 WLR 2355 [74] (Laddie J).
[55] *Douglas v Hello!* [2008] 1 AC 1 [252]. Carty refers to this ongoing control as a 'collateral concern' in publicity: Carty (n 9) 210.
[56] Their claims in court have been described as 'witness-box performances', indicating that they were perhaps aware of the need to convince the court of this element of personal distress. W Cornish and D Llewellyn, *Intellectual Property: Patents, Copyright, Trade Marks and Allied Rights*, 5th edn (London, Sweet & Maxwell, 2003) para 8–59, fn 58.
[57] *Douglas v Hello!* [2003] 3 All ER 996 [10].

OK!—there does appear to have been a significant personal aspect to their action. Loss of control of their dignitarian interests resulted in a successful claim for compensation for the 'real distress' they suffered from the publication of paparazzo photographs which left them 'devastated and shocked'.[58] Dignitarian interests and economic interests appear to co-exist for these claimants.

Madow questions the contention that celebrities suffer dignitarian harm from the unauthorised use of their persona where they actively seek publicity. Whereas unknown individuals could legitimately protest at unwanted publicity:

> Claims of such emotional injury were not nearly as convincing when they came from celebrities, however. After all, how could a movie star or professional athlete, who had deliberately and energetically sought the limelight, complain of embarrassment or hurt feelings when an advertiser or merchandiser simply gave his face some *additional* publicity?[59]

Yet this is contradicted by the evidence of celebrities such as Irvine and the Douglases. Even if allowance is made for the possibly strategic motivations of the parties in asserting this dignitarian distress, it does seem unlikely that there will never be embarrassment or distress. Furthermore, such reaction is deeply subjective, and it is difficult to legislate for this. Although not all celebrities will be embarrassed on all occasions, we should not rule out the potential for such emotional distress and dignitarian harm.

C. The Economic and Dignitarian Interests in Other Areas of Law

Legal recognition of these interests is not novel, as dignitarian and economic concerns are protected by law in other contexts. Perhaps the closest analogy is with copyright.[60] Here, a statutory right protects an intangible asset, the copyright. The copyright is created by the individual and can frequently be seen as a personal expression of the individual and his or her creativity. The author's dignitarian interests are protected by the moral rights granted. These rights, which are inalienable, entitle the author to object, for example, to derogatory treatment and false attribution of the work.[61] The statutory regime also offers protection for the author's economic interests, as copyright can be exploited for commercial gain through assignation[62] and licensing[63] of the right to copy. Further, the very fact that no-one is entitled to copy the work without the

---

[58] ibid [82]–[84].
[59] Madow (n 5) 168–69.
[60] As well as providing a point of comparison here, copyright will be referred to in future chapters as a right which shares much with publicity—and for that reason, copyright (and intellectual property) justifications may have a role to play in justifying a right of publicity.
[61] Copyright, Designs and Patents Act (CDPA) 1988 ss 80–84.
[62] ibid s 90.
[63] ibid.

owner's[64] consent[65] arguably recognises the economic and dignitarian interests of the owner. Whether the work is plastered on every hoarding in the country or left languishing in a cupboard is, to some extent, a matter for the owner, and this choice can be exercised for dignitarian as well as economic reasons.

Contract law similarly enables individuals to further their economic interests and to fulfil their dignitarian interests by living their life in the manner of their choosing, through the control and certainty that derives from enforceable contracts. So too with property rights, which are most commonly equated with economic interests. Thus, the right of ownership enables owners to use their land or goods in the manner of their choosing, including to make money. However, property rights are also capable of respecting individuals' dignitarian interests. The fact that the law enables individuals to control the use of their possessions or land enables them to make their own choices, thus respecting their autonomy. Indeed, earlier justifications for the recognition of private property were based on notions of respect for individuals and the necessity of some means for individuals to express their personality.[66]

The interests that would be protected by a publicity right are recognised and protected in other areas of law. There can be nothing controversial per se about the protection of (i) economic or commercial interests, looking to realise the value in persona and control its future economic potential; and (ii) dignitarian interests, looking to dignity, autonomy, and control.

D. Dignitarian and Economic Interests: Mutually Exclusive or Mutually Compatible?

Although there is widespread recognition of both economic and dignitarian interests in publicity, one question is whether a single right of publicity could or should protect *both* the dignitarian and economic elements. This is reminiscent of the debate between monistic and dualistic protection, but must be considered here in light of the different legal systems in the United Kingdom. This question arises in Scots and English law in part because of the very nature of current protection. Where a celebrity has attempted to shoehorn his or her claim for infringement of a 'publicity right' into a breach of confidence/article 8 action, concerns arise as to whether this inherently personal privacy-based action should be used to protect what is seen as an economic interest.

---

[64] It is necessary to distinguish between author (as creator of the work) and owner (who has control of the work, subject to the author's moral rights).

[65] As per s 16 *et seq*, subject to the permitted uses in ch III of the CDPA 1988.

[66] For an analysis of Lockean and Hegelian justifications for property, see for example J Hughes, 'The Philosophy of Intellectual Property' (1988) 77 *Georgetown Law Journal* 287; M Radin, 'Property and Personhood' (1982) 34 *Stanford Law Review* 957; and CB MacPherson, *Property – Mainstream and Critical Positions* (Oxford, Basil Blackwell, 1978).

This concern was reflected in Lord Walker's dissenting speech in *Douglas v Hello!*:

> it is not obvious why a claimant should be able to invoke the law's protection for the confidentiality of his or her private life (this claim being based on the high principle of respect for human autonomy and dignity) and also to invoke its protection for the commercial confidentiality of the same or similar material, as a trade secret, until it is to be disclosed for profit at a time of his or her own choosing.[67]

These concerns are legitimate so far as they go. Whilst it is indeed 'not obvious' why a legal right designed to protect one set of values should be used to protect others which are apparently 'at odds' with them, this does not mean that both types of value can never co-exist. Indeed, the monistic right in German law proves that it is possible for one right to protect both economic and dignitarian interests.[68] As copyright illustrates, it is possible for both interests to be protected in one legal scheme, where that scheme has been specifically developed to address them.[69] The concern here arguably arises only where there is no such tailored scheme and individuals instead manipulate an existing legal action to meet their needs. This is a valid concern, but it does not mean that no such tailored protection can ever exist. Instead, it could be addressed by the creation of a coherent scheme of publicity rights in law specifically intended to protect the interests involved. This would enable individuals to protect both their economic and dignitarian interests, as appropriate, without attempting to shoehorn a claim for one into an action designed to protect the other.

My conclusion therefore is that the two interests are not mutually exclusive: they are equally relevant and compatible. This reflects the reality of publicity practice: 'looking at the problem purely from a commercial appropriation perspective, or from an exclusively dignitary right of privacy perspective, distorts the true picture. Both economic and dignitary interests have to be taken into account.'[70]

III. Accepting Three Rebuttals of Publicity Rights

Before turning to justifications in support of publicity rights, it is necessary to acknowledge and reject three arguments which are commonly advanced *in favour* of a right of publicity, but which in fact fail to justify such a right. These are the

---

[67] *Douglas v Hello!* [2008] 1 AC 1 [275] (Lord Walker). See also the written submissions, 'Case for the Respondents' [21] (J Price QC, G Fernando, November 2006).
[68] See the analysis of the monistic and dualistic protection in Civilian jurisdictions in chapter two, section III.
[69] CDPA 1988.
[70] Beverley-Smith et al (n 34) 62.

incentive justification, the labour-desert justification, and the consumer protection justification. In brief, these justifications contend that:

(i) individuals will not develop valuable identities unless there is an incentive to do so, and legal protection provides that incentive by ensuring that control and the potential for commercial gain is vested in the individual;

(ii) the individual has laboured to create a valuable persona, and a legal right is the individual's desert or reward for doing so;

(iii) control by the individual over use of his persona in advertising, merchandising and the media is necessary for public protection, to ensure that consumers are not misled by false advertising or publicity.

Part of the problem with the first two of these arguments is that there is a tendency to confuse the subject matter under review. While the analysis in chapter three showed that the subject matter of protection is persona—name, image, and reputation—these incentive and labour-desert arguments often look to justify protection for the *value* in persona. Instead, the value is a separate consideration which does not affect the existence of the persona (since we all have a persona), nor should it affect the recognition of a right of publicity. As with copyright, where the value of the work may vary enormously, the existence of the right and justifications for it are not predicated on that value. Instead, the value of the copyright work is relevant when assessing remedies.

Madow's dismissal of the incentive argument is comprehensive. The idea that people will labour for some end only if there is a sufficient incentive, or 'some measure of assurance that they will be able to reap what they sow'[71] does not apply in publicity. McCarthy appears to advance this justification, on the basis that even a slight inducement enriches us all, but concedes that it is 'hypothetical' since the degree of incentive 'can probably never be proven either in the abstract or in any particular case'.[72] Madow, however, shows that the incentive justification is severely flawed:

> Farmer Brown might give up growing corn and turn to hunting if marauders were free to invade his land and steal his crop. Novelist Brown might give up writing mysteries and turn to investment banking if others were free to copy and sell his books. But will Quarterback Brown give up professional football and his multimillion dollar salary if others are free to use his picture on posters or T-shirts without paying him for the privilege? Not likely.[73]

---

[71] Madow (n 5) 205.

[72] T McCarthy, *The Rights of Publicity and Privacy*, 2nd edn (United States, West Group, 2001) para 2:6. A further weakness is that he accepts that the incentive justification only operates in the case of celebrities, rather than non-famous individuals (para 2:6).

[73] Madow (n 5) 210. See also De Grandpre (n 26) 102; Carty (n 9) 251; and Westfall and Landau, who point out that the incentive effect is reduced when celebrities are already wealthy, in Westfall and Landau, 'Publicity Rights as Property Rights' (2005–2006) 119.

Vaver also questions the incentive justification on a broader front when he asks whether the incentive of copyright protection has really made any difference to creative output:

> Are we sure that much of what the law vigorously protects would not have been created anyway, with no, or at least much less vigorous, protection? In crude terms, would I write less or worse letters or articles if my work was protected for, say, only 10 years? Or even not protected at all?[74]

The need for an incentive is frequently lacking in publicity, and therefore cannot act as a justification for recognition of a legal right.[75] Further, the opportunity to profit from publicity often arises—as Vaver and Madow recognise—regardless of whether or not there is a specific legal right of publicity. This is most obviously the case in the United Kingdom, where there is a strong market for publicity exploitation, regardless of the ad hoc legal basis for it. There is therefore nothing to be gained from anchoring the grant of a right of publicity to claims that an individual needs such a legal right to act as an incentive to develop his or her persona. Further, even if it were agreed that a legal right would provide an incentive to individuals to develop valuable persona, the question remains whether such an incentive is necessary or desirable—and that question requires its own response. On these grounds, looking to law to provide an incentive fails to provide a justification for publicity rights.

Closely related to the incentive justification is that of labour-desert, whereby a legal right to exploit persona is seen as the individual's reward for his or her labour in creating a valuable persona.[76] An initial point to note is that this justification is frequently tied to the *value* in persona (rather than the persona itself) whereas publicity exploitation can rely upon any persona, not only valuable ones.

In any event, the labour-desert justification fails to support a publicity right because there is frequently no evidence that the individual has laboured to create his or her persona.[77] Justifications based on Locke's theory of labour are inappropriate since '[t]he labor justification cannot account for the idea whose inception does not seem to have involved labor'.[78] A popular persona is 'sometimes the result of hard work towards securing a public image based on an internal vision. But quite often they are creations of pure chance, perhaps the only "intellectual property" without intentionality'.[79] Labour may well play a critical role in creating the value in the persona, as demonstrated by industry

---

[74] D Vaver, 'Intellectual Property: the State of the Art' (2000) 116 *LQR* 621, 631.

[75] And even less so for the portion of the right, if any, that endures post mortem: see Westfall and Landau (n 10) 88.

[76] The fact that we are all born with a particular image does not preclude individuals labouring to enhance or develop that image—thus there may well be labour in particular cases.

[77] Coombe notes the distinct lack of empirical data on this point: Coombe, *The Cultural Life of Intellectual Properties* (1998) 94 and, more generally, 92–100.

[78] Hughes, 'The Philosophy of Intellectual Property' (1988) 365.

[79] ibid 341 fn 220.

players such as Milligan: in *Brand it Like Beckham,* he makes very clear reference to the level of labour and effort that goes into creating and maintaining the valuable Beckham brand. For every Beckham, however, it is possible to point to other individuals who have exploited their persona on the back of little or no effort.[80] As Madow suggests, such justifications are 'a bit quaint', being tied 'normatively and conceptually, to a picture of individual creation and originality, and of self-authorship as well'.[81] Further, even for those individuals who do labour at their persona, Madow suggests that their attempts may not succeed in such a direct manner:

> No matter how long and conscientiously he 'labors' to create and maintain a preferred public image, and no matter how adept and shrewd his advisors and handlers are, he cannot make his persona 'mean' precisely and solely what he wants it to mean.[82]

Thus, the value in persona is not always within the individual's control and the product of the individual's labour. While evidence reveals that some individuals do labour very carefully to maximise the appeal of their persona, it is hard to deny that in other instances '[t]he notion that a star's public image is nothing else than congealed star labour is just the folklore of celebrity, the bedtime story the celebrity industry prefers to tell us and, perhaps, itself'.[83]

Further, the correlation between the labour and the fame is too uncertain and unreliable to operate as a suitable incentive, since there is usually no direct correlation between labour invested and celebrity status. As Madow notes, 'Fame does not play fair; it plays favorites'.[84] The economic consequence of this is that 'the market structure will often make it nearly impossible for a contestant to assess rationally the marginal revenue of an additional hour of training'.[85]

Another concern is that highlighted by Coombe, amongst others. She points to the 'studios, the mass media, public relations agencies, fan clubs, gossip columnists, photographers, hairdressers, body-building coaches, athletic trainers, teachers, screenwriters, ghostwriters, directors, lawyers and doctors'[86] who are all involved in the 'creation' of the persona—especially the fame of celebrities. With reference to Marilyn Monroe, she also assigns some of the credit for persona to the general public.[87] Again, this is not necessarily unique to publicity:

---

[80] Typical examples are winners of reality television shows such as Big Brother, and celebrities such as Paris Hilton, who are commonly said to be 'famous for being famous'. For US examples, see R Coombe, 'Publicity Rights and Political Aspiration: Mass Culture, Gender Identity, and Democracy' (1991–1992) 26 *New Eng L Rev* 1221, 1229. The Ninth Circuit has noted that celebrities may achieve fame 'out of rare ability, dumb luck, or a combination thereof': *White v Samsung Electronic America Inc* 971 F.2d 1395, 1399.

[81] Madow (n 5) 198.

[82] ibid 192.

[83] ibid 184.

[84] ibid 189.

[85] De Grandpre (n 26) 102.

[86] Coombe (n 26) 94; endorsed by Beverley-Smith (n 9) 295–96. Also Klink, '50 Years of Publicity in the US' (2003) 365; Carty (n 9)249.

[87] Coombe (n 26) 94. Also Madow (n 5) 193–96; Carty (n 9)249.

JK Rowling's creation of Harry Potter was presumably assisted by editors, publishers, illustrators, public relations managers, and possibly friends, yet the copyright is only vested in one person. Similarly, those who argue that celebrities are derivative (that Madonna owes her image to Marilyn Monroe, for example) may have a point, but they need to address the fact that art and literature may well be derivative, yet still benefits from copyright protection.

As this brief review shows, individual labour may often be present and it may often be extensive, but it need not be. Even where labour can be demonstrated, it does not follow that it was exclusively the labour of the individual in question, nor can it be proven that there is a direct correlation between labour invested and the resulting persona. Labour therefore cannot operate to justify a general right of publicity.[88]

Consumer protection justifications on the other hand turn the focus from the individual to the public at large. On this analysis, publicity rights are needed to 'protect consumers from deceptive trade practices, especially false representations of endorsement or sponsorship'[89] or to clamp down on 'advertisers of dangerous or shoddy products… manipulat[ing] consumers by exploiting powerful celebrity images'.[90] While a publicity right would ensure that all exploitation would be authorised, and therefore not confusing in that regard, Madow disputes the need to introduce a publicity right simply for these purposes. Members of the public are no longer, if they ever were, likely to believe wholeheartedly that a celebrity uses or believes in the product she advertises.[91] Madow also notes that a right of publicity would far exceed the consumer protection function ascribed to it, by applying in a much wider range of situations.[92] A further objection is that protecting consumers is a concern, and therefore a justification, only where they are exposed to *unauthorised* exploitation: in instances where the individual agrees to the use of his or her persona then there can be no risk of consumer confusion through false or misleading use of persona.[93] One final point is that, even if the

---

[88] A detailed analysis of the role of the labour justification in intellectual property in general is provided by Gordon. One of the points she makes in criticising over-reliance on labour as a justification is that labour can be destructive as well as constructive: 'in the abstract [labour] yields no necessary claim to reward'. W Gordon, 'On Owning Information: Intellectual Property and the Restitutionary Impulse' (1992) 78 *Virginia Law Review* 149, 170.

[89] Madow (n 5) 228.

[90] ibid 228. Consumers are of course still at risk of such practices where the celebrity *does* consent to the use of his or her persona to promote such shoddy products.

[91] ibid 229, fn 478. This is a point also made by Milligan who notes a sea-change in the style and public perception of advertising: 'Gone are the days of "Hi, I'm Kevin Keegan. Let me tell you why I use Brut." The Pepsi ads [featuring Beckham] were far more sophisticated.': Milligan, *Brand it Like Beckham* (2004) 122. See also De Grandpre (n 26) 89.

[92] Madow (n 5) 233.

[93] Although the advertisement itself may still be false or misleading—such practices are regulated through, for example, the Consumer Protection from Unfair Trading Regulations 2008 SI 2008/1277 or by the Advertising Standards Agency's Codes of Practice (available online at www.asa.org.uk/asa/codes/).

above arguments were ignored, the consumer protection justification only operates to justify a right which protects the public—it does not constitute a justification of a right for the individual to control his or her persona. Thus, consumer protection ends could be secured by a right against misleading use of persona, which is enforced by the state.

It is clear that consumer protection concerns alone cannot justify the creation of a publicity right,[94] and especially not in the case of the positive power to exploit. Where publicity is otherwise justified, however, then its contribution to consumer protection can be seen as an additional advantage. Although consumer protection may be one consequence of a right of publicity, it should properly be regarded as an incidental benefit rather than a driver for the right.

While each of these justifications may have something to offer in support of a right of publicity, it is clear that they are insufficient as they stand. Other justifications must be sought.

---

[94] McCarthy accepts that the falsity justification operates as a very limited justification of publicity, if at all: McCarthy, *The Rights of Publicity and Privacy* (2001) para 2:8.

6

Order, Autonomy and Efficiency: Justifying a Right of Publicity

I. Advancing Justifications for Publicity Rights

WITH THE REJECTION of three commonly-advanced arguments now established, we can turn to those justifications which seek to demonstrate that a carefully constructed publicity right can be justified and is certainly desirable, not least when contrasted with the two alternatives: the unsystematic status quo or no right at all.

At the outset, it should be acknowledged that publicity is not a right which is especially easy to justify. It is not a right which is clearly 'good' or beneficial: it is not a right which tackles poverty or outlaws torture or makes a notable contribution to scientific endeavour. On the other hand, neither is it a prejudicial or dangerous or oppressive right. It does not promote racial segregation or discrimination against women, for example. Despite the fact that publicity practice is neither inherently notable nor inherently dangerous, it is something of a Marmite right—commentators either love it or hate it.

A publicity right is, all things considered, a right to regulate a specific practice—and that practice benefits all parties concerned: the individuals who retain control of their persona, while gaining a financial advantage; their commercial exploiters whose custom and reputation is increased; and the populace at large who enjoy the 'fun',[1] colour and human interest that exploitation brings. As McCarthy observes, 'the human mind is more fascinated by people than by ideas... most of our social conversation concerns people'.[2] A publicity right may

---

[1] Carty, who is opposed to a publicity right, accepts that the use of a celebrity in advertising can be fun and eye-catching—'but that is all': H Carty, 'Advertising, Publicity Rights and English Law' [2004] *IPQ* 209, 258.

[2] T McCarthy, 'Public Personas and Private Property: The Commercialization of Human Identity' (1989) 79 *TMR* 681, 682. He demonstrates this by starting his article with the tale of the dispute between Bette Midler and Ford, to awaken the reader's interest in the legal issues at stake.

not feed the world, but nor is it intrinsically harmful.[3] This is a useful perspective to maintain throughout this chapter.

The first justification takes a rather pragmatic approach, by recognising the reality of the practice and the uncertainty of the existing unsystematic legal response. The second and third justifications look respectively to the dignitarian and economic interests inherent in publicity, to demonstrate why a right is necessary. Although objections to these justifications have been made, and will be considered below, it is submitted that these objections are not fatal: rather than leading to the conclusion that there should be no such right, they instead provide a basis for recognising limitations to a right of publicity. These three justifications operate to show that a publicity right is legally and practically desirable, while also forming the basis for limits on that right.

II. Ordering the Chaos

Publicity exploitation is something which happens extensively, as was seen in chapter three. The available evidence shows that individuals and exploiters treat publicity exploitation as a valid commercial practice like any other. There is a large industry built around brand management, licensing, celebrity endorsement, and public relations. The positive practice of publicity exploitation is alive and well. Conversely, there is also a visible trend of unauthorised use followed by litigation to prevent or recover for this use. The courts have been willing to protect the interests of both the individual[4] and the authorised exploiter.[5] Cases such as *Irvine v Talksport Ltd* and *Douglas v Hello!*[6]—despite the many critical analyses of their doctrinal bases—demonstrate that lawyers and the courts are prepared to recognise the practice and provide remedies. The door to publicity rights protection is therefore ajar, if not standing open.

This can be seen as the logical progression of legal development. De Grandpre, who provides an economic justification for publicity, refers to 'the evolution of the right of publicity in the last one hundred years or so, from not being recognized at all, to being recognized as an inalienable personal right, to becoming, in many jurisdictions, a form of property'.[7] The social practice has

---

[3] See also Westfall and Landau, who state that the right of publicity is 'both hard to object to and hard to support': in Westfall and D Landau, 'Publicity Rights as Property Rights' (2005–2006) 23 *Cardozo Arts and Ent LJ* 71, 121.

[4] In England: *Douglas v Hello!* [2006] QB 125; *Irvine v Talksport Ltd* [2003] 2 All ER 881. In the US: *Midler v Ford Motor Company* 849 F 2d 460 (9th Cit 1988).

[5] In England: *Douglas v Hello!* [2008] 1 AC 1. In the US: *Haelan Laboratories v Topps Chewing Gum Inc* 202 F 2d 866 (2nd Cir 1953).

[6] *Irvine v Talksport Ltd* [2003] 2 All ER 881; *Douglas v Hello!* [2006] QB 125.

[7] V de Grandpre, 'Understanding the Market for Celebrity: An Economic Analysis of the Right of Publicity' (2001–2002) 12 *Fordham Intell Prop Media and Ent LJ* 73, 78. Also Westfall and Landau, 'Publicity Rights as Property Rights' (2005–2006) 72–74.

driven the legal change, and with the increasing practice of publicity comes a crystallisation of the law, as 'general principles of fairness and equity… give way, in their maturity, to more certain legal rules'.[8] This need for certainty results in the drawing of

> … ever sharper lines around our entitlements so that we can identify the relevant players and so that we can trade instead of getting into confusions and disputes – confusions and disputes that would otherwise only escalate as the goods in question became scarcer and more highly valued.[9]

Although publicity is not tangible, it is potentially exposed to scarcity and exhaustion nonetheless, as will be examined in section IV. C. below. Thus, in publicity, as in other areas of law, the evolution of social practice can be seen to drive the evolution of law.

Law as a response to social reality arguably takes us only a limited way towards a justification for publicity. Indeed, some would contend that it does not even achieve that, since reliance on commercial practice alone is on one view 'hardly a satisfactory basis on which to analyse the development of the law'.[10] It is certainly the case that other activities are prohibited by law despite the brisk trade and social participation that they generate. The fact that there is supply and demand for cocaine and heroin is, on its own, unlikely to convince the public that these drugs should be legalised. There are of course arguments that legalisation of these drugs would enable more effective control by the Government, as some arguably 'undesirable' activities (such as the production and sale of alcohol) are licensed to enable them to be regulated. This analogy is not exact, however, since even if the desirability of legal protection is not universally accepted, publicity is not obviously socially undesirable in the same manner as drugs (one cannot overdose on Hello! magazine). Nonetheless, it does demonstrate that there must be more to a legal right than the simple fact of social and commercial practice in that area. In the words of Coombe (in the context of property): 'the decision to allocate particular property rights is a prior question of social policy that requires philosophical and moral deliberations and a consideration of social costs and benefits'.[11]

Consideration of the social costs and benefits follows in sections 3 and 4 below but, for the present, law's response to the practice of publicity provides the first justification for a right of publicity. The fact that most legal systems have, so far, recognised a right of publicity through a wide range of causes of action, produces a twin-pronged justification for a clearer, more coherent right.

---

[8] de Grandpre, 'Understanding the Market for Celebrity' (2001–2002) 76.
[9] CM Rose, *Property and Persuasion* (Colorado, Westview, 1994) 199–200.
[10] Carty, 'Advertising, Publicity Rights and English Law' (2004) 246, fn omitted.
[11] R Coombe, 'Author/izing the Celebrity: Publicity Rights, Postmodern Politics, and Unauthorized Genders' (1991–1992) 10 *Cardozo Arts & Ent LJ* 365, 368.

In the first place, publicity rights do exist in many jurisdictions, and even in those jurisdictions where there is no publicity right, claimants can usually obtain some measure of protection through an amalgam of rights, including registered trade marks, passing off and privacy laws.[12] If the onus is on the 'advocates of change' to prove the benefits[13] then this works both ways: not only do those in favour of a right of publicity have to prove why such right is necessary, but those who are opposed to publicity rights have their own justificatory mission, in order to show why these existing rights should be denied altogether in publicity cases. Those who wish to reject publicity entirely must make a case for this. Westfall and Landau note that the critics of publicity rights are 'good at tearing down positive arguments for the right of publicity, [but] they are not nearly as good at building their own positive case against those rights'.[14] Even Madow, who persuasively argues *against* the justifications for a publicity right, acknowledges this and claims that '[t]here is work to do on the other side of the question as well. A definite argument for the outright abolition of the right of publicity cannot be made on the present state of the record.'[15] It is not sufficient to do this simply on the grounds that the existing method of protection is inappropriate for the task of protecting publicity. For example, many English commentators argue that passing off is not suited to protect publicity interests.[16] I would certainly agree with this assertion, but not with the subsequent claim that rejecting passing off (or any other specified doctrine) as a home for publicity rights equates to the rejection of publicity rights in all circumstances. Rejecting a specific doctrine does not equate to rejecting the underlying premise of protecting publicity rights. It is therefore not sufficient for critics of publicity rights to challenge them on the basis that the current method of protection is inappropriate: legal protection per se must be addressed.

Closely allied to this is the second prong of this justification. Both proponents and opponents of publicity rights point to the typically chaotic and incoherent nature of current publicity protection. The current UK and US approaches—the latter reliant on a wide range of state legislation, case law, federal jurisprudence, tort and unfair competition restatements—are certainly not an ideal coherent whole. The protection for publicity rights in the United States is not necessarily to be envied or emulated.

---

[12] As for example in England. See chapters two and three.

[13] As advocated by the Adelphi Charter, adopted by the Royal Society for the Arts, 13 October 2005.

[14] Westfall and Landau (n 3) 121.

[15] M Madow, 'Private Ownership of Public Image: Popular Culture and Publicity Rights' (1993) 81 *Cal L Rev* 125, 239.

[16] Leading critics of this use of passing off are H Beverley-Smith et al, *Privacy, Property and Personality* (Cambridge, Cambridge University Press, 2005) 15–34 and Carty (n 1) 235–237, but note her acceptance of the use of passing off where 'real endorsement is being misrepresented in the advertising', at 258. At the Fordham Intellectual Property Conference on 28 March 2008, Professor Laddie stated in person that he viewed *Irvine* as a straightforward passing off case and that it did not involve issues of publicity (a right with which he disagreed).

Yet, this does not mean that publicity rights could never have such coherence. Although some critics use the unsystematic or chaotic nature of legal protection as an argument to reject publicity rights in principle, the opposite conclusion is at least equally valid. Instead of being advanced as an argument *against* publicity rights, these concerns of chaos and incoherence can be seen as an argument *for* publicity rights. The dangers of allowing rights to develop through ad hoc litigation, as is currently the case in the United Kingdom, and the advantages of strategic and deliberate legislative development are demonstrated by Hughes in his consideration of intellectual property in general:

> There is a very simple reason why the legal doctrines of unfair competition and trade secret protection are inherently oriented toward the value-added theory: they are court-created doctrines and people rarely go to court unless something valuable is at stake. *When intellectual property is created more systematically, such as through legislation, the resulting property doctrines seem less singularly oriented toward rewarding social value.*[17]

Any rejection of publicity rights based on its incoherent development to date can be countered by advocating the advantages of legislation. Criticism of the status quo should not result in the automatic rejection of publicity rights as a whole.

It is possible to advance a counter-argument, by claiming that the rationalisation of the existing ad hoc protection through legislation only holds good where there is a prior justification in favour of a statutory right. However, this argument is capable of working equally for and against statutory protection: the chaos and incoherence of ad hoc measures cannot be advanced as a ground for abolishing any such right(s) without a prior justification for the abolition either.

The reality is that publicity practice—and legal acceptance of that practice—is a feature of life. This operates as a justificatory sword *and* shield. The internal incoherence of that 'right', or series of rights, demonstrates just why a single, purpose-built right is needed, thereby attacking the status quo. However, the current practice also shields publicity rights from opponents who wish to cut it down altogether, since they too must provide a justification for such a course of action.

This rather pragmatic justification, based on the need to impose some order on the incoherence that is existing publicity rights protection, is supported by two substantive justifications, which appeal to dignitarian and economic considerations.

---

[17] J Hughes, 'The Philosophy of Intellectual Property' (1988) *77 Georgetown Law Journal* 287, 306, emphasis added.

III. The Dignitarian Rationale for Publicity

The second justification in favour of a right of publicity is based upon fundamental notions of autonomy and dignity: a right of publicity enables control of persona, which is an inherent part of each individual.

A. Autonomy and Dignity

Autonomy is the notion that individuals should be free to make their own life choices, with as little regulation from external sources as possible, subject to the need for each individual to respect the self-respect and bodily integrity of others.[18] The exercise of autonomy enables each individual to take responsibility for his or her own life choices and pursuit of the 'good life'.[19] Such is the importance of autonomy in the Western legal tradition that MacCormick says '[i]f there is any fundamental moral value, that of respect for persons as autonomous agents seems the best candidate for that position'.[20] The role of law is, in part, 'to prevent the violation of a citizen's autonomy, dignity and self-esteem'.[21]

In fact, MacCormick argues that the fundamental human right to privacy is based on the prior acceptance of individual autonomy:

> the value upon which privacy rests is, surely, the value of autonomy in shaping a personal, as distinct from a public, dimension of one's life. The wrong of intrusion is the wrong of infringing that aspect of an individual's autonomy contrary to his wish and without his permission.[22]

This argument is made in the context of privacy, and it is not my intention to predicate a right of publicity on a prior right of privacy. Nonetheless, the recognition of autonomy as the principle underlying privacy, and its importance in enabling the individual to control that right of privacy together with recognition of the corresponding wrong done by unauthorised intrusion, is of relevance when justifying a right of publicity.

Alongside autonomy, and complementing it, is the notion of dignity.[23] The right to autonomy is seen as contributing to an individual's dignity:

---

[18] And also (although of less relevance in this context) to avoid causing damage to public institutions. See N MacCormick, *Legal Right and Social Democracy* (Oxford, Clarendon Press, 1982, reprinted 1986) 37.

[19] See N MacCormick, *Institutions of Law: An Essay in Legal Theory* (Oxford, Oxford University Press, 2007) ch 14, especially at 249.

[20] MacCormick, *Legal Right and Social Democracy* (1982, reprinted 1986) 35.

[21] *Mosley v News Group Newspapers Ltd* [2008] EWHC 1777 (QB) [7].

[22] MacCormick (n 18) 178. See also *Campbell v MGN* [2004] 2 AC 457 [51] (Lord Hoffmann).

[23] Oliver identifies five key values which she claims underlie both public and private law, as being dignity, autonomy, respect, status and security: D Oliver, 'The Underlying Values of Public and Private Law' in M Taggart (ed), *The Province of Administrative Law* (Oxford, Hart, 1997) 218.

> The right to make one's own decisions about many aspects of one's fate, and to contribute to decisions made by others which affect one's life can be seen as a major contribution to an individual's dignity, likening the notion [of dignity] to a Kantian perspective on morality.[24]

In this way, dignity works to 'bolster individual freedom by making it desirable to enhance autonomy and moral integrity or to provide social and political rights to an infrastructure which enables people to live in a dignified way'.[25]

The correlation between autonomy and dignity—and their fundamental place in our society—gains further support from article 8 of the European Convention on Human Rights (ECHR), which states that '[e]veryone shall have respect for his private and family life, his home and correspondence'. Eady J recently affirmed the correlation between privacy and dignity in *Mosley v News Group Newspapers Ltd*, wherein he held that the infringement of Mosley's privacy by the *News of the World* 'has taken away or undermined the right of another – in this case taken away a person's dignity and struck at the core of his personality'. As Moreham argues, the Convention jurisprudence on article 8 reveals five sub-categories of private life interest and one of these is the 'right to live autonomously'.[26] Although Moreham's focus is on infringement of autonomy and personal freedom in sexual and familial relationships and medical treatment,[27] she recognises that 'all interferences with private life will affect autonomy to some extent'.[28]

Respect for autonomy is not restricted to human rights: it affects every area of life. Radin assesses the relationship between property and personhood, in particular in relation to objects so 'closely related to one's personhood [that] its loss causes pain that cannot be relieved by the object's replacement'.[29] Objects which fall into this class 'could be described as simply a category of property for personal autonomy or liberty'.[30] Although she goes on to develop this theory in much greater detail than can be related here, her starting point is worth noting, whereby individuals can become connected with the external world through

---

[24] D Feldman, 'Human Dignity as a Legal Value: Part 1' [1999] *PL* 682, 685.

[25] ibid.

[26] NA Moreham, 'The Right to Respect for Private Life in the European Convention on Human Rights: a Re-examination' [2008] *EHRLR* 44, 71.

[27] For further detail on personal autonomy in the context of medical treatment, see K Mason and G Laurie, 'Personal Autonomy and the Right to Treatment' (2005) Vol 9 *Edin LR* 123; G Laurie, 'Personality, Privacy and Autonomy in Medical Law' in NR Whitty and R Zimmermann (eds), *Rights of Personality in Scots Law: A Comparative Perspective* (Dundee, Dundee University Press, 2009).

[28] Moreham, 'The Right to Respect for Private Life' (2008) 71. This interpretation is echoed in Feldman's analysis of dignity in the context of human rights, where he notes that article 8 is as much about protecting autonomy as dignity, but that this affords indirect protection for dignity. See D Feldman, 'Human Dignity as a Legal Value: Part 1' [1999] *PL* 682, 694.

[29] M Radin, 'Property and Personhood' (1982) 34 *Stanford Law Review* 957, 959.

[30] ibid 960.

being bound up with external 'things' which 'they feel are almost part of themselves'.[31] Property can therefore be a very necessary expression of an individual's autonomy and dignity.

However, autonomy is not sacrosanct: not all interferences with the exercise of autonomy will be prohibited. In some cases there may be a valid (albeit potentially paternalistic) restriction on individual actions, in order to protect the interests of other individuals or society in general.[32] A good example of this is the French ban on dwarf-throwing competitions, because 'it was an affront to human dignity to put on a spectacle devoted to allowing spectators to throw a person selected by reason of his suffering from a physical handicap'.[33] The need to respect the human dignity (of society in general) was given priority over the interests of the dwarf in question, who was in fact keen to participate in such competitions in order to make a living. Accordingly, dignity here was placed 'above the freedom of an individual member of the group to choose how to exploit his or her physical form'.[34] Objective conceptions of dignity can therefore be used as a ground on which to interfere with the exercise of (possibly subjective standards[35] of) personal autonomy.

B. The Significance of Image for Autonomy

The critical importance of image has recently been emphasised by a decision of the European Court of Human Rights (ECtHR), *Reklos v Greece*.[36] The action was raised by the parents of a child, claiming a breach of their article 8 right to private and family life. The day after the birth of their son, the applicants (his parents) were offered the opportunity to purchase photographs of him, taken by the professional photographer in the private clinic. The photographs were taken face-on to the baby. Not only had the parents not consented to the taking of these pictures, but it also revealed that the photographer had been into the sterile unit where their son was being treated, despite the fact that access to the unit was

---

[31] ibid 959.

[32] See for example MacCormick (n 18) chs 2 and 9.

[33] Feldman, 'Human Dignity as a Legal Value: Part 1' (1999) 701. Manuel Wackenheim, the dwarf, challenged the French ban in front of the UN Human Rights Committee on the grounds that the ban was discriminatory and that allowing dwarf-tossing actually upheld his dignity, since dignity consists of having a job. He was unsuccessful, with the UN Committee holding that the ban was not discriminatory and that it was based on reasonable and objective criteria. *Manuel Wackenheim v France*, UN Human Rights Committee Communication No 854/1999 of 15 July 2002.

[34] ibid.

[35] For example, N Whitty, 'Overview of Rights of Personality in Scots Law' in N Whitty and R Zimmermann (eds), *Rights of Personality in Scots Law, a Comparative Perspective* (Dundee, Dundee University Press, 2009) para 3.4.11.

[36] *Reklos v Greece* (App no 1234/05) (2009), [2009] EMLR 16.

restricted to doctors and nurses. The parents complained to the clinic management, but their request that the negatives be handed over was refused. After exhausting their domestic remedies in Greece, they then raised an action under the ECHR.

It is important to note that this is very much a claim under article 8 for invasion of private life and, moreover, there was no attempt to publish or disseminate the photographs.[37] There was in fact specific reference by the Government that there had been no commercial exploitation of the images. Thus, for the reasons examined in chapter four, this is a privacy case and not a publicity case.

However, the opinion of the ECtHR is highly relevant, because the question of 'private life' (not privacy) includes 'the right to identity and the right to personal development, whether in terms of personality or of personal autonomy, which is an important principle underlying the interpretation of the article 8 guarantees'.[38] Autonomy therefore lies at the heart of the wider article 8. In a key passage, the Court stated:

> A person's image constitutes one of the chief attributes of his or her personality, as it reveals the person's unique characteristics and distinguishes the person from his peers. The right to the protection of one's image is thus one of the essential components of personal development and presupposes the right to control the use of that image. Whilst in most cases the right to control such uses involves the possibility for an individual to refuse publication of his or her image, it also covers the individual's right to object to the recording, conservation and reproduction of the image by another person. As a person's image is one of the characteristics attached to his or her personality, its effective protection presupposes, in principle and in circumstances such as those of the present case, obtaining the consent of the person concerned at the time the picture is taken and not simply if and when it is published. Otherwise an essential attribute of personality would be retained in the hands of a third party and the person concerned would have no control over any subsequent use of the image.[39]

This is a very strong statement of the importance of an individual's image and its significance for personal development (and thus autonomy), with the corresponding need to ensure that it is protected from unauthorised use.

C. Autonomy and Dignity in the Context of Publicity

How does this understanding of autonomy and dignity apply to publicity rights? Central to the exercise of autonomy and dignity are the notions of personal choice and control, and these are the very notions which are jeopardised where there is no right of publicity. Lacking a right of publicity, individuals can attempt

---

[37] The fact that there had been no publication was advanced as a defence by the Greek Government, but rejected.
[38] *Reklos v Greece* (App no 1234/05) (2009), [2009] EMLR 16, [39], references omitted.
[39] ibid [40], reference omitted, emphasis added.

to control when and where their persona—their very identity—is used, and by whom, but there is no certainty of success. Coombe acknowledges the fundamental connection between an individual and his or her persona, whereby individuals 'never lose their autonomy from the objects that circulate in their likeness'.[40] Kwall also recognises the 'damage to the human spirit'[41] which can arise from publicity infringements and which, for her, necessitates a role for moral rights in publicity. Critically, lack of control over persona makes it difficult to prevent unauthorised or unsought use. It is the *unsought* intrusion which MacCormick identifies (above) as the heart of intrusion into privacy, and there seems to be no reason for reaching a different conclusion in the case of publicity. Thus, autonomy and dignity operate to justify a right for each individual to control the use of his or her persona.[42]

Control, and thus autonomy, lies at the heart of McCarthy's justification of a publicity right:

> the [justification] that appeals the most to me is the simplest and most obvious. It is the natural right of property justification. It is an appeal to first principles of justice. *Each and every human being should be given control over the commercial use of his or her identity.* Perhaps nothing is so strongly intuited as the notion that my identity is mine – it is my property, to control as I see fit. Put simply, my identity is 'me'. The existence of a legal right to control identity would seem to be essential to any civilized society.[43]

This is a powerful and emotive argument, and underlies the 'natural rights of property' school of thought.[44] As the added emphasis in the above quotation shows, McCarthy identifies *control of identity* as the core notion to be protected by a publicity right, and this is inherent in the rights to autonomy and dignity.[45]

McCarthy's justification is made in the context of a Common law jurisdiction, and there is even greater evidence of the primacy of the individual and personal choice in Civilian jurisdictions. Neethling starts his review of personality rights by noting that they 'recognize a person as a physical and spiritual-moral being

---

[40] R Coombe, *The Cultural Life of Intellectual Properties: Authorship Appropriation, and the Law* (Durham and London, Duke University Press, 1998) 102.

[41] RR Kwall, 'Preserving Personality and Reputational Interests of Constructed Personas through Moral Rights: a Blueprint for the Twenty-First Century' [2001] *U Ill L Rev* 151, 152.

[42] Interestingly, Carty's main objection to this justification is that it is 'not part of the Anglo-American tradition' (Carty (n 1) 250), but autonomy is increasing relevant in English law, thanks in part to the influence of the ECHR. See *Mosley v News Group Newspapers* [2008] EWHC 1777 (QB) [7]; *Wood v Commissioner of Police for the Metropolis* [2009] EWCA Civ 414 [20]; *Reklos v Greece* (App no 1234/05) (2009), [2009] EMLR 16.

[43] McCarthy, 'Public Personas and Private Property' (1989) 685, emphasis added. See also T McCarthy, *The Rights of Publicity and Privacy*, 2nd edn (United States, West Group, 2001) para 2:5, where he repeats this and adds that, if this control is denied, then 'the law is an ass'. (Quoting Dickens, *Oliver Twist*.)

[44] I am not seeking to advocate a natural right of property for publicity however: whether or not property is indeed the most appropriate legal classification will be examined in later chapters.

[45] *Reklos v Greece* (App no 1234/05) (2009), [2009] EMLR 16. Also O Weber, 'Human dignity and the commercial appropriation of personality: towards a cosmopolitan consensus in publicity rights?' (2004) 1:1 *SCRIPT-ed* 160.

and guarantee his enjoyment of his own sense of existence'.[46] In the context of German law, Beverley-Smith et al explain that §823 I BGB, which protects absolute subjective personality rights,[47] is

> based on a theory of subjective rights which has its roots in the legal philosophy of Immanuel Kant and the legal theory of Savigny: subjective rights delimit certain spheres in which each individual can act according to his or her free will'.[48]

Further, the protection of autonomy and dignity can be seen clearly in the protection of other intangible attributes of personhood: one's beliefs, emotions and relationships, and education. These are attributes that Western legal systems are committed to protecting, and they all enable autonomous action and self-determination. Article 8 (respect for family and private life), article 9 (right to freedom of thought, conscience and religion), and article 2, protocol I (right to education) of the ECHR guarantee these intangible aspects of an individual.

An analogy can also be drawn between persona and the *tangible* aspects of each individual. Just as my hands and kidneys are mine to control,[49] so is my persona. Although this raises the spectre of ownership of the body and body parts, it can in fact be addressed without resolving this complex moral and ethical question. Whether or not I can truly be said to 'own' my hands or my kidneys does not detract from the fundamental principle that no one else has any better right to control what I do with them than I do. My right to dignity and autonomous action necessitates that I have control over my hands and my kidneys, and my body in general. Thus, whether hands or kidneys are susceptible to ownership does not need to be definitively answered to be able to answer the primary question: who controls them? I do.[50]

D.   Denial of Autonomy and Dignity in Publicity

Not only do autonomy and dignity require each individual to have control of his or her life and life choices, but they also illustrate the harm caused when that right to control is denied, unless there is a legitimate reason for such denial, as in

---

[46]   Neethling, 'Personality Rights' (2006) 530.

[47]   Comprising the rights to life, body, health, freedom, property or 'any other right of another person'. See §823 I BGB (www.gesetze-im-internet.de/englisch_bgb/) and the analysis thereof in Beverley-Smith et al, *Privacy, Property and Personality* (2005) 97.

[48]   ibid 97, fn omitted.

[49]   At least, this is certainly the case while they are still attached to me and I am still alive. (For discussion as to rights after severance, see NR Whitty, 'Rights of Personality, Property Rights and the Human Body in Scots Law' (2005) 9 *Edin LR* 194.) Whether persona can be separated and whether it can survive post mortem will be examined in chapters eight and nine.

[50]   Although slavery has existed in different societies at different times, thereby showing that 'ownership' and control of one's body *can* be asserted by another person, in the twenty-first century it is non-controversial to assert that the only person who *should* control the use of a body is that particular individual. This is enshrined in article 4(1) of the ECHR: 'No one shall be held in slavery or servitude.'

the case of the dwarf-throwing competition. Whether or not such good reasons exist in cases of publicity will be considered in chapter 10. The present examination will focus on the consequences of denying individuals the right to control the use of their persona.

Where an individual is unable to control the use of his or her persona, it impacts on both the individual's negative right to prevent use and positive power to exploit his or her persona. Since there is no right for the individual to give or withhold such consent, persona becomes freely available for use by others,[51] without the need to seek the consent of the individual.

Yet, a specific wrong occurs where the individual's persona is used without the individual's consent. Spence analyses the consequences of unpermitted use of a trader's brand name in the context of passing off.[52] Although the current discussion does not focus on use of corporate identity in passing off, the points he makes hold good. The starting point for Spence's argument is that where a company uses a rival trader's brand without the consent of that trader, it is making an untruthful representation and 'a community that claims to value truthfulness, must be reluctant to allow one party to suffer harm, or indeed another party to benefit, as a consequence of an untruthful statement'.[53]

In a passionate claim, Spence emphasises the attack on autonomy that results when unauthorised (and therefore 'untruthful') use is made of the rival brand, such that it becomes a mask that is used by the unauthorised exploiter:

> The maintenance of a society of autonomous persons must involve at least some prevention of others, unauthorised, speaking on their behalf. In this way, the wrong in passing off not only parallels the wrong in plagiarism, it also somehow parallels the wrong in torture. As De Grazia has pointed out, one of the wrongs involved in torture is the appropriation of another's voice, the unauthorised assumption of the right to speak on his behalf. It is arguably precisely this right that is involved when one trader claims to speak through the identity of even a corporate rival.[54]

The claim here is that just as torture is used to subjugate the voice of the victim to that of the torturer, so the unauthorised use of the brand suppresses the brand owner's voice and imposes upon his or her brand the voice or 'message' of the unauthorised user. McCarthy refers to a similar analogy drawn by Cobb J, whereby the unauthorised use of image enslaves the individual: the individual's loss of control means he or she is no longer free.[55]

What is particularly interesting about Spence's argument is that it is made in the context of one company passing itself off as another *juristic* person, yet it can

---

[51] MacCormick, *Institutions of Law* (2007) 126. MacCormick illustrates this with the example of Neil Armstrong being sued in a Scottish court for trespass upon the moon: 'the absence of any prohibition in Scots law entails a (passive) right in Mr Armstrong that the action against him be summarily dismissed' (at 126).

[52] M Spence, 'Passing Off and the Misappropriation of Valuable Intangibles' (1996) 112 *LQR* 472.

[53] ibid 497.

[54] ibid 498.

[55] McCarthy, *The Rights of Publicity and Privacy* (2001) para 2:5, and references therein.

be applied to the use of an individual's brand, his or her persona, as well. Where this happens, the individual has lost control of his or her persona and thus his or her autonomy is infringed, because the individual's persona is used to convey the message of another party without his or her consent or control. Further, although passing off is traditionally seen as an action to protect the economic interests of the trader, Spence's arguments here reveal the dignitarian interests that are also present in a misrepresentation of the company through misuse of its trade mark. These arguments, made in the context of passing off disputes between companies, arguably apply with even greater force in the case of publicity rights, where the subject of the misrepresentation is a natural person whose very identity is being abused and misappropriated.

Nonetheless, it is difficult to accept that there is much in common between Eddie Irvine and victims of torture throughout the world. While the analogy between torture and passing off put forward by Spence is thought-provoking, it is too extreme to command much sympathy in this context. Its underlying message can instead be applied through a less emotive analogy.

The real harm done in such cases, Spence argues, is the unauthorised use, and consequent suppression, of someone else's voice. This results in harm both to the individual (or company) *and* to the society which receives the 'untruthful' message. A similar, yet less extreme, analogy for the suppression of voice and subsequent harm can be found in the right to vote.[56] This is an intangible right of every adult, and is recognised as fundamental in a democratic society. The unauthorised 'use' of someone else's vote would deprive that individual of his or her voice in a democratic society and be an affront to the individual's autonomy. If an individual's vote were to be commandeered or confiscated, harm would be done to the individual and to the wider society and the process of democracy. Not only would the individual have lost his or her voice and, consequently, the ability to speak on his or her own behalf and autonomy, but society's interest in truthfulness (and democracy) would also be tarnished if it failed to stop the misuse.

The association of identity with truthful communication which underlies Spence's argument can also be found in the Civilian right to identity. Neethling defines the right to identity as arising from a person's 'uniqueness which individualizes him as a particular person and this distinguishes him from others... A person's identity is infringed by falsification, i.e. where indicia are used in a way which cannot be reconciled with his true identity.'[57] Although the identity right which Neethling is discussing is a personal, non-patrimonial right, the importance of the right of the individual to prevent false use is evident here.

---

[56] Many local authorities encourage their residents to join the Electoral Register with phrases such as 'Don't lose your voice – register to vote' and 'Make your voice heard'. There is a clear link between voting and voice in Western democracies.
[57] J Neethling, 'Personality Rights' in Jan M Smits (ed), *Elgar Encyclopaedia of Comparative Law* (Cheltenham, Edward Elgar, 2006) 540.

This concept of using persona to deceive can also be found in Logeais' analysis of the French image right. She states:

fame is best conveyed through the name or picture which are inherent to the person and therefore their use or perfect imitation makes identification certain. *Because these intrinsic 'marks' are so personal and inseparable from the person, their use implies some necessary deliberate involvement of the person, that is, the likelihood of deception or implied endorsement,* unless the use is too blatantly inconsistent with their status or position to imply a likely consent on the part of the celebrity.[58]

This echoes Spence's concern that, unless the use is blatantly false, it is potentially deceptive and harmful to society and to the individual.[59] Even Madow, who argues that publicity protection is largely unjustified, accepts that use which *does* constitute a misrepresentation is not to be permitted, since he argues (in the context of a specific example) that the actor Robert Young cannot 'cry foul when someone markets a T-shirt emblazoned with his smiling, benign face and the slogan "Father Knows Nothing" – *provided, of course, it is clear to consumers that Young himself has neither approved nor sponsored the product.*'[60] Thus, Madow appears to concede that use which is misrepresentative, and purports to use the individual's persona—the individual's 'voice'—with his or her consent, when in fact there has been no consent, should not be permitted. However, where there is no misrepresentation then, on this analysis, we should be slower to accept that there is a problem. One situation where Madow would contend that there is no misrepresentation would be where the publicity use is 'blatantly inconsistent' with the individual's status. This might arise in some cases of subversive or parodic cultural communication, where there is a cultural or artistic use of persona. However, it is possible to accept Madow's position, that there are competing uses of persona which should be permitted, without leading inevitably to the conclusion that *any* uses of persona are valid. Instead, co-existence may well be possible—and this will be explored in chapter 10.

The conclusion remains: right to control use of persona is essential in any society which professes to respect dignity and autonomy. Failure to protect this harms the individual and society as a whole.

---

[58] E Logeais, 'The French Right to One's Image: a Legal Lure?' [1994] *Ent LR* 163, 169, emphasis added.

[59] This is a more serious concern than the consumer protection justification considered in the previous chapter. Whereas consumer protection aims to protect the consumer from being misled, and the consequent damage to his or her economic interests, this is concerned with the harm that arises to individuals and to society as a whole when an identity is used, without consent, to communicate a deceptive message, thereby depriving that individual of his or her own 'voice'.

[60] Madow, 'Private Ownership of Public Image' (1993) 200, emphasis added.

E.   Autonomy and Dignity in the Economic Interest

Although this justification relies on fundamental notions of each individual's personhood, and innate rights, it should not be taken to limit a right of publicity to protection of dignitarian interests. Protection of autonomy and dignity enables control of economic, as well as dignitarian interests.

This stance contrasts with Madow's, for example.[61] As shown in the previous section, he is prepared to accept that justifications based on personal interests could operate to justify a publicity right, but declines to consider them, since they 'can at most, I think, justify a *personal* right against certain kinds of unauthorized commercial appropriation'.[62] Madow's primary reason for reaching this conclusion appears to be that the damage done to interests such as dignity is not damage to the individual's wallet, or economic interests, 'but to her interest in not being misrepresented or cast in an offensive "false light"'.[63]

However, it is not obvious that the economic and dignitarian interests can be so clearly separated. As discussed in chapter five, they are parts of the same whole, and that whole is the individual's persona. Where there is control there can be exploitation (for profit or otherwise), as well as the right of non-exploitation. To some extent, this is the same as the basis for employment. Where an individual has the right to control the use of his or her hands and intellect, the individual can choose to exploit them commercially by seeking employment, and he or she has control over the nature of that employment. No other private party[64] has the right to control the individual's choice of employment or unemployment, and whether the individual chooses to pursue the highest salary, the most rewarding career, or the most interesting lifestyle is a matter for the individual. It does not make sense to say that where the individual controls his or her body and intellect for the purposes of a career which meets his or her dignitarian interests then that control will be respected, but not where the individual chooses to exercise that control for the economic rewards that employment brings. Further, economically- and emotionally-fulfilling careers are not mutually exclusive, and this also applies to publicity rights. The ability to control the use of my persona—to publish in OK! instead of Hello!—may be as rewarding to my dignitarian as to my economic interests. The fact that both OK! and Hello! offered the Douglases the same fee suggests that there was indeed an

---

[61]   And also Beverley-Smith, who makes the brief observation that autonomy and dignity 'obviously do not justify protecting predominantly economic interests in personality'. H Beverley-Smith, *The Commercial Appropriation of Personality* (Cambridge, Cambridge University Press, 2002) 314.

[62]   Madow (n 15) 181, note 271, emphasis in the original.

[63]   ibid 182, note 271.

[64]   Article 4(3) of the ECHR does recognise that the state may impose work on an individual in the course of detention or as part of compulsory military service (or, for conscientious objectors, as an alternative to that military service).

additional, non-monetary, deciding factor between the two magazines: a dignitarian factor, perhaps? Support for the protection of dignity and autonomy in an economic context can also be drawn from the Restatement of the Law on Unfair Competition, 3d, which focuses on the commercial value in identity and states that '[l]ike the right of privacy, the right of publicity protects an individual's interest in personal dignity and autonomy'.[65]

Thus, economic interests, as well as dignitarian ones, can be protected through a right of publicity.

F. Waiver of Autonomy and Dignity in Persona?

One common argument advanced against publicity protection is that, through their own conduct, celebrities have waived their rights to autonomy, dignity or privacy. As one journalist put it, following the revelations of Tiger Woods' infidelities: 'Put simply, it is not credible for anyone to trade lucratively on their public image and to expect the press to leave them be when there is evidence of behaviour (albeit behind closed doors) that directly contradicts that image.'[66] The fact that an individual has courted publicity in the past means that the individual can have no complaint when his or her image, or another aspect of the individual's persona, is used in the future.[67] On this interpretation, dignity and autonomy cannot justify a legal right to control persona where the individual has provided a general waiver through his or her own conduct.

There are two responses to this. The first is simply that, even if this argument were to be accepted, it does not negate a right to control persona at all: it can only operate in individual cases. Thus, if it is possible to waive a publicity right, it must be determined on a case by case basis, according to the actions of the individual (usually a celebrity). Of course, this approach gives rise to its own problems. How is such waiver to be identified? Does the fact that I have consented to merchandise bearing my image mean that I have waived my rights regarding promotion or media use of my persona? Or must the waiver be 'like for like'? Or is the waiver much broader than that, whereby any famous person is deemed to have waived his right to control persona by virtue of being famous, regardless of the source of that fame?

However, a second objection can be advanced against this 'waiver' claim, which is that we do not deny legal rights in other spheres solely on the basis of past behaviour, least of all rights which strike at something as fundamental as autonomy and dignity. A waiver of the right to private life in the context of a medical examination does not constitute a waiver either in respect of all future medical examinations or any other invasion of bodily integrity. Likewise, a waiver

---

[65] American Law Institute's Restatement of the Law, Unfair Competition, 3d, ch 4, para 46.
[66] Matthew Syed, 'Tiger Woods has Forfeited his Right to Privacy' *The Times* (9 December 2009).
[67] Madow (n 15) 168–169.

of copyright on one occasion cannot be taken as a perpetual waiver for all future work produced by that person. Where a person chooses to appear in a public arena— singing at a concert, competing at a sporting event—that should not be seen as consent to all other public uses.

There are, of course, those celebrities who are famous for being famous, and who do appear to court fame and notoriety, seemingly with little dignity.[68] While it may be difficult to have much sympathy for the voracious appetite of some for exposure at any cost, it should not impact upon the basic principles of autonomy and dignity, which require respect for image and identity. Where there is self-seeking exposure, it would be appropriate to consider defences or permitted uses of identity—a point to be addressed in future chapters.

G. Summary

Respect for autonomy and dignity are two principles at the heart of our legal tradition, and reflect the importance of allowing each individual to make his or her own life choices and pursue his or her own concept of the morally good life. In the context of publicity rights, autonomy and dignity require that each individual has control over something as inherently personal and inseparable as persona. This is not a 'lofty' basis for protecting persona,[69] but a fundamental one.

The denial of a right of publicity therefore interferes with autonomy and dignity in two ways, reflecting the positive and negative aspects of publicity identified in chapter three. In the first place, the individual loses the certainty of control in cases of self-exploitation of persona. While it is always open to the individual to enter into contracts for exploitation of persona, the legal right behind such agreements remains uncertain, absent a recognised publicity right. Second, the lack of a right effectively places each individual's persona in the public domain, where it can be used by anyone, without seeking the consent of the individual. As Spence shows, the misrepresentation that arises from use of an individual's persona—his or her 'voice'—without the individual's consent harms society as well as the individual, not least because of the infringement of the individual's autonomy and dignity. However, it would be erroneous to conclude that a justification based on autonomy and dignity can only justify use of persona in a dignitarian context. The right to control persona results in protection for the individual's economic interests as well as his or her dignitarian interests.

---

[68] The tabloids are frequently full of these minor celebrities, and the lack of dignity can be illustrated by the recent voyeuristic trend for paparazzi 'crotch shots', taken as the (female) celebrity gets into or out of a car.
[69] Beverley-Smith, *The Commercial Appropriation of Personality* (2002) 313.

IV. The Economic Rationale for Publicity

In addition to the dignitarian justification, two separate, but mutually re-enforcing, arguments can be made to show why a right of publicity is also justified on economic grounds. The first draws on considerations of economic efficiency, while the second relates to the benefits derived from striking a balance between private rights and the public domain. This economic rationale constitutes the third justification to be advanced in favour of a publicity right.

A. Economic Efficiency

This justification is predicated on the argument that the practice of publicity is economically and socially valuable, and that formalised legal protection will enhance these values through certainty and order, to ensure the maximum utility of persona. An efficient market will, of course, serve the wider public interest.

Economic arguments in the context of intellectual property were most famously advanced by Posner.[70] However, they have been applied to publicity by Grady[71] and de Grandpre[72] in two key articles which show why a right of publicity is justified on economic grounds.[73] In the words of Grady:

> Under the theory presented in this article, the right of publicity is needed to ensure that publicity assets are not wasted by a scramble to use them up as quickly as possible. The right of publicity privatizes a public good (in publicity) and thus encourages a more sensible use of this type of social asset.[74]

This is akin to the tragedy of the (traditional) commons, whereby the scramble to use resources adversely impacts on their long-term availability. The first challenge for this justification therefore is to identify the 'social asset' or 'public good' that will be protected from such over-consumption through a publicity right, and the second is to assess whether over-consumption of this asset is likely.

[70] See for example, WM Landes and R Posner, 'An Economic Analysis of Copyright Law' (1989) 18 *Journal of Legal Studies* 325; R Posner, 'Trademark Law: An Economic Perspective' (1987) 30 *Journal of Law and Economics* 265; and more generally, R Posner, *Economic Analysis of Law*, 7th edn (New York, Aspen Publishers/Wolters Kluwer, 2007) particularly para 3.3.

[71] M Grady, 'A Positive Economic Theory of the Right of Publicity' (1994) 1 *UCLA Ent L Rev* 97.

[72] de Grandpre (n 7).

[73] McCarthy also discusses the economic justification for publicity, drawing heavily on Grady's work, amongst others. He concludes that '[t]o many people, the economic justification for a right of publicity... is of marginal persuasiveness... But to those who demand rigorous social utility logic, the economic justification may be just their cup of tea.' McCarthy (n 43) para 2:7.

[74] Grady, 'A Positive Economic Theory of the Right of Publicity' (1994) 98.

B. Identifying the Social Asset

In respect of the first question, the social asset to be protected is persona. As discussed in chapters two and three, persona is valuable for the 'eyeball appeal' it engenders and the economic value of that appeal.

In addition to the economic value in persona, it is also a socially valuable asset. Persona plays a central role in our cultural experience, through the creation and communication of meaning[75] and by the addition of common human interest.[76] Celebrities are a critical part of the creative commons in popular culture, since 'star images are widely used in contemporary American culture to create and communicate meaning and identity'.[77] Image and identity play a significant role in our daily lives—on posters, t-shirts, merchandise, advertisements, and in the media—and in each case they function to communicate a message. Celebrity images are therefore not simply marks of identity or commodities, but 'are constitutive of our cultural heritage'.[78] Use of existing cultural imagery (whether of individuals or otherwise) is at the core of postmodernist music and art, where 'pre-existing works and images are consciously and openly appropriated, reworded and recycled'.[79] In this world, celebrities 'provide meaningful resources for the construction of identity and community'.[80]

What is especially important about this social use of persona is that it is not restricted to commercial uses by corporate entities. Communities and groups can annexe celebrities as short-hand for the message they seek to share. Coombe cites a number of examples, including Judy Garland, who 'had a special place in gay culture as the symbol gay men used in the pre-Stonewall period to speak to each other about themselves'.[81] More recently, Kylie Minogue can be seen as symbolic of certain gay culture, so much so that she was used as a point of reference in a Supreme Court decision regarding the human rights of gay men seeking asylum in the United Kingdom:

> To illustrate the point with trivial stereotypical examples from British society: just as male heterosexuals are free to enjoy themselves playing rugby, drinking beer and talking

---

[75] See chapter seven, and Madow (n 15) 143–145; de Grandpre (n 7) 96 and 123; Coombe, *The Cultural Life of Intellectual Properties* (1998) and Coombe, 'Author/izing the Celebrity' (1991–1992).

[76] See chapter seven, and McCarthy (n 2) 682–683; Carty (n 1) 258.

[77] Madow (n 15) 142; see also discussion at 143; see also Carty's reference to image as a 'vehicle for social comment or criticism', Carty (n 1) 252.

[78] Coombe (n 40) 89.

[79] Madow (n 15) 198. See also W Gordon, 'On Owning Information: Intellectual Property and the Restitutionary Impulse' (1992) 78 *Va L Rev* 149 157–58.

[80] Coombe (n 40) 89.

[81] RJ Coombe, 'Publicity Rights and Political Aspiration: Mass Culture, Gender Identity, and Democracy' (1991–1992) 26 *New Eng L Rev* 1221, 1256. Other examples provided by Coombe include Madonna, Elvis Presley and (although not directly relevant here) Star Trek.

about girls with their mates, so male homosexuals are to be free to enjoy themselves going to Kylie concerts, drinking exotically coloured cocktails and talking about boys with their straight female mates.[82]

Given the extensive social, political and commercial use of celebrity persona by corporations and by the public, they are correctly regarded by Grady as 'socially valuable publicity assets'.[83] The available evidence also suggests that such exploitation is not limited to the persona of celebrities.[84]

The second question, regarding the likelihood of over-consumption, requires more detailed analysis.

C. Over-Consumption of Persona Leading to Tragedy?

Just as fish can be safeguarded by requiring a licence to fish, Grady argues that a 'legal right of publicity can be understood as a fishing license designed to avoid races that would use up reputations too quickly'.[85] Whereas uncontrolled public use of persona would lead to this exhaustion, a right for the individual to control such use would minimise this risk. Evidence in support of this can be drawn from Milligan's comparison between George Best and David Beckham. Milligan shows that, even lacking a formal legal right, Beckham's greater awareness of the need for management of image has successfully avoided Best's rapid burnout of the value and meaning in his image through overexposure.[86]

Madow, however, challenges this notion of the tragedy of the commons as applied to individuals. He concludes that there is no comparable limited commons which could be exhausted: advertisers will always be able to find a new celebrity or individual to promote their goods. Thus, in Madow's words, 'there would be no "tragedy" in the classic parable if the herdsmen, after depleting their common pasture, could simply move on to another one'.[87] Celebrities act as 'pastures' for the herdsmen advertisers and publishers, and the grazing public can be moved from one pasture to another, with no limitation or depletion of the herdsmen's supply. Given the limitless number of celebrities and individuals in general, there would seem to be no risk of exhaustion—and, in any event, Madow asks whether exhaustion of *all* the available celebrities would be any cause for concern.[88]

Yet this approach is open to challenge. In the first place, Madow queries whether total exhaustion of all available celebrities would be problematic, since

---

[82] *HJ (Iran) v Secretary of State for the Home Department* [2010] UKSC 31 [78] (Lord Rodger).
[83] Grady (n 71) 126.
[84] See for example chapters two and three and Appendix 1.
[85] Grady (n 71) 103.
[86] A Milligan, *Brand it Like Beckham* (London, Cyan, 2004) 61–63.
[87] Madow (n 15) 224.
[88] ibid. This argument is repeated and apparently endorsed by Westfall and Landau (n 3) 120.

'the promotional values'[89] attaching to celebrities could be replaced by 'the myriad other techniques'[90] currently used by advertisers to attract attention. However, he does not address the loss to the public arising from such over-exhaustion. He himself has drawn attention to the valuable social role played by persona, in allowing the communication of meaning in social and cultural contexts.[91] If all available personas are over-exploited to the point of becoming meaningless, there will be no cultural commons left to provide a stock of communicable meaning. Thus, if we accept the role that Madow assigns to celebrities in the creation and communication of meaning, it *would* be a cause for concern if, in extreme circumstances, all available celebrity personas were to be exhausted. Importantly, this cultural concern remains even if the advertising value of persona could be replaced by another technique. The likelihood of complete exhaustion may be remote, but the question remains: if celebrity persona is so valuable to cultural communication, surely it is in the public interest to ensure that this source of meaning and expression is not devalued through over-exposure and exhaustion?

The second objection to Madow's challenge is that it relies on addressing scarcity from the angle of the herdsman, which in this case would be the user or advertiser. This is the approach in the classic parable, not least because the pasture is inanimate. However, in our case, the 'pasture' of the commons is an individual and it is possible to exhaust his or her persona, to that individual's detriment. Over-grazing and exhaustion becomes a more serious concern when the pasture itself has interests and rights. The advertisers, or herdsmen, may be free to move on to fresh pastures, but the individual/pasture is left with a depleted, and valueless, identity if it is over-exploited. The ongoing individual behind the persona is acknowledged by Coombe:

> Arguably the celebrity evokes the fascination she does because however endlessly her image is reproduced, her substantive duration, that is, her life, never becomes wholly irrelevant. *She never loses her autonomy from the objects that circulate in her likeness.*[92]

If the objects that circulate in his or her likeness become depleted and valueless, the individual behind them also suffers, since the persona and individual are of course inextricably linked.

While this over-grazing may not be a tragedy for the herdsman-exploiters, it is still a loss to the individuals/pastures themselves: '[i]n economic terms, personalities should be regarded as scarce resources since, although there is a fairly high degree of substitutability, the use of a personality by one person will diminish its usefulness to other users'.[93] If its usefulness to others is diminished, this is a loss

---

[89] Madow (n 15) 225.
[90] ibid.
[91] ibid 142; see also discussion at 143.
[92] Coombe (n 11) 375, emphasis added.
[93] T Frazer, 'Appropriation of Personality – a New Tort?' (1983) 99 *LQR* 281, 303.

in itself, as well as diminishing its economic value. This analysis is supported by a number of sources providing an insight into the practical side of exploitation. Evidence presented to the Court of Appeal in *Irvine v Talksport* included a statement from Irvine that 'an endorser cannot in practice endorse more than one product or service in any one particular field'.[94] Where unauthorised use is made of an individual's persona in one field, it effectively closes the gate on other, authorised, exploitation in that same field. In this sense, the individual's persona is exhausted in much the same way as the original pasture. Individuals have a vested interest in preventing exhaustion resulting from unauthorised use and in ensuring that the meaning and value attached to their persona is preserved.[95]

To this extent, the tragedy of the commons becomes the 'tragedy of the pastures': an argument which may have little relevance where the pasture is inanimate, but which deserves more serious consideration where the pasture has rights and interests. Whereas Madow argues that the celebrity pasture is (effectively[96]) inexhaustible, it is in fact the case that, although the total number of pastures may be limitless, each individual pasture is certainly exhaustible.[97] For Frazer, this individual scarcity provides a reason to protect identity:

> Purely in terms of economic efficiency, therefore, there may be a justification for converting personality from no-ownership to private property. Since an over-use of personality may permanently depress its value, it is most important that such property right be protected by way of injunction as well as by damages.[98]

As the law has responded to protect tangibles from over-exploitation, so it can also respond to the risk of over-exploitation of persona: '[w]e can ration the use of highways by imposing tolls. We grant celebrities a property right to ration the use of their names in order to maximise their value over time.'[99]

Doing so also recognises the dignitarian value, as well as the economic value, of persona to the individual. While it may not be a great tragedy to an individual advertiser if Beckham's persona is rendered meaningless through over-exploitation, it is most certainly a personal tragedy for Beckham—and arguably a tragedy for that section of the population which uses his persona for communication and symbolism. This over-exploitation would negatively impact on Beckham's dignitarian interest identified above, regardless of the consequences for his economic interest.

Whereas Madow favours the unprotected free use of such valuable imagery, de Grandpre and Grady argue that unprotected use typically results in a net loss to

---

[94] *Irvine v Talksport* [2003] 2 All ER 881 [91].

[95] Again, this management can be seen in Milligan's comparison between the (mis)management of George Best in the 1960s and the more controlled approach taken by and on behalf of David Beckham in recent years. Milligan, *Brand it Like Beckham* (2004) 61–63.

[96] Although note his position regarding the possibility of complete exhaustion—a position I have sought to challenge above. See section IV. C.

[97] Grady (n 71) 101.

[98] Frazer, 'Appropriation of Personality' (1983) 306.

[99] Grady (n 71) 112, citing a 1994 decision of the Fifth Circuit.

society, since over-exploitation results in the degradation and exhaustion of any meaning in that image to the detriment of the individual, the public, and ultimately the exploiters:

> the public also tires of celebrities; many become stale, the buzz surrounding them giving way to fatigue and even contempt. For this reason, becoming and remaining a celebrity requires careful management, for it depends on constantly evoking the right impressions and remaining in the public's unaided memory.[100]

D. Allowing Net Positive Externalities

However, this economic argument does not necessarily produce a right of publicity which creates a private stranglehold. Madow makes the point that not all uses of persona will necessarily result in a diminution in the value of that persona.[101] In fact, with reference to the property right of publicity in the United States, de Grandpre claims that 'the current right of publicity is overbroad'[102] and grants more protection than is required to satisfy the economic case for a publicity right. Instead, any right to control must be balanced against positive uses of publicity which promote or enhance the value, or at least which do not cause damage to it. De Grandpre challenges the need for publicity to be recognised as a property right, since this gives excessive control to individuals:

> As Ronald Coase suggested, why not simply give everyone an absolute property right in her identity and let the market decide who should control what rights over whose identity? As one might suspect, the problem lies with transaction costs, which can be sizable and may not be passed on to consumers.[103]

These transaction costs include, for example, negotiating a licence with the individual and the fee to be paid. Instead, transaction costs for 'beneficial' uses can be minimised or excluded by enabling the public to use persona in certain cases without breaching the prior publicity right. This, in effect, acts as a defence to a claim for breach, or operates to remove any individual right in that situation. In the language of economic analysis, 'the law of publicity should prohibit unauthorized uses of identity that harm it – that result in net negative externalities – but would allow unauthorized uses that result in net positive externalities – informative or recoding uses, for example'.[104]

This is a balancing exercise, in order to achieve the promotion of 'net positive externalities' while preventing 'net negative externalities'. A right to control use of persona is necessary on economic grounds to prevent the exhaustion of these valuable social images as discussed in the previous section, but the economic

---

[100] de Grandpre (n 7) 100.
[101] Madow (n 15) 221–22.
[102] de Grandpre (n 7) 79.
[103] ibid 109.
[104] ibid 114.

justification also recognises that any such right should not be absolute. Exceptions are necessary to enable certain beneficial or net-gain uses. Not only would such exceptions for 'beneficial' uses be to the public's advantage, but in some cases they would benefit the individuals too. This is because an absolute right of control

> is unlikely to result in an optimal production of fame because our understanding of celebrity suggests that the media must be able to publicize it and the public must have meaningful opportunities to use it creatively, in formal and informal contexts.[105]

These balances will be considered in chapter 10.

E. Maximising Efficiency through a Balance of Rights

The need for a balance to be struck between private interests and public interests is also reflected in the second economic justification to be considered. Commentators typically favour either control of property through private rights or the freedom of public use associated with the public domain. An alternative to the either/or approach is posited by Howkins, who disagrees with the view that private rights are the 'sole source' of innovation and economic growth:

> I regard both the public domain and private rights as capable of generating economic activity. They are both economically efficient. They are both tools. They are not ends in themselves. They are tools to achieve ends – creativity, innovation, growth and knowledge.[106]

Treating private rights and the public domain as tools to be used to achieve certain ends makes it easier to understand that neither one nor the other is always the best or most efficient answer: instead, a balance is required. Where an appropriate balance is achieved, the ends served by these tools will be enhanced. Thus, as Howkins argues, it is 'the balance that is efficient (or not): neither the public domain nor a private right on its own'.[107] This approach is echoed in the Adelphi Charter, which states that '[t]he public interest requires a balance between the public domain and private rights. It also requires a balance between the free competition that is essential for economic vitality and the monopoly rights granted by intellectual property laws'.[108]

In searching for justifications for a publicity right, it is important to remember that seeking an either/or outcome may not be the most efficient one: public and private interests may both be best served through a balance of rights and

---

[105] ibid 115, emphasis added.

[106] J Howkins, 'Is it Possible to Balance Creativity and Commerce?' in Fiona MacMillan (ed), *New Directions in Copyright Law Volume 2* (Cheltenham, Edward Elgar, 2006) 312.

[107] ibid. For an analysis of the 'contours of copyright' and the balance with human rights, see C Waelde, 'Copyright, Corporate Power and Human Rights: Reality and Rhetoric' in Fiona MacMillan (ed), *New Directions in Copyright Law Volume 2* (Cheltenham, Edward Elgar, 2006).

[108] The Adelphi Charter, adopted by the Royal Society for the Arts (13 October 2005) para 3.

freedoms. This reflects the conclusion drawn in the previous section that a property right of publicity is 'overbroad', and that net positive externalities should be recognised as limitations or exceptions to a right.

In fact, the interaction of rights and freedoms is arguably essential for *both* camps, as Coombe demonstrates. She discusses the role of legal regulation of private rights in enhancing and advancing the interests of the public domain. Her analysis of the role of celebrity in popular cultural expression (a use which she undoubtedly supports) highlights the complexity of the interaction between private rights and cultural use:

> The law of publicity rights, by prohibiting reproductions of the celebrity image for another's advantage, promotes the mass circulation of celebrity signifiers by ensuring that they will have a market value. If the image were freely available for mass reproduction, there would, presumably, be less of an incentive to engage in the investments necessary to disseminate it through media channels. *Ironically, then, the law creates the cultural spaces of postmodernism in which mass media images become available for signifying practices.* It produces fixed, stable identities authorised by the celebrity subject, but simultaneously creates the possibility of places of transgression in which the signifier's fixity and the celebrity's authority may be contested and resisted.[109]

Coombe's analysis suggests that de-regulation would not lead to a freeing up of celebrity image for general cultural consumption, but that it would lead to an increased scarcity not only through over-use (as addressed above) but also through reduced production. Arguing for persona to be part of the public domain would not necessarily bring the advantages of free use that its advocates seek. Without the legal regulation to create 'the cultural spaces of postmodernism' in which celebrity persona flourishes, the possibility of cultural re-configuration of that persona will be diminished[110]—something which Madow would, presumably, regret.

F. Summary

If the economic aspect of publicity practice is accepted (and even opponents of publicity rights concede the practical economic value of persona), there is considerable support for striking a balance between private and public interests. A legal right of publicity can help to engender the very social and cultural practice which Coombe, Carty and Madow support. As Grady and de Grandpre acknowledge, however, an exclusive private right of publicity is not necessarily the answer either. Howkins suggests that striking a balance can be the most

---

[109] Coombe (n 11) 386–87, emphasis added. Note that this theory holds good even in the absence of a specific publicity right, so long as there is some legal mechanism for enforcing these interests, such as passing off or privacy.
[110] A point Coombe also makes in Coombe, 'Critical Cultural Legal Studies' (1998) 10 *Yale JL & Human* 463, 469: 'The rights bestowed by intellectual property regimes... play a constitutive role in the creation of contemporary cultures and in the social life of interpretive practice.' See also 479–81.

efficient solution. In the case of publicity, this would recognise the value of persona to the public domain where freedom of expression or cultural communication is at stake, but enable the necessary private control to ensure that over-exploitation does not diminish either the economic or dignitarian interests in persona.

V. Two Further Objections Considered

These dignitarian and economic arguments advanced in favour of publicity allow us to consider two objections commonly advanced against publicity rights. The arguments from free-riding and from wealth allocation can be challenged, thereby strengthening the case in favour of publicity rights.

A. The Argument from Free-Riding

The argument from free-riding is expressed by Madow as the idea that 'society has a strong and independent moral interest in preventing people from free riding'.[111] If such misuse is not prevented, then the exploiter will receive something for nothing, or, in classic intellectual property terminology, will have reaped without sowing.[112] According to Madow, the problem with such contentions is that 'there is still no *general* common law prohibition against benefiting from the commercial efforts of others'.[113] He provides several examples of situations where one person's creativity is enjoyed and exploited by others since, once it has been voluntarily placed in the market, it effectively becomes freely appropriable.[114] Gordon makes the point that there is at least a balance to be struck: where all free riding is identified as wrongful, such 'a prohibition is itself potentially destabilizing, and, though it may express one community norm, important contrary community norms exist as well'.[115]

Although there may be no common law rule against free-riding in the abstract, it is nevertheless a practice which the World Intellectual Property Organisation (WIPO) has criticised. The WIPO Intellectual Property Handbook deals with unfair competition[116] and the problem of free-riding, which it defines as 'any act that a competitor or another market participant undertakes with the intention of

---

[111] Madow (n 15) 200.

[112] See for example, A Kamperman Sanders, *Unfair Competition Law: The Protection of Intellectual and Industrial Creativity* (Oxford, Clarendon Press, 1997) 13–15. See also Carty (n 1) 247.

[113] Madow (n 15) 201.

[114] ibid at 201–03.

[115] Gordon, 'On Owning Information' (1992) 278.

[116] Free-riding can be seen as one aspect of unfair competition, which Kamperman Sanders describes as the 'misuse of another's exploits' (Kamperman Sanders, *Unfair Competition Law* (1997) 22). For a detailed analysis of unfair competition in Common law and Civilian jurisdictions, see ibid.

directly exploiting another person's industrial or commercial achievement for his own *business* purposes without substantially departing from the original achievement'.[117] WIPO addresses this problem principally from the perspective of free-riding on a competitor's achievements, rather than specifically the problem of free-riding on an individual's persona. However, whether a business free-rides on a juristic person's reputation or a natural person's reputation, through persona, the action remains the same where the free-rider's business is insufficiently distinguished from the original 'achievement'. WIPO states that unfairness arises from

> the obvious exploitation of the notoriety of the indication [that is, trade mark]... without any proper effort being made to depart substantially from the characteristic features of that particular achievement, but also from the risk of damage to the reputation of the existing business.[118]

There is therefore a twofold wrong: (i) the initial undifferentiated use by the exploiter and (ii) the subsequent risk of damage to the original reputation.

Applying the language of economic analysis used by Grady and de Grandpre above, the net economic costs of commercial free-riding on persona are negative, that is to say, the exhaustion or degradation of the particular identity, together with the potential consumer confusion, will outweigh any benefit to the public. Free-riding is therefore not an activity that should constitute a permitted exception to a right of publicity.

There is also a moral or dignitarian ground on which to reject free-riding, reflecting the concerns expressed above regarding honest use and the dangers of taking another's voice. WIPO states that free-riding is 'contrary to honest business practice'.[119] While free competition is encouraged by WIPO, unfair competition is not.[120] WIPO thus sanctions measures to combat unfair competition, which would arguably include measures to prevent free-riding on another's reputation, even where that does not cause consumer confusion. The connection between free-riding and unfair competition in this context is emphasised by the recognition of a right of publicity in the Third Restatement of the Law of Unfair Competition.[121]

Further, free-riding can be challenged in the particular context of publicity, where there is use of part of the individual against his or her will. Here, the unauthorised use does not exploit a separate creation in which I have invested my personhood: the thing exploited *is* my personhood. Regardless of the additional

---

[117] *WIPO Intellectual Property Handbook: Law, Policy and Use*, 2nd edn (Geneva, WIPO, 2004: www.wipo.int/about-ip/en/iprm/) para 2.843.
[118] ibid para 2.842.
[119] ibid para 2.847.
[120] ibid para 2.751.
[121] American Law Institute Restatement of the Law of Unfair Competition, 3d, chapter 4, paras 46–49.

'meaning' which fame, celebrity or society may have imposed upon an individual's persona, it remains a representation of a human being which is used for gain by another without any consideration for that individual's interests, whether commercial or dignitarian. A comparison can be drawn here with slavery: 'we cannot alienate the whole of our labour because then we would be made slaves'.[122] It is difficult to justify an institution which condones the commercial exploitation of another individual without that individual's consent, and free-riding does just that. As one American court stated in a publicity case: 'Let the word go forth – there is no free ride. The commercial hitchhiker seeking to travel on the fame of another will have to learn to pay the fare or stand on his own two feet.'[123]

B.   The Argument from Wealth Distribution

The second counter-justification is that of wealth distribution. Madow questions the role of publicity in distributing wealth *upwards*, to those who already have wealth:

> Why, we may properly ask, should the law confer a source of additional wealth on athletes and entertainers who are already very handsomely compensated for the primary activities to which they owe their fame?[124]

This rhetorical question is echoed at a much later stage in his article, where he addresses the issue of whether the law should play a role in allocating wealth.[125] Questions such as this were considered by economists like Adam Smith, who conceded that limited monopolies might have a beneficial role in allowing creators and inventors to reap the economic rewards, if any, of their creation or invention.[126]

Two observations can be made in response to Madow's objection. In the first place, it is arguably not solely the law that confers this additional source of income. The social practice and corresponding market demand—the fact that there are willing 'buyers' and 'sellers' of publicity, even if there is nothing in law to buy and sell— creates the value. As Madow himself accepts, if

> sneaker makers were free to use Michael Jordan's picture in their advertisements... Jordan would still be able to command a price, maybe a hefty one, for wearing a particular brand of sneaker in the Big Game or for touting or demonstrating its virtues

---

[122]   S Maniatis, 'Trade Mark Rights – a Justification Based on Property' [2002] IPQ 123, 158. See the reference above to this point, made by McCarthy with reference to Cobb J, McCarthy (n 43) para 2:5.

[123]   Grady (n 71) 110, citing a 1994 decision regarding Jackie Onassis.

[124]   Madow (n 15) 137.

[125]   ibid 220 et seq.

[126]   RL Meek, DD Raphael and PG Stein, *Adam Smith, Lectures on Jurisprudence* (Oxford, Clarendon Press, 1978, reprinted 1987) ii.31–ii.34.

in a television commercial. Or suppose T-shirt makers were free to use Bruce Springs-teen's picture without his permission. Some consumers would probably choose to purchase the T-shirt 'officially authorized' by Springsteen – because they would expect him to monitor its quality, because they would want their money to go to him, or because they would derive a closer sense of identification with him in this way.[127]

As demonstrated in chapter three, publicity value is predominantly derived from authorised exploitation, and this exploitation is not solely reliant on legal sanction, as we have seen. It is not the legal right but the marketplace which creates the value:[128] a commercial practice does not need the sanction of law to 'create' the value. Legal recognition may provide certainty, which in turn may *enhance* the value,[129] but this is not the same as creating the initial value.[130] A clear example of a lucrative market without the sanction of law is the cocaine trade. Not only is cocaine not recognised as a legitimate trade, it is positively prohibited. Despite this, it is still worth a staggering amount of money.

Thus, to suggest that it is the legal protection which creates and confers the publicity value is misleading. Legal recognition may well benefit individuals by creating certainty in their dealings for authorised exploitation, but the commercial evidence suggests that law is not solely or even primarily responsible for creating that value in the first place. The only additional source of wealth for individuals that would arise from a legally-sanctioned right of publicity comes from compensation for unauthorised exploitation. Although these figures may be high in the United States, in the United Kingdom the Douglases' compensation for unauthorised use was less than £15,000, compared with the £1 million price tag for the authorised deal.[131] Madow's claim that adopting a legally enforceable right is responsible for this value can therefore be disputed: it may *enhance* it by the greater legal and commercial certainty which would come from a legal right, but it does not *create* the value at the outset.

A second observation about Madow's wealth distribution point is that it is made in isolation about publicity. He questions why we should expect the state to provide publicity rights which would 'operate to channel additional dollars to the very people – Einstein rather than Bohr, Vanilla Ice rather than Too Short – who happen to draw first-prize tickets in the fame lottery'.[132] However, arguably a patent right rewards people who have drawn winning tickets in the intelligence lottery, while those who are blessed with sporting prowess are rewarded in preference to those who are not, no matter how hard the latter may try to gain that coveted Olympic gold. Further, some individuals benefit from windfalls by

---

[127] Madow (n 15) 211.
[128] S Halpern, 'The Right of Publicity: Maturation of an Independent Right Protecting the Associative Value of Personality' (1995) 46 *Hastings LJ* 853 858.
[129] Users may be prepared to pay higher prices for a right which they know can be enforced, particularly where the right is good against third parties.
[130] See McCarthy (n 43) para 2:2.
[131] *Douglas v Hello!* [2006] QB 125.
[132] Madow (n 15) 189.

virtue of birth: our society does not demand a 100 per cent inheritance tax in order to ensure there are no undeserved or unearned gains. The capitalist economy is not concerned with the equal or communal distribution or redistribution of wealth. As McCarthy argues, if we accept Madow's argument in respect of publicity, 'consistency would demand that we refuse property rights in Rolls Royce and Mercedes automobiles, personal swimming pools, expensive personal jewelry, and the like'.[133]

McCarthy raises a further objection in relation to Madow's assertion that publicity channels wealth to stars who are already wealthy. Giving the example of a former Olympian whose name is being used to promote cereal, McCarthy points out that allocating the value to the retired athlete rather than the cereal conglomerate is not a redistribution 'upwards'.[134] Madow's argument may therefore have a certain egalitarian appeal but, in the context of a capitalist society, it is insufficient to operate as an argument against publicity rights.

VI. The Alternative Question

Whereas this chapter has so far sought to justify the recognition of a right of publicity, there is in fact an alternative question that can be posed. It is possible to suggest that this entire justificatory project can be replaced with a single question such that, even if all the above arguments advanced in favour of publicity rights were to be rejected, this question and answer can resolve the matter in favour of the creation of a publicity right. By addressing both the primary question and this secondary question, and by answering both in favour of a right of publicity for the individual, the case in favour of publicity rights becomes even stronger.

This alternative question is posed by Reiter:

> the crucial question for the law is not the unanswerable moral question, 'Do celebrities deserve the earning power their status commands?' but rather the factual question, 'Given that celebrities command considerable commercial power, who should benefit?'[135]

Goodenough chooses to address this question and provides a rational, and personal, answer:

> If there were no control over the persona, as Madow advocates, then the values inherent in it would be at the full disposal of capital-rich companies... *as between a star whose*

---

[133] McCarthy (n 43) para 2:3. Also Westfall and Landau (n 3) 121, who ask why publicity should be singled out in this way.

[134] T McCarthy, 'The Human Persona as Commercial Property: the Right of Publicity' (1995) 19 *Colum-VLA JL & Arts* 129, 141.

[135] E Reiter, 'Personality and Patrimony: Comparative Perspectives on the Right to One's Image' (2001–2002) 76 *Tulane L Rev* 673, 726.

name is to be used and a huge manufacturing company making the use, I, at least, would rather see the star control the value of the use of her identity than leave the benefit solely to the company.[136]

There cannot be many who would disagree with Goodenough here.[137] Even Madow acknowledges that 'caution' is required since 'in a "free use" world… it is not only *popular* cultural practice that would be liberated. Large corporate actors would also be set free to "graze" on the celebrity commons.'[138] While these corporate actors would still seek to differentiate themselves from the rest of the herd, the unlimited use of persona would be a part of that—especially for businesses, like Talksport, Hello! and Anabas, which are keen to exploit popular figures of the day.

Denying a legal right of publicity does not cancel out the commercial value inherent in persona or award it to some party who is more deserving (however such a party could be identified). Instead, it means that the value becomes a free-for-all and this, in turn, means that, realistically, it is most likely to be annexed for the benefit of 'capital-rich companies'. In the absence of legal protection, the commercial value in persona is as likely to fall to the 'huge manufacturing company' or the media enterprise—neither of which are likely to be more deserving or have any greater demands on our sympathy than the individual in question. It is certainly most unlikely to benefit the man in the street or the small creative enterprise.

The practical reality of the creation of a legal right is that it assigns whatever value there may be in persona to the individual. This is echoed in Hughes' work on intellectual property, where he observes that '[p]roperty rights in the persona *give the individual the economic value derived most directly from one's personality*. As long as the individual identifies with his personal image, he will have a personality stake in that image.'[139]

On this analysis, the question of justification becomes an issue not of determining whether or not we need a right, but how we respond to the undeniable commercial practice which exists. As Reiter contends, the question under this analysis moves from the moral to the factual. Despite this, the answer to his factual question, as with the moral one, remains the same: the individual is entitled to the control (both economic and dignitarian) of his or her persona which a right of publicity would formally recognise, subject always to defences to recognise the competing interests—which are the subject of the next chapter.

---

[136] O Goodenough, 'Re-Theorising Privacy and Publicity' [1997] IPQ 37, 60, emphasis added.
[137] Support also comes from McCarthy (n 43) para 2:2; and Halpern, who, in a choice between 'scavengers', favours the 'scavenger who has at least some colourable connection to the phenomenon': Halpern, 'Publicity: Maturation of an Independent Right' (1995) 871–872.
[138] Madow (n 15) 240, footnotes omitted. Emphasis in the original.
[139] Hughes, 'The Philosophy of Intellectual Property' (1988) 341, emphasis added.

VII. Conclusion

This chapter has explored the 'reasons or considerations likely to sway the free understanding of the participants in social life in favour of the institution that is being defended'.[140] Whether one looks to the question of whether an individual should be entitled to a publicity right—a right to control use of his or her persona—or the alternative question of who should benefit from the undeniable value of the commercial practice, the answer is the same: a right of publicity, vested in the individual, can demonstrably be justified.

Individuals, whether famous or not, have certain dignitarian and economic interests in their persona, which can only be protected through control. Where their persona is used without consent, they suffer harm to those interests. Not the least of these harms is the risk of adulterated 'free' speech through misuse of persona, which challenges the integrity of persona and the very notion of free speech or freedom of expression. A society which professes to respect autonomy and dignity cannot deny the individual's right to control and protect something as inherently personal as his or her image, indicia, information and reputation. Parallels have been drawn between the harm resulting from unconsented use of persona and the harm arising from unauthorised use of one's vote, where the individual's 'voice' is appropriated for unauthorised purposes.

However, these justifications are not absolute. It is also necessary to look at the competing interests for use of and control over persona—interests which are, moreover, informed by these very justifications. The following chapter will examine competing interests to be protected and attempt to reconcile these two positions.

---

[140] HM Spector, 'An Outline of a Theory Justifying Intellectual and Industrial Property' [1989] *EIPR* 270, 270, as quoted in chapter five, n 1.

7

The Competing Interests

I. Introduction

ALTHOUGH ACADEMIC ATTENTION has traditionally focused on individuals and unauthorised exploiters, the interests of other parties—such as users/exploiters and the public in general—can be discerned through some of the arguments made against publicity rights. In fact, two such interests soon become apparent.

The first of these is the right to freedom of expression, as embodied in article 10 of the European Convention on Human Rights (ECHR) or in the American first amendment right to free speech: 'one of the most difficult areas of this body of law is when the right of publicity must be balanced against the free speech concerns of the first amendment'.[1] The second competing interest is that of the creative commons, specifically the commons of cultural imagery. Celebrities derive their meaning from, and contribute meaning to, the cultural tradition, such that 'celebrities often cannot be viewed as a separate phenomenon, a discrete item of creativity'.[2] In borrowing from and becoming part of our 'cultural commons',[3] celebrities and their persona become part of the public domain and should arguably be available for others to draw upon, without the restrictions created by a right of publicity. Both these interests will now be examined in more detail.

II. Freedom of Expression

Freedom of expression, or free speech, is fundamental in our society. The right to freedom of expression, as protected by article 10 of the ECHR, provides for the right to receive and impart information and ideas. It is therefore potentially

---

[1] JT McCarthy, 'Public Personas and Private Property: The Commercialization of Human Identity' (1989) 79 *TMR* 681, 696.
[2] H Carty, 'Advertising, Publicity Rights and English Law' [2004] *IPQ* 209, 252.
[3] ibid 252.

opposed to the grant of a right of publicity, which may deprive certain parties of the right to use someone else's persona in their own speech or expression, thus curtailing their freedom of expression.[4]

In the United States, the constitutional right to free speech under the First Amendment acts as a defence to, amongst other things, a claim for infringement of publicity rights.[5] Even those who support a right of publicity accept the importance of freedom of expression.[6] Goodenough, for example, suggests that it would be wise 'to allow unfettered freedom for the expression of information about people on matters of public interest, no matter whose ox it gores, and considerable freedom for the creative use of persona'.[7]

However, there is a need to strike a balance. Free speech does not entail the right to say freely *anything* one wishes.[8] In fact, balancing freedom of expression with private interests is not a new endeavour, and courts in Europe and the United States are now well versed in this exercise. As McCarthy observes, 'such line drawing is the stock in trade of the law'.[9] Although article 10 is accorded 'a conspicuously elevated status in the human rights framework',[10] it is not an automatic trump over other rights.[11] Article 10(2) recognises the existence of other rights which may require to be balanced against the right to freedom of expression, in particular (in this context) for the protection of the reputation or the rights of others, for preventing the disclosure of information received in confidence. As has been seen in previous chapters, English case law to date has involved the courts in carrying out a balancing exercise between the right to privacy under article 8 and the right to freedom of expression under article 10.[12] This jurisprudence has clearly established that once the claimant's article 8 right

---

[4] As noted in chapter three, Halpern states that '[b]y its nature, the right of publicity implicates speech'—this can refer both to communication by persona and publicity use and also its impact on the free speech of others. SW Halpern, 'The Right of Publicity: Maturation of an Independent Right Protecting the Associative Value of Personality' (1995) 46 *Hastings LJ* 853, 867.

[5] See, for example, JT McCarthy, *The Rights of Publicity and Privacy*, 2nd edn (United States, West Group, 2001) section 3:6 and 3:47; O Goodenough, 'Re-theorising Privacy and Publicity' [1997] *IPQ* 37, 51–53; and Carty, 'Advertising, Publicity Rights and English Law' (2004) 223.

[6] One exception is Halpern, who believes that free speech issues are at the 'outer edge' of publicity rights, since exploitation of 'the hard economic commercial value of an individual's identity' is primarily commercial. Consequently, free speech issues 'have little impact on the avowedly commercial appropriation of identity': SW Halpern, 'The Right of Publicity: Maturation of an Independent Right Protecting the Associative Value of Personality' (1995) 46 *Hastings LJ* 853, 868.

[7] Goodenough, 'Re-theorising Privacy and Publicity' (1997) 70.

[8] For an analysis of post-Human Rights Act 1998 case law regarding 'insulting' expressions (of controversial religious or political beliefs), see R Reed and J Murdoch, *A Guide to Human Rights Law in Scotland*, 2nd edn (Edinburgh, Tottel, 2008) para 7.44; A Geddis, 'Free Speech Martyrs or Unreasonable Threats to Social Peace? – 'Insulting' Expression and Section 5 of the Public Order Act 1986' [2004] *PL* 853.

[9] McCarthy, *The Rights of Publicity and Privacy* (2001) para 2:4.

[10] C Angelopoulos 'Freedom of Expression and Copyright: the Double Balancing Act' [2008] *IPQ* 328, 329.

[11] *Campbell v MGN* [2004] 2 AC 457 [113] (Lord Hope); *In re S* [2005] 1 AC 593 [17] (Lord Steyn).

[12] Chapter five, section II. D.

is engaged, there must be a balancing between that article 8 right and the defendant's article 10 right. In each case, the question of which right takes precedence is dependent on the particular circumstances and facts of that case.[13]

Whilst this need for balance is well-established as regards article 8, we are not directly concerned with privacy here, as was concluded in chapter four. The question becomes what other rights, if any, must be balanced against article 10? Article 10(2) allows for restrictions on the exercise of freedom of expression to accommodate, amongst other things, the rights of others.[14] This would include intellectual property rights, for example, since the very purpose of intellectual property is to regulate the use (and prevent unauthorised use) of literary works, trade marks and otherwise publicly available icons and culture.[15]

Thus, intellectual property rights may necessitate legal protection for one individual (by way of copyright, for example) which adversely interferes with the freedom of expression of others. Freedom of speech will clash with copyright where 'it might be necessary – because adequate alternative means of expression do not exist – to use a protected text to achieve an expressive goal that it would not otherwise be possible to achieve'.[16] Where this is also the case with publicity (that is to say, where the particular speech required can be achieved only through the use of a particular individual's persona) then article 10 should enable this. This is subject, however, to balancing article 10 against the publicity right since, in Spence's words (regarding intellectual property in general): '[i]t may be that I can only contribute to public debate if I have the right both to be identified with my speech and to prevent it from being distorted'.[17] Any distortion of persona in this speech may thus reduce the weight to be accorded to freedom of expression.

The law should be slow to protect untruthful expression, especially where it infringes the rights of another party, such as the right to autonomy and dignity. Civil rights and criminal wrongs exist to prevent or deter the making of untruthful statements, by way of defamation and perjury for example, while misrepresentations can be challenged by way of an action for passing off.

There is of course a grey area between a blatant lie and the purest truth; an area of half truths, misleading associations and even silence. For Hughes, however, the right to freedom of expression should exist only on the truthful side of this divide: '*freedom of expression is meaningless without assurances that the expression will remain unadulterated. Free* speech requires that speech be guaranteed some

---

[13] See for example *Mosley v News Group Newspapers Ltd* [2008] EWHC 1777 (QB) [11]; chapter five, section II. D.

[14] For a detailed discussion of the scope of the article 10(2) provision for interference with the right, see Reed and Murdoch, *Human Rights Law in Scotland* (2008) paras 7.29 *et seq.*

[15] Angelopoulos provides an analysis of why copyright and freedom of expression are capable of working together 'like a well oiled machine, enhancing each other in the process'. C Angelopoulos, 'Freedom of Expression and Copyright: the Double Balancing Act' [2008] *IPQ* 328, 353.

[16] M Spence, 'Intellectual Property and the Problem of Parody' (1998) 114 *LQR* 594, 610, fn omitted.

[17] ibid 609.

integrity'.[18] Where the unauthorised use of persona is misleading, we should be slow to protect it through freedom of expression. In *Irvine v Talksport*,[19] for example, the image of Irvine used by Talksport was misleading because it had been doctored. Talksport's use of Irvine's image was therefore an adulterated expression which could not, and should not, be protected by a defence of freedom of expression—and arguably, as a commercial use with no wider public benefit, should not be accorded the protection of article 10 anyway.

The converse of course is that the individual cannot hide behind a publicity right in order to project a misleading persona. This forms the basis of one of Carty's objections to the grant of a publicity right:

> the celebrity image may be used as a vehicle for social comment or criticism. Free speech is threatened when the publicity right is seen as allowing the celebrity to impose his 'preferred meaning' not allowing different interpretations by others, though those interpretations may be used for powerful social criticism.[20]

This use of persona to project a 'preferred meaning' is well illustrated by the case of *Campbell v MGN*,[21] where Campbell's lies regarding her use of drugs were exposed by the defendant newspaper. The need to correct the misleading impression projected by Campbell formed a fundamental part of the *Daily Mirror's* defence.[22] In doing so, the right to freedom of expression under article 10 of the ECHR was balanced against Campbell's rights under article 8.

What is critical in the ECHR jurisprudence and other civil rights is that the right to freedom of expression and communication is not supreme: it must be balanced. As with privacy, there is no single answer to the problem of balancing private rights with the right to freedom of expression, and it is never possible to provide a definitive guide as to which right takes precedence on any occasion.[23] Instead, the courts need to balance the rights of each party on a case-by-case basis, by making 'a sensitive, nuanced and contextually specific examination of the particular factual circumstances of each case, incorporating an evaluation

---

[18] J Hughes, 'The Philosophy of Intellectual Property' (1988) 77 *Georgetown Law Journal* 287, 359, his emphasis, fn omitted.

[19] *Irvine v Talksport* [2003] 2 All ER 881.

[20] Carty (n 2) 252, fn omitted.

[21] *Campbell v MGN* [2004] 2 AC 457.

[22] Although see Gordley's alternative contention that in some cases a lie to promote virtue is preferable to the honest disclosure of vice. See J Gordley, *Foundations of Private Law: Property, Tort, Contract, Unjust Enrichment* (Oxford, Oxford University Press, 2006) 236.

[23] Section 12 of the Human Rights Act 1998 appears to encourage the courts to give priority to freedom of expression, but this reading would run into difficulties since, as Reed and Murdoch note, 'if the courts were to construe the provision as adversely affecting the application of countervailing Convention guarantees (for example, article 8's requirement of respect for private life), a litigant who was unsuccessful in the domestic courts could bring proceedings in Strasbourg'. Reed and Murdoch (n 8) para 7.33. Reed and Murdoch provide a detailed discussion of judicial consideration of section 12 at para 7.34.

and attachment of weight to both of the competing interests'.[24] If the balance is not achieved, there is a risk that 'tenuous property interests [may be allowed] to outweigh substantial expression rights'.[25] Conversely, failure to achieve balance may result in expression rights subjugating private rights to control persona, to the detriment of the individual's autonomy and dignity.

Two final observations reinforce the point that the article 10 right is strong but not unlimited. In the first place, article 10(2) expressly states that the exercise of the right 'carries with it duties and responsibilities'. This encompasses, for example, the duty to ensure that any opinions have a reasonable factual basis.[26] Second, even where the unauthorised user successfully relies upon his or her article 10 right to counter the individual's publicity right, the court may still award compensatory damages to the individual for the use made of his or her persona, since '"Freedom of expression should not normally carry with it the right to make free use of another's work", to profit from it without compensation.'[27]

It is suggested that freedom of expression must be balanced against a right of publicity. Article 10 is an important limit on the right of publicity, but it remains a qualified limit—it does not and should not operate as an outright ban.

III. Creative and Communicative Use

The second relevant public interest which opposes a private right over persona is the cultural 'creative commons'. This arises where a persona (typically a celebrity persona) is used as a cultural short-hand or to create meaning or pass quasi-political comment on the existing meaning of a persona. Popular culture relies on celebrity image and identity, and 'star images are widely used in contemporary American culture to create and communicate meaning and identity'.[28] Examples given in the previous chapter include Judy Garland and Kylie Minogue, who operate as reference points and communicative iconography for the gay community. This cultural communication may be subversive or political or simply fun.

Against this background, the right of publicity

---

[24] Charlotte Waelde and Niall Whitty, 'A Rights of Personality Database' in Niall Whitty and Reinhard Zimmermann (eds), *Rights of Personality in Scots Law, a Comparative Perspective*, (Dundee, Dundee University Press, 2009) para 11.5.

[25] *Laugh if Off v SAB* 2006 (1) SA 144 [74].

[26] Reed and Murdoch (n 8) para 7.32.

[27] C Angelopoulos, 'Freedom of Expression and Copyright: the Double Balancing Act' [2008] *IPQ* 328, 342. The unattributed quotation is from *Ashdown v Telegraph Group* [2002] Ch 149 [46].

[28] M Madow, 'Private Ownership of Public Image: Popular Culture and Publicity Rights' (1993) 81 *Cal L Rev* 125, 142; see also discussion at 143; see also Carty's reference to image as a 'vehicle for social comment or criticism': Carty (n 2) 252.

chills commercial, expressive uses of already famous people. In this light, a central challenge of the right of publicity consists in balancing rights in personal identity with the necessity of allowing everyone to dip into a rich common cultural pool.[29]

Madow expresses the concern that a right of publicity (certainly where it is cast as a property right) fails to achieve this balance, and instead transfers this 'semiotic value' of celebrity image into private ownership.[30]

To illustrate the damage that this transfer to private ownership would potentially cause, Madow explores the use of celebrity persona to create and communicate meaning, and the resultant conflict between different interest groups:

> popular culture remains what it long has been: a struggle for, and over, meaning. It is a contest in which dominant groups try to naturalize the meanings that best serve their interests into the 'common sense' and 'taste' of society as a whole, while subordinate and marginalized groups resist this process with varying degrees of effort and success.[31]

The two groups who are competing to annexe popular culture and impose their own meanings upon it are identified by Madow as the 'culture industries' and subcultures. Some of the latter can be 'relatively powerless' yet still able to generate meanings to compete with the 'dominant ideology'[32] promoted by the culture industries. In this contest it is impossible, Madow argues, for the law to remain neutral: it can act either to 'strengthen the already potent grip of the culture industries over the production and circulation of meaning, or it can facilitate popular participation, including participation by subordinate and marginalised groups, in the processes by which meaning is made and communicated'.[33]

Creating a legal right over the substance of the cultural commons—the celebrity images which populate it—denies the subordinate groups access to that commons and thereby deprives them of the ability to create and communicate cultural meaning. De Grandpre shares Madow's concerns 'for what he [Madow] perceived to be the courts' privatization of popular culture through the commodification and appropriation to celebrities of socially constructed meanings'.[34] While the public at large apparently stands to lose, celebrities and the big-business interests of the culture industries appear to gain through such a right.

On this analysis, protection of publicity rights interferes with freedom of expression and creative expression, not least by removing celebrity persona from the 'rich pool' of the cultural commons. Given these competing interests against

---

[29] V De Grandpre, 'Understanding the Market for Celebrity: An Economic Analysis of the Right of Publicity' (2001–2002) 12 *Fordham Intell Prop Media and Ent LJ* 73, 106. See also R Coombe, 'Publicity Rights and Political Aspiration: Mass Culture, Gender Identity, and Democracy' (1991–1992) 26 *New Eng L Rev* 1221, 1234.

[30] Madow, 'Private Ownership of Public Image' (1993) 142.

[31] ibid 141.

[32] ibid 141.

[33] ibid 141–42. This emphasises the control exercised by corporations in the intellectual property arena.

[34] De Grandpre, 'Understanding the Market for Celebrity' (2001–2002) 123.

publicity rights, it becomes necessary to seek some factor which will justify favouring one set of interests over the other, that is to say granting the legal right of publicity or withholding it.

Perhaps the first point to note is that where the use of persona is necessary to enable the communication of opinions and ideas, this is likely to be protected by article 10 of the ECHR. Thus, where there is a genuine communicative purpose served by the use of persona, which cannot be met in any other way, then the individual's publicity right will be matched by the countervailing right of expression, as discussed in the previous section.

In other cases, where the use is indeed part of cultural communication, intended for social or subversive comment, this should be recognised as a valuable contribution to our society. This is articulated in the copyright debate by MacMillan, who supports 'a distinction between productive and reproductive uses of another's copyright work. The former involving a creative use of existing copyright work, whilst the latter involves a merely exploitative use of someone else's intellectual property.'[35] This distinction can also be applied to publicity to help protect genuine creative use of persona: a productive use being more worthy of protection than a reproductive use. This would protect the interests of those who use persona to create new meaning or pass quasi-political comment on existing meaning, in the manner of *Laugh It Off v South African Breweries*.[36] This balance can be achieved by recognising a right of publicity for individuals, to enable them to control use of persona, which is then countered by a defence of parody and fair use.

Nonetheless, as discussed in chapter six, Coombe and Howkins refer to the need to be wary of over-reliance on the concept of cultural communications at the expense of the prior private right. Use of publicity, on both sides of the fence, needs a framework in which to flourish. It is submitted that, since the practice of cultural communication depends upon the prior practice of publicity, this exception to publicity should be treated not as a countervailing right, which exists on its own merits, but as a subsequent right, being a permitted use of persona. Only where a right of publicity is first recognised is it necessary or indeed possible to recognise a right of cultural communication dependent on use of persona.

---

[35] F MacMillan, 'Striking the Copyright Balance in the Digital Environment' [1999] *ICCLR* 350, 351, fn omitted.

[36] *Laugh It Off v South African Breweries* 2006 (1) SA 144. The applicant company printed t-shirts bearing an image and slogan based on the registered trade mark of the respondent, having changed certain words in order to parody them and pass social comment. Thus, the words 'Black Label' in 'Carling Black Label' were replaced with the words 'White Guilt', while 'America's lusty lively beer' was changed to 'Africa's lusty lively exploitation since 1652'. The respondent unsuccessfully sought to rely on its registered trade marks to stop the use of its marks on these t-shirts.

The cultural commons has a role to play as a countervailing right to a monopoly right over persona.[37] Accordingly, the public interest in cultural communication can be accommodated through a series of permitted uses, most notably the public interest, which allow unauthorised use of persona where it serves a cultural function. These permitted uses require closer consideration, and will be examined in chapter 10.

IV. Conclusion

The analysis in chapter six demonstrates that the justifications from autonomy and dignity and the economic rationale operate to support a legal right granting control of persona to the individual.

These justifications do not, however, claim that a publicity right is inviolate and should trump all other interests at stake: an unfettered property right in publicity is 'overbroad', as de Grandpre recognised. On the other side of the fence is the public interest in freedom of expression and cultural communication—interests which may be adversely affected by a private right of publicity.

However, these competing interests do not operate to defeat claims to publicity, but are correctly to be viewed as limitations to any such right. Freedom of expression and cultural communication should be recognised as important limitations on a publicity right. Accordingly, they will form the basis for permitted uses to the right, and will be examined in greater detail in chapter 10. Before that stage is reached, the nature and scope of the right itself needs to be examined.

---

[37] This also reflects the fifth ideal of copyright as identified by Chafee, being that copyright 'should not stifle independent creation by others'. Cited in G Davies, *Copyright and the Public Interest*, 2nd edn (London, Sweet & Maxwell, 2002) para 9–002.

8

The Nature of Publicity Rights

I. Introduction

THE JUSTIFICATIONS ADVANCED in favour of a right of publicity—
and those against it—allow us to draw three important conclusions
about the fundamental nature of a publicity right. Moreover, these
conclusions are relevant for all jurisdictions: they are not tied to the assessment of publicity in any one legal system. They are:

— the identity of the holder of the right;
— the inalienability of the right; and
— the monopoly status of the right.

II. Identifying the Individual

Accepting the justification from autonomy and dignity impacts upon the question of who can exercise a publicity right in two important ways. In the first
place, it operates to exclude fictional characters. Where a right of publicity is
justified on the grounds that it protects the inherently personal image and
identity of an individual, fictional characters are excluded from its scope. Thus,
the cartoon characters Teenage Mutant Ninja Turtles[1] would be excluded from
publicity rights, whereas Eddie Irvine would not. As noted in chapter two, this
boundary is somewhat blurred in the case of individuals who are strongly
identified with a particular fictional character, such as Paul Hogan/Crocodile
Dundee. Although the distinction may be less clear-cut in these cases, nonetheless
the right of publicity would extend to Paul Hogan as an individual, thereby
encompassing his activities in character (subject always to any independent
copyright issues arising in the creation of the character).

---

[1] The subject of *Mirage Studios v Counter-Feat Clothing* [1991] FSR 145, discussed in chapters
two and three.

The second consequence of the dignitarian justification is that it answers the question whether the right should be limited to celebrities or available to all. I have predominantly used 'individual' to refer to the holder of any publicity right, while recognising that the majority of those who will benefit and exercise the right will be celebrities: the signal importance of reputation was discussed in chapter three. The lure of fame transforms persona into a valuable 'asset' and reputation is at the core of publicity exploitation. On this analysis, the conclusion would be that only celebrities could or should benefit from a publicity right. Yet it has already been noted that the subject matter is persona, not the value in that persona. The consequence of this, together with the justification from autonomy, is that *every* individual should benefit from any legally recognised publicity right in the individual's persona.

As would be expected from his emphasis on the inherently personal nature of a publicity right, McCarthy is very strongly in favour of a universal right:

> Does the right of publicity cover only celebrities? The answer is clearly no. The right of publicity is an inherent right of identity possessed by everyone at birth. While the commercial value of a celebrity's identity is understandably greater than that of a non-celebrity, this does not mean that only celebrities have a right of publicity.[2]

As Nimmer rather pragmatically notes '[i]t is impractical to attempt to draw a line as to which persons have achieved the status of celebrity and which have not; it should rather be held that every person has the property right of publicity'.[3]

Vaver also agrees that 'personality protection surely should not depend on how rich or famous a person is'.[4] Unsurprisingly, authors in the Civilian personality rights camp also favour a universal right. As Logeais says, '[e]veryone gets an image at birth... there is no reason to discriminate between a celebrity and an anonymous individual'.[5] Neethling couches this in even stronger terms: person-ality rights are highly personal and are therefore 'non-transferable, uninheritable, incapable of being relinquished or attached, they cannot prescribe, *and they come into existence with the birth and are terminated by the death of a human being*'.[6] There is certainly no suggestion that such rights are exercisable by some persons but not by others.

---

[2] JT McCarthy, 'Public Personas and Private Property: The Commercialization of Human Identity' (1989) 79 *TMR* 681, 688; also T McCarthy, The Rights of Publicity and Privacy, 2nd edn (United States, West Group, 2001) paras 1:3 and 4:15–4:16.

[3] M Nimmer, 'The Right of Publicity' (1954) 19 *Law and Contemporary Problems* 203, 217. Halpern notes that the right is 'peculiarly celebrity based' but concludes that a final resolution is perhaps unnecessary since the debate is 'largely academic': S Halpern, 'The Right of Publicity: Maturation of an Independent Right Protecting the Associative Value of Personality' (1995) 46 *Hastings LJ* 853, 854.

[4] D Vaver, 'Advertising Using an Individual's Image: A Comparative Note' (2006) 122 *LQR* 362, 365.

[5] E Logeais, 'The French Right to One's Image: a Legal Lure?' [1994] *Ent LR* 163, 168.

[6] J Neethling, 'Personality Rights: a Comparative Overview' (2005) XXXVIII *CILSA* 210, 534, emphasis added.

If publicity rights are to be recognised by virtue (at least in part) of their inseparable link to the individual upon whose persona they depend, then they should be recognised equally for all individuals. The dignitarian justification has this consequence: it ensures the availability of the right to all individuals.

However, while all individuals are entitled to a publicity right by virtue of their inherent image, the impact of fame potentially makes itself felt when it comes to assessing damages. This can be seen in arguments advanced by McCarthy, Nimmer and Vaver, amongst others. Thus, McCarthy accepts that the commercial value of the celebrity's persona is 'understandably greater' than that of an anonymous individual. Nimmer's position is revealed by the full extent of the quotation cited above, where he goes on to argue that:

> ... it should rather be held that every person has the property right of publicity, but that the damages which a person may claim for infringement of the right will depend upon the value of the publicity appropriated which in turn will depend in great measure upon the degree of fame attained by the plaintiff.[7]

So too with Vaver who observes that, in New York at least,

> it did not matter one jot on the issue of liability whether the plaintiff was a private person or a public person. *When one came to consider damages, the factor was relevant*; the nature and extent of recovery could quite properly differ depending upon the circumstances of a particular plaintiff.[8]

These sentiments are also echoed by Madow in a footnote, where he states:

> [s]trictly speaking, everyone, obscure as well as famous, 'has' a right of publicity... As a practical matter, however, as Nimmer himself conceded, the right of publicity 'usually becomes important only when the plaintiff (or potential plaintiff) has achieved in some degree a celebrated status'... this is because the damages recoverable for infringement of the right depend on the commercial value of the publicity that has been appropriated... Very rarely will the economic value of a noncelebrity's persona be sufficient to support a lawsuit for infringement.[9]

The justification from autonomy and dignity therefore serves to shape the extent of the right in two ways. In the first place, it demonstrates that the right should be available to all individuals, by virtue of the universal nature of personhood and persona. In the second place, it draws out a secondary factor which impacts at the stage of compensation for unauthorised use and licence fees for authorised use. Reputation may affect the size of the licence fee and the calculus of damages, but it should not impact on the prior creation of the right. The role of reputation in the quantum of damages will be discussed in more detail in chapter 11.

---

[7] Nimmer, 'The Right of Publicity' (1954) 217, emphasis added.

[8] D Vaver, 'What's Mine is Not Yours: Commercial Appropriation of Personality under the Privacy Acts of British Columbia, Manitoba and Saskatchewan' (1981) 15 *U Brit Colum L Rev* 241, 257, emphasis added.

[9] M Madow, 'Private Ownership of Public Image: Popular Culture and Publicity Rights' (1993) 81 *Cal L Rev* 125, 137, fn 39, references omitted.

III. Inalienability and the Property Status of Publicity

Professor MacCormick considers the right to a horse, to shares in a company and to a house, all of which are the subject of property rights. As property, they

> are conceived as durable objects existing separately from and independently of other objects and of persons, subject to being used, possessed, and enjoyed by persons, and capable of being transferred from one person to another without loss of identity as that very thing.[10]

This definition of a thing gives us three criteria for property rights and ownership: (i) the thing must be durable; (ii) it must exist separately from and independently of a person; and (iii) it must be capable of being transferred from one person to another without loss of identity. For an individual's persona to be the subject of a property right, and be owned, it must meet these criteria of durability, separability and transferability. If this is the case, then the persona becomes subject to the usual consequences of property ownership.

Only the durability criterion presents no problems (at least during life): both the separability and transferability criteria do. It is meaningless to talk of one's image, for example, being separate or separable from one's corporeal body or capable of transfer without loss of identity. The very notion of persona is so clearly bound up with the individual that to attempt to separate out, and transfer on, the constituent (and intangible) elements of a publicity right is a thankless task. This inherent connection is emphasised by the justification for protecting persona advanced in chapter six, which arose from the autonomy and dignity of each individual in controlling the use of his or her image and identity.

The consequence of this is that persona (and therefore publicity) cannot be protected as property, and subject to ownership—at least under the property doctrines of Civilian systems and also the mixed system Scots law. While a more pragmatic approach can be found in Common law systems, whereby the value in persona may give rise to a property right, this too has been criticised. It is suggested that the temptations of classifying publicity as property should be resisted.

To strengthen this argument, it is helpful to look to the consequences of treating persona as the subject of property rights, in which case it would be subject to the usual consequences of ownership. It could be assigned outright (not simply licensed) or used to satisfy the debts of a creditor. Yet to contend that an individual's persona could pass to his or her spouse on divorce or form part of the individual's estate on bankruptcy fails to reflect the reality of the situation— yet these are both obvious consequences of ownership and property rights. The

---

[10] N MacCormick, Institutions of Law: An Essay in Legal Theory (Oxford, Oxford University Press, 2007) 136, fn omitted.

considerable problems experienced in the United States from treating publicity as a property right in this context have been examined in detail by Westfall and Landau, who conclude that 'it seems relatively clear that publicity rights should not be treated as property for purposes of bankruptcy'.[11] Beverley-Smith, also writing in the Common law tradition, makes a similar observation that '[t]he fact that a right is labelled as "property" or "proprietary" is not inherently significant and does not mean that the right will have all the characteristic incidents of full ownership.'[12] In fact, in legal systems in the Civilian or Romanistic tradition, that is indeed what a 'property' label signifies. The pragmatism of the Common law approach, whereby publicity is property for some purposes but not for others, may meet with commercial approval, but for many it lacks the coherency and consistency which is sought in law.

Further, there would be very serious concerns with treating persona (not least the subset of persona which comprises personal information) as subject to ownership. Doing so would create a far-reaching right, beyond any requirement of publicity rights. Even those writers who are in favour of a publicity right accept that a property right grants 'overbroad'[13] protection for publicity. If individuals were to be granted property rights in their name, stage name, nick-name, image, voice, characteristics and 'trade mark' gestures or catch-phrases, private information, together with reputation and goodwill, if any, then their right to control would far exceed anything currently recognised or even required. The analysis of publicity rights so far emphasises the value of these attributes when they are exploited, typically commercially. Yet, to recognise them as property would take legal protection far beyond the exploitation of persona in the publicity uses. Instead, a property right would enable an individual to control *any* use of her persona, including use in a wide range of government, administrative, health, and employment contexts, and in news reporting. It would be possible to limit protection by requiring 'commercial use' of persona, but reliance on the notion of commercial use to delineate the right is not satisfactory, as explored in chapter three, section II. A. Such a broad and exclusive right would be an extreme and unprecedented development, and would require extensive exceptions, defences and permitted uses.[14] The advantage of providing an individual with a strong right to control the use of his or her persona is far outweighed by the damaging impact that would be caused by the grant of such a right, or the complications involved in minimising this impact. The repercussions would be much wider than simply the protection of an individual's publicity rights.

---

[11] D Westfall and D Landau, 'Publicity Rights as Property Rights' (2005–2006) 23 *Cardozo Arts and Ent LJ* 71, 117, and see discussion at 99–117, in the context of divorce and bankruptcy.

[12] H Beverley-Smith, The Commercial Appropriation of Personality (Cambridge, Cambridge University Press, 2002) 287.

[13] V De Grandpre, 'Understanding the Market for Celebrity: An Economic Analysis of the Right of Publicity' (2001–2002) 12 *Fordham Intell Prop Media and Ent LJ* 73, 79.

[14] Frazer describes a 'complete prohibition of unconsented use' as 'unjustifiable, undesirable and impracticable'. See T Frazer, 'Appropriation of Personality – a New Tort?' (1983) 99 *LQR* 281, 312.

Persona is inseparable from the individual and inalienable. It therefore cannot be 'owned', but this is not the same as saying that its commercial value is abandoned or homeless, as will be seen. Curiously, as a final point, the inalienability of persona, which precludes outright transfer, in life does not necessarily do so on death. At that point the indicia of the individual becomes reliant on representation in much the same way as a trade mark, and *can* be separated out from the individual. Further, the justification from autonomy ceases to operate to protect the individual (although it may operate in favour of heirs) and persona will be incapable of further change or development at the hands of the individual.[15] Thus, Marilyn Monroe and James Dean are still iconic figures today, decades after their deaths, and, while the public perception of them may evolve over time, their names and images remain fixed as they were at the time of their deaths. Accordingly, while the concept of inalienability in the Civilian tradition typically prevents transfers both *inter vivos* and *post mortem*, publicity should be inalienable only as regards lifetime transfers, leaving an economic right which is freely transferable after death.[16] In this regard it would be akin to copyright, for example, where the inalienable moral rights cease on death, leaving the fully transferable economic rights.

IV. Publicity as a Monopoly

The right identified so far has resisted classification as a right of privacy, does not fit well with passing off and, doctrinally at least, cannot be owned or subject to property rights, since persona is inalienable. Protection which is anchored in tort law is also unsatisfactory, not least since (as the privacy/ breach of confidence discussion in chapter four demonstrated) it fails to take account of the very real need to exploit the right. Tort remedies, such as passing off and breach of confidence, typically focus on achieving remedies for unauthorised use of the goodwill or confidential information—but this only addresses one side of publicity practice.[17] Publicity is therefore a difficult right to classify, because of (i) the tension caused by the need to protect its economic and dignitarian interests equally; and (ii) the importance of enabling authorised use as well as defending against unauthorised use. Yet there is one category of legal right which has the potential to address these problems, and provide a coherent and rational basis for a right of publicity: monopoly rights.

---

[15] Society's 'interpretation' or attitude towards the deceased may, of course, continue to evolve.

[16] See further chapter nine, section III.C.

[17] And, as the comparisons in chapter three demonstrated, unauthorised use is typically worth considerably less than authorised use.

A monopoly, or exclusive privilege, is 'an exclusive, and valuable, right to do something and, hence, to stop others from doing the same thing'.[18] This is exactly what the individual is seeking to do in relation to persona: to use it and prevent others from using it. Intellectual property too is a monopoly, and publicity has a number of striking similarities with intellectual properties, especially copyright, since both rights look to protect dignitarian interests (persona or creative expression) on the one hand, while recognising the economic benefits to be derived from exploitation on the other.

While intellectual property today is frequently classed as a property right,[19] not least because the intellectual property statutes declare that it is,[20] historically the picture was not so clear. Baron Hume classed patents and copyright as exclusive privileges,[21] that is to say monopolies. Of the historical debate, MacQueen has stated that in Scotland 'the firm view came to be that copyright was not a right of property but a form of statutory monopoly, restricting for reasons of public policy what would otherwise be the natural liberties of mankind'.[22] Deazley's analysis of the origins of copyright supports this assessment. He concludes that the evolution of copyright in the eighteenth century, from the Statute of Anne to the case of *Donaldson v Beckett*,[23] has been subject to a 'back-reading'.[24] This has created a myth regarding the origin of copyright, which advances the view that the Statute of Anne was passed to protect the labour of authors and their property in that labour. In doing so, the Statute allegedly overturned the

---

[18] K Reid, 'Property', in *Stair Memorial Encyclopaedia* Vol 18, Pt I (1993), para 5, with reference to Adam Smith and Baron Hume. In Scots law, exclusive privilege is classed as a real right, as is ownership, yet it is the only real right which does not have a 'thing' as its subject matter. It is identified by Reid as the eighth real right. (ibid) Its status as a real right is supported by earlier writers in Scots law, including Adam Smith (Meek et al, *Adam Smith, Lectures on Jurisprudence* (Oxford, Clarendon Press, 1978, reprinted 1987) i.16–17, i.20 (10–11) and ii.27– ii.41 (81–85)) and Baron Hume (D Hume, *Baron David Hume's Lectures 1786–1822 vol IV*, edited by G Campbell and H Paton (Edinburgh, Stair Society, 1955) vol 17, ch IV.) As a real right, it is 'good against the world'—a further advantage in comparison to personal rights such as delicts and contractual rights.

[19] F Easterbrook, 'Intellectual Property is Still Property' in A Moore (ed), *Information Ethics Privacy, Property, and Power* (Seattle, University of Washington Press, 2005) 114; H MacQueen, 'Property', in *Stair Memorial Encyclopaedia* Vol 18, Pt II (1993), para 802; N MacCormick, 'General Legal Concepts', in *Stair Memorial Encyclopaedia Reissue* (2008), para 121. There is still some doubt, however, and there are those who favour the view of intellectual property as distinct from tangible property. Beverley-Smith, for example, concludes that 'in the case of intellectual property, the term "property" is used in a purely metaphorical way'. Beverley-Smith, *The Commercial Appropriation of Personality* (2002) 278 and more generally at 277–83; see also K Reid, 'Property', in *Stair Memorial Encyclopaedia* Vol 18, Pt I (1993), para 5.

[20] The Copyright, Designs and Patents Act 1988 opens with the statement that 'Copyright is a property right' (section 1(1)); the Trade Marks Act 1994 states that a 'registered trade mark is a property right' (section 2(1)); and sections 30 and 31 of the Patents Act 1977 assert the property status of a patent as regards England and Scotland respectively.

[21] Hume, *Hume's Lectures IV* (1955) 59–72.

[22] H MacQueen, *Copyright, Competition and Industrial Design*, Hume Papers on Public Policy, 2nd edn (Edinburgh, Edinburgh University Press, 1995) vol 3 no 2, 3.

[23] *Donaldson v Beckett* (1774) 2 Bro PC 129 [139]–[140], and the Scottish case on the same point: *Hinton v Donaldson* (1773) Mor 8307.

[24] R Deazley, *On the Origin of the Right to Copy* (Oxford, Hart, 2004) xxiii.

'common law' notion of copyright in published works[25] and replaced it with a limited monopoly right for authors of 14 years. Deazley seeks to show that there was no comparable concept of copyright or author's rights prior to the Statute of Anne, and that this notion of the common law rights of authors has been constructed, post-legislation, in the eighteenth century and thereafter.[26] He concludes that '[a] statutory phenomenon, copyright was fundamentally concerned with the reading public, with the encouragement and spread of education, and with the continued production of useful books'.[27] Copyright was therefore never intended to protect the proprietary interests of the author, but was indeed a limited statutory grant of a right to encourage the dissemination of learning. What came after was an attempt to impose sense and order on the complex and non-linear progression of copyright in the eighteenth century,[28] coupled with the evolving scope of copyright, and drew strength from the notions of property in one's labour, as popularised by Locke.[29] Deazley's analysis would support the notion of copyright as a right of exclusive privilege, created by statute, rather than a property right arising at common law.

In view of the similarities between intellectual property rights and publicity rights, it is not difficult to conclude that they also share a legal classification as monopoly rights, or exclusive privileges. In fact, arguably the strongest support for this conclusion as regards publicity can be drawn from the leading American case, *Haelan Laboratories v Topps Chewing Gum*.[30] Although the subsequent commentaries have focused on the reference to the property status of publicity rights, Judge Frank in fact referred to the right to control publication of a photograph as one of exclusive privilege: 'a man has a right in the publicity value of his photograph, i.e., the right to grant the *exclusive privilege* of publishing his picture... Whether it be labelled a "property" right is immaterial'.[31]

It is interesting to speculate on how publicity rights might have developed in the United States if subsequent jurists had concentrated on Judge Frank's reference to exclusive privilege rather than his 'property' observation.

Thus, while privacy, tort and property rights fail to reflect all the varied attributes of a publicity right, monopoly rights, or rights of exclusive privilege, can address these issues. A monopoly, as the exclusive right to control the use of persona and, hence, to stop others from doing the same thing, enables both exploitation and defence. Monopolies are also not unlimited in the way that

---

[25] Unpublished works remained subject to different principles until their regulation under the Copyright Act 1911 and their eventual assimilation to published works in the Copyright, Designs and Patents Act (CDPA) 1988. See, for example, Deazley, *On the Origin of the Right to Copy* (2004); H MacQueen et al, *Contemporary Intellectual Property* (Oxford, Oxford University Press, 2007) paras 2.4–2.6.

[26] Deazley (n 23) 221–226.

[27] ibid 226.

[28] ibid, particularly at 221–26.

[29] ibid.

[30] *Haelan Laboratories v Topps Chewing Gum* (1953) 202 F.2d 866.

[31] ibid 868 (Frank J), emphasis added.

property rights (in theory[32]) are, thus enabling exceptions and restrictions to be accommodated and even to be expected.

A final point of interest is the support that writers such as Hume and Smith gave to monopolies such as intellectual properties—support which can be conveyed to publicity. Despite being opposed to monopolies in general, as being 'extremely detrimental'[33] and tending to 'promote the poverty or, which comes to the same thing, the uncomeatibleness of the thing so monopolized',[34] Smith acknowledged that the privileges of copyright and patents 'can do no harm and may do some good, [and] are not to be altogether condemned'.[35] Hume likewise appeared to support these rights, despite criticising the abuse of other monopolies in particular commodities.[36] However, the support given to a monopoly right of copyright by Hume, Smith and others, was qualified by the need to ensure that the monopoly was as short as possible, while still securing the benefits of the right.[37] This too reflects the conclusions already drawn regarding publicity, whereby the private right needs to respect competing public interests, notably expression and cultural communication.

V. The Likelihood of Legislation

While the above discussion has advanced publicity rights as monopoly rights (primarily in the context of the Scottish and English legal systems), rather than torts or privacy or property rights, it is necessary to concede the difficulties in achieving this outcome in reality. There is no evidence than monopolies can emerge from common law jurisprudence—the closest comparators with publicity are intellectual property rights, all of which are statutory in origin. It is acknowledged that any monopoly right of publicity, to protect the private right to control persona subject to necessary limitations and exceptions, would require legislative intervention. And if the relevant governments are unwilling to legislate on privacy, how much more unlikely is it that they will turn their attentions to publicity?[38] To this extent, these conclusions are certainly more relevant for

---

[32] It is accepted that the unbounded nature of property rights is more theoretical than actual. Nevertheless, the mantra of unlimited property rights is still very powerful.

[33] Meek et al, *Adam Smith Lectures*, at ii.33. See also N MacCormick, 'On the Very Idea of Intellectual Property: an Essay According to the Institutionalist Theory of Law' [2002] IPQ 227, 237.

[34] Meek et al, *Adam Smith Lectures* (1978) ii.34. The use of 'uncomeatibleness' in these lectures is probably a neologism referring to the exclusivity of any item subject to a monopoly. Thanks to Professor John Cairns for his help with my interpretation of the *Lectures* in this regard.

[35] ibid ii.33.

[36] Hume (n 17) 60.

[37] For example, G Davies, *Copyright and the Public Interest*, 2nd edn (London, Sweet & Maxwell, 2002) para 4–005, citing Lord Macaulay's speeches in the Houses of Parliament, 1841.

[38] Beverley-Smith, for example, comments on the 'preponderance of opinion [which] suggests that any initiative in protecting interests in personality which do not fall under the existing heads of liability will be judicial rather than legislative'. Beverley-Smith (n 12) 328.

theory than practice at present, and this is also true of the following chapters, which outline the scope of a right of publicity with reference to its monopoly classification. Despite the remote likelihood of legislation,[39] the project is still valid: if the theoretical basis and scope of publicity rights is not explored, any future legal development will be hampered, whether statutory or judicial.

VI. Conclusion

This short chapter has attempted to draw out certain fundamental characteristics of any legal right of publicity. Where the law does recognise a right to control the use of persona, that right should be vested in the individual—and all individuals, not only celebrities, should be entitled to this right. The right in persona cannot be owned since it is inherently inalienable, at least during life, nor can it be comprehensively treated as a privacy right or within the class of torts. The most apt categorisation of publicity is as a monopoly right, or exclusive privilege, albeit such a right would need a statutory basis, however unlikely this may seem. These conclusions, together with the justifications in chapter six and competing interests in chapter seven, do much to shape the functional aspects of the right, and it is these functional aspects which will be explored in the remaining chapters.

---

[39] Whilst remote, it is nevertheless not impossible.

Part III

Shaping Publicity Rights

9

The Scope of Publicity Rights:
Formation, Duration and Transfer

I. Introduction

T HE PURPOSE OF this chapter is to consider the scope of a right of publicity which has emerged from the foregoing study. The justifications in favour of a right and the need to balance the right against the legitimate competing interests of other parties both operate to shape the right.

There are five elements which operate to limit the extent of the right or its exercise:

1. formalities in respect of creation;
2. duration of the right;
3. transfer and transmission of the right;
4. countervailing rights; and
5. permitted uses.

In the case of an action for publicity infringement, these five elements operate to establish:

— whether or not there is a right (have all formalities been complied with?);
— whether there is any limitation on enforcement (has the right expired or been transferred?); and
— whether there is a countervailing right which operates to prevent reliance on the right (is there a permitted use?).

The first two questions will be considered in this chapter, while chapter 10 will examine the nature of permitted uses. The rights of other interested parties, notably authorised users, will also be considered where relevant.

II. Formalities

The law often imposes formalities which must be complied with before a right comes into existence. With patents and trade marks, for example, registration is necessary to benefit from statutory protection.[1] What formalities, if any, should apply in the case of publicity?

A. Labour or Creativity

One option, which can be swiftly dismissed, would be the need for a minimum standard of labour or creativity in 'creating' the persona which is to be protected by the right of publicity. As was shown in chapter five, the need for prior labour, and the extent and quality of that labour, are problematic concepts, and it is frequently impossible to determine in any given case whether there has been labour expended in creating the persona and, if so, by whom.[2] More fundamentally, a labour or creativity prerequisite is contrary to the dignitarian justification for the right of publicity, which refers not to the need to protect (or provide an incentive for) labour expended on persona, but to protect the individual's autonomy in his or her persona.

Further, even if we were to assume that (a) a labour requirement could be defined and (b) an identifiable point of creation could be determined, we would still be faced with the issue of an ever-evolving image for each individual. Would the right be recreated with each new achievement or hairstyle of the individual? The consequences of extending a right through reworking the original subject matter can be seen in early copyright debates. MacQueen notes that Sir Walter Scott (who died in 1832) was able to extend copyright protection in certain works until at least 1870 as a result of revising and reissuing those titles.[3]

In any event, as copyright shows, where there is a requirement for some degree of labour or creativity (or originality in the case of copyright), this requirement is frequently eroded over time to a bare minimum: 'mundane' compilations such as

---

[1] See for example the Patents Act 1977 ss 7–9 and 14–20; the Trade Marks Act 1994 s 2(1).

[2] Madow says that '[t]he notion that a star's public image is nothing else than congealed star labour is just the folklore of celebrity, the bedtime story the celebrity industry prefers to tell us and, perhaps, itself'. M Madow, 'Private Ownership of Public Image: Popular Culture and Publicity Rights' (1993) 81 *Cal L Rev* 125, 184.

[3] H MacQueen, *Copyright, Competition and Industrial Design*, Hume Papers on Public Policy, Vol 3, No 2, 2nd edn (Edinburgh, Edinburgh University Press, 1995) 3. Copyright duration was only tied exclusively to the life of the author by the Copyright Act 1911. See also WM Landes and R Posner, 'An Economic Analysis of Copyright Law' (1989) 18 *J Legal Stud* 325, 363; R Posner, *Economic Analysis of Law*, 7th edn (New York, Aspen Publishers/Wolters Kluwer, 2007) para 3.3.

a timetable index and the listing of programmes to be broadcast have been held sufficient to attract copyright protection.[4]

B. Registration

An alternative formality, and one which requires more detailed consideration, is whether or not the right of publicity should come into existence only on the registration of persona, in a manner similar to the trade mark and patent registration systems. In their analysis of the emergence of modern intellectual property law, Sherman and Bently argue that the evolution of the modern system of registration for designs, patents and trade marks is one of the hallmarks of the modern intellectual property regime.[5] Focusing on the administrative aspects of registration (such as form-filling, providing a two-dimensional representation of the mark or design, and so on) means that registration becomes an end in itself, rather than being seen as 'a poor imitation of the "true" property – one which was twice removed from the essence of the intangible property'.[6] So long as the invention, design or trade mark could be reduced to the required descriptive and illustrative form, protection would be granted: theoretical debates as to the role of creativity and the merits of treating intangibles as property were superseded by this administrative 'closure' of intangible property rights.[7] Intellectual property disputes likewise moved away from matters of creativity and originality, to concentrate on interpretation of the registration documents.[8]

In turning the focus from the abstract to the concrete, registration performs a number of beneficial functions. First, it marks the creation not of the intangible but of the legal right over the intangible. The subject of the patent or trade mark may exist, but the existence of the legally enforceable patent or trade mark right is dependent on registration. Second, registration marks priority, making it easier to determine which party was first to acquire the legal right (if not the underlying subject).[9] The third advantage is that registration enables the owner of the right to be identified with some certainty.[10] A final benefit—and one often cited as the rationale behind granting the legal right in patent cases—is that registration of

---

[4] W Cornish and D Llewelyn, *Intellectual Property: Patents, Copyright, Trade Marks and Allied Rights*, 5th edn (London, Sweet & Maxwell, 2003) para 11–05, and cases cited therein.

[5] B Sherman and L Bently, *The Making of Modern Intellectual Property Law: the British Experience 1760–1911* (Cambridge, Cambridge University Press, 1999) 180–86. See also 67–76.

[6] ibid 185.

[7] ibid 180 and see also 182–83.

[8] ibid 186.

[9] ibid 68.

[10] ibid 68.

the patent, design or trade mark provides a source of public information to inform and inspire future work in the field.[11]

Registration often works in tandem with unregistered rights at common law. For example, where an inventor chooses not to register his or her invention to obtain a patent, the inventor can, in certain circumstances, rely on commercial confidence in trade secrets to protect the invention. Similarly, the law of passing off provides a remedy for misrepresentative use of an unregistered trade mark. One option for publicity rights would therefore be to restrict the exercise of the right to those who have registered their personas, while existing rights (such as passing off and the article 8 right to privacy) could operate to provide protection insofar as they can in unregistered cases. This would have the advantage of providing certainty as to when a statutory (registered) right of publicity could be exercised, albeit with the risk that the unregistered right(s) may develop over time to offer wider protection than that of the registered right.[12]

There are four arguments against imposing a registration requirement for a statutory right of publicity, however. The first consideration is derived from the personal nature of the subject: the individual's persona. As was concluded in chapter six, persona is something which inheres to the individual. Writing in the Common law tradition, McCarthy says 'The right of publicity is an inherent right of identity possessed by everyone at birth.'[13] This attitude is even more strongly held in Civilian systems, where Neethling argues that personality rights, as a category, 'come into existence with the birth and are terminated by the death of a human being'.[14] Since every individual has, from birth, a persona, it is counter-intuitive to impose a registration requirement before a right over persona can be enjoyed.[15]

A further consequence of the personal nature of the subject is that the main benefits of registration are not easily applied to a right which is so intimately associated with the individual. Unlike patents, designs and trade marks, for example, publicity rights do not give rise to doubt as to the original owner,[16] nor is there any need to establish priority or to share information about the subject

---

[11]   ibid 69. See also, for example, Cornish and Llewelyn, *Intellectual Property* (2003) para 3–37; H MacQueen et al, *Contemporary Intellectual Property* (Oxford, Oxford University Press, 2007) paras 10–16–10–18.

[12]   Carty discusses the risks of an expansive application of the doctrine of breach of confidence, whereby it offers wider protection for inventions than that offered by patents: H Carty, 'An Analysis of the Modern Action for Breach of Commercial Confidence: When is Protection Merited?' [2008] *IPQ* 416, particularly 433.

[13]   T McCarthy, 'Public Personas and Private Property: The Commercialization of Human Identity' (1989) 79 *TMR* 681, 688.

[14]   J Neethling, Johann, 'Personality Rights: a Comparative Overview' (2005) XXXVIII *CILSA* 210, 534. Also E Logeais, 'The French Right to One's Image: a Legal Lure?' [1994] *Ent LR* 163, 168.

[15]   This can be distinguished from the administrative requirement to registers births and deaths: subsequent rights, such as human rights, are not dependent on having registered one's birth.

[16]   The position of subsequent owners, if any, will be considered in section IV. B. below (Transmission of the Right Post Mortem).

for the benefit of the world at large. The typical benefits of registration (which help justify its use) are therefore lacking in publicity rights.

Third, as was seen in chapter six, the need for a *sui generis* right of publicity is, in part, based on the lack of protection at common law and the need to ensure a more coherent, rational system of protecting economic and dignitarian interests. To limit this system to those who have chosen to register their persona is disadvantageous to individuals and to other parties alike. Where there has been no registration, both the individual and prospective (or actual) users are left with the incoherent and potentially ad hoc protection provided for in the United Kingdom by passing off and article 8—protection which was criticised on a number of grounds in the foregoing chapters. There may also be judicial doubts as to the merits of allowing a pursuer to recover through doctrines such as passing off, where he or she could have achieved the legal protection he or she seeks through registering his or her persona. These factors add to the already existing uncertainties as to the availability and extent of such common law rights.

The fourth objection is that registration brings costs for both parties: the individual who has to pay to register his or her persona[17] and, to a lesser extent, the user who has to check the register to see if there has been a registration. These costs are particularly problematic in the case of a right which is intended, in part, to protect dignitarian interests. Requiring an individual to register (and to pay for such registration) in order to protect these interests contradicts the basic need to safeguard them.

Simplicity and certainty have much to offer all interested parties and, given that all individuals have a persona which can be the subject of publicity rights, that simplicity and certainty is more likely to be found by creating a standard right applicable to all. The universal nature of persona and publicity requires a universal right.

The analogy has already been drawn between the right of publicity and copyright and it is interesting to note that copyright is one of the few intellectual property rights not dependent on registration. There are two practical obstacles to imposing a registration requirement on copyright works, namely the large volume of copyright works and the low value of many of them.[18] These objections are also relevant to publicity where, for many individuals, persona will have a low (albeit rarely negligible) economic value. Further, since all individuals have a persona, the large volume of possible applications could prove a considerable administrative burden if registration were required. A third reason why copyright is not well suited to registration is that 'unlike the situation with patents, designs and trade marks where applicants had to describe what it was that they were claiming, in the case of copyright it was the object *itself*, the libretto, the score, or the book, rather than a representation of it, which was

---

[17] This will often incur legal costs, as well as the registration costs, in doing so.
[18] Sherman and Bently, *The Making of Modern Intellectual Property Law* (1999) 183–184.

deposited at Stationers' Hall'.[19] Copyright is not susceptible to further reduction.[20] Again, the same can be said of publicity, where the persona is not easily reduced to registrable criteria in the same manner as patents, designs or trade marks. Further, unlike any of the other intellectual property rights, no guarantor of originality is required, since persona, by its very nature, cannot be pirated. Individuals may imitate another person[21] but they cannot *be* another person.

The conclusion that can be drawn is that there should be no formalities as to either labour or registration attaching to the proposed statutory right of publicity. In the same way as copyright comes into existence with the expression or fixation of the idea, publicity rights should come into existence with the individual.[22] A further advantage of this joint birth date is that the date of creation of the right can be ascertained with precision.

III. Duration

A. Introduction

Careful consideration must be given to the term of a right of publicity. Setting the appropriate duration is essential to ensure that the benefit to the individual is not procured at society's expense. In the context of monopolies it has been observed that the 'privilege involved should be seen as a derogation from the order of natural liberty, and thus as one to be extended only so far as the justification for it runs'.[23] Once the justification for granting a right of publicity has been served, the right should expire. As with other intellectual property rights, at that point the subject of the right will lapse into the public domain to be available to all.[24] In

---

[19] ibid 184, emphasis in original. Footnote omitted.

[20] This difference between copyright and the other intellectual property rights is indicative, according to Sherman and Bently, of the 'pre-modern' nature of copyright protection: Sherman and Bently
(n 5) 193. The differences between copyright and trade marks and patents become more explicit if one uses the term 'industrial property' rather than intellectual property, since the origins and rationales for legal protection of industrial property do not easily apply to copyright. For a discussion of these differences see H MacQueen, 'Property' in *Stair Memorial Encyclopaedia* Vol 18, Pt II (1993) paras 801–02.

[21] See Coombe, *The Cultural Life of Intellectual Properties*, at 96–97; Madow, 'Private Ownership of Public Image' (1993) 197; H Carty, 'Advertising, Publicity Rights and English Law' [2004] *IPQ* 209, 249–50. The consequences of fraudulent imitation in commercial transactions are examined in cases such as *Shogun Finance Ltd v Hudson* [2004] 1 AC 119 and (proving that identity fraud is not a new problem) *Morrison v Robertson* 1908 SC 332.

[22] Infancy is no barrier to publicity: see the advertisement in Appendix 1; also Suri Cruise: www.out-law.com/page-7274.

[23] N MacCormick, *Institutions of Law: An Essay in Legal Theory* (Oxford, Oxford University Press, 2007) 236.

[24] J Hughes, 'The Philosophy of Intellectual Property' (1988) 77 *Georgetown Law Journal* 287, 324.

creating a right to protect persona, it is necessary to consider what time limits should be placed upon that right to protect the 'order of natural liberty'.

B. Duration in Life

Determining the duration of the right requires the identification of both the start date and the end date. These are separate issues but, in the case of publicity, are inextricably linked to the life of the individual. As was concluded above, the date of creation of the right should be the date of birth of the individual.

The next issue to be determined is therefore the end-point of the right. In America, where publicity is regarded as a property right, the various statutory rights of publicity typically provide for a lifetime duration.[25] In the United Kingdom, one comparator might again be the statutory intellectual property rights, which all have fixed terms. Each is different not only in length, however, but also in its potential for renewal. Patents expire 20 years after the application was made and are non-renewable.[26] In contrast, trade marks have a shorter lifespan of 10 years, but this is subject to the right to renew the registered mark for a further period of 10 years, which is exercisable indefinitely.[27] When copyright was first introduced as a monopoly right by the Statute of Anne 1709, the grant was limited to 14 years, followed by a renewed grant of a further period of 14 years if the author was still alive at the expiry of the first period. In the 300 years since then, the duration of the copyright has been revised and now currently exists for the life of the author plus 70 years.[28]

Landes and Posner state that these fixed terms not only reduce the adverse consequences of monopolies, they also reduce tracing costs, being the costs incurred with the necessary effort and expense to trace the owner of a prior intellectual property right in order to seek consent to use the right.[29]

---

[25] A detailed analysis of the statutory protection is given by T McCarthy, *The Rights of Publicity and Privacy*, 2nd edn (United States, West Group, 2001) chapter 6. He notes that each statutory response is 'one of a kind', para 6:6. See also the US legislation cited below.

[26] The Patents Act 1977 s 25(1), states that the 20-year period shall begin with the date of filing the application for the patent 'or such other date as may be prescribed'.

[27] Trade Marks Act 1994 ss 42 and 43. However, marks which are not used can be removed on application, if five years' non-use can be proved, per s 46(1). Subject to this, it is possible for trade marks to last indefinitely: Trade Mark 1, registered on 1 January 1876, is still in force today: www.ipo.gov.uk/tm/t-find/t-find-number?detailsrequested=C&trademark=1.

[28] Copyright, Designs and Patents Act (CDPA) 1988 s 12. Note that this is in fact the length of copyright protection for literary, dramatic, musical or artistic works: other periods are in place for sound recordings and films, as per ss 13A, 13B, 14 and 15. Moral rights have separate terms (s 86). Until the CDPA 1988 came into force, there were a limited number of rights which lasted in perpetuity. These were unpublished literary, dramatic and musical works, together with unpublished engravings and photographs. The CDPA 1988 implied an expiry date of 31 December 2039 for the copyright in any such works in existence at the time of the Act, per Schedule 1, para 12(4).

[29] WM Landes and R Posner, 'An Economic Analysis of Copyright Law' (1989) 18 *J Legal Stud* 325, 361.

Where should publicity rights fall on this spectrum of term? The need for a limit does not provide any further guidance as to what that limit should be. There is no underlying principle which dictates that monopolies must expire after x years, although, following Adam Smith, there is an argument that any monopoly created should be of the shortest possible duration to fulfil its intended purpose,[30] and Landes and Posner point to the costs involved in tracing the right's owner several decades after the first creation. Thus, a patent should secure a viable return to the inventor within 20 years and is also one of the hardest rights to trace, given its likely incorporation and development in many other products. Trade marks, in contrast, protect the trading name and goodwill of a business and therefore need to last for as long as the business name does, but with the proviso that they lapse where the business fails to renew it or use it. Other than making reference to these economic factors, the duration of intellectual property rights is entirely a matter for the legislature, dependent on the purpose to be served by the monopoly and the competing interests.

As demonstrated above, the purpose of publicity rights is to enable individuals to control and manage their persona, thereby protecting their dignitarian *and* economic interests. Publicity is therefore a right which combines the personal values and economic values arising from the individual's persona. Although the economic interests could be met with a time-limited monopoly, a fixed term duration does not reflect the dignitarian element of the right. This leads to the conclusion that publicity rights should endure for the life of the individual.[31]

C. Post Mortem Duration

While the right of publicity should endure for the life of the individual, the extent of any post mortem duration requires separate consideration. The exploitation associated with publicity does not necessarily cease when the individual does:

> A person may not live for long, but his or her beliefs, personality and image can live on and be passed down from one generation to another. Decades after their deaths, the images of Marilyn Monroe and James Dean continue to sell posters and T-shirts.[32]

Although not specifically derived from exploitation of persona, Michael Jackson generated $1 billion in the year after his death, through record and film sales and

---

[30] See chapter eight, section IV; N MacCormick, 'On the Very Idea of Intellectual Property: an Essay According to the Institutionalist Theory of Law' [2002] *IPQ* 227, 237.

[31] This reflects both the statutory right of publicity in the US and the Civilian personality rights approach: see chapter two.

[32] A Milligan, *Brand it Like Beckham* (London, Cyan, 2004) 177. For a short commentary on post mortem celebrity, see Neil Steinberg, 'Death, Career Move: Image Management doesn't Stop at the Pearly Gates Anymore' at www.forbes.com/media/2008/10/27/death-career-move-biz-deadcelebs08-cx_ns_1027steinberg.html.

publishing.[33] This has led to speculation that he will shortly be the 'top earning dead celebrity', although to ensure Jackson's name 'continues its run of good fortune, executors will have to keep a tight rein on his image and a close eye on anyone else who tries to slap his face on so much as a mug'.[34] There is clearly ongoing, if not increased, demand for celebrities after their death. The question therefore arises whether there should be any post mortem right over persona.[35] If so, how long should such rights last and who should enjoy and enforce them?

There is certainly truth in Beverley-Smith's comment that 'reputation and injured dignity are generally of no concern to a deceased person'.[36] While arguably *nothing* is of concern to a deceased person, nevertheless both dignitary and economic issues which may occur after death routinely concern individuals while still alive. It is presumably this which motivates people to leave wills which deal with both financial and personal matters after their death.[37]

The Civilian position is summarised by Waelde and Whitty, as being that

> personality rights generally are not actively transmissible by succession on the victim's death but that after death relatives (or universal successors) of the deceased may have remedies in their own rights under rules prohibiting any interference with a deceased person's body or reputation.[38]

However, while this may be the starting point, Beverley-Smith et al note that:

> A trend is emerging in French case law according to which the non-economic element of personality rights is indescendible, but the economic element devolves on the heirs in accordance with the ordinary rules of the law of succession.[39]

In Germany there is also a division between the economic and non-economic interests. Following the leading case regarding the rights of Marlene Dietrich's heirs, it was accepted that 'personality rights, as far as they protected economic interests, were descendible'.[40] In contrast, the non-economic, or ideal, interests

---

[33] Even his aborted tour generated significant income, since many fans apparently opted to keep their tickets as souvenirs, rather than returning them for a refund: 'Jackson: Life after death?' *BBC News Online* (25 June 2010).

[34] ibid; see also Harris, 'Michael Jackson: after the Mourning comes the Earning' *The Observer* (18 October 2009).

[35] This is different from the right of the individual's successors to continue, or to initiate, any legal action for wrongs committed while the individual was alive, which is a valid course of action.

[36] H Beverley-Smith, *The Commercial Appropriation of Personality* (Cambridge, Cambridge University Press, 2002) 124.

[37] Wills often provide for matters such as funeral instructions and the distribution of items of sentimental value, as well as financial and material matters, indicating that most individuals do wish to plan for some element of ongoing economic *and* dignitary autonomy even after death.

[38] C Waelde and N Whitty, 'A Rights of Personality Database' in N Whitty and R Zimmermann (eds), *Rights of Personality in Scots Law, a Comparative Perspective* (Dundee, Dundee University Press, 2009) para 11.4.3(e).

[39] Beverley-Smith et al, *Privacy, Property and Personality* (Cambridge University Press, Cambridge, 2005) 204.

[40] ibid 104, referring to *BGHZ* 143, 1 December 1999 – *Marlene Dietrich*.

can be enforced post mortem but only by relatives, rather than being freely available for testamentary disposal.[41] This approach in German law is supported by Beverley-Smith et al.[42]

Neethling, in his review of personality rights, gives brief consideration to personality rights post mortem. He contrasts the approach of what he terms the 'traditional school' of France and Switzerland, whereby all personality rights are terminated by death and 'the idea of post-mortem personality rights is rejected',[43] with the German and Austrian approaches, for example, whereby (as discussed above) an individual's personality rights 'continue after his death and are maintained by his relatives as fiduciaries'.[44] In the specific case of publicity rights, Neethling concludes that '[i]n so far as this right or interest is patrimonial'[45] it should fall into the owner's estate on death, but this should be seen as 'part of the immaterial property right to the advertising image (of the deceased)',[46] thus meriting different treatment from the owner's extra-patrimonial personality rights.

The US approach embraces a post mortem right, which reflects the predominant classification of publicity as a property right.[47] Westfall and Landau argue that the initial classification of publicity as a property right resulted in syllogistic reasoning, which drove the subsequent recognition of post mortem protection for publicity.[48] This was despite considerable arguments against post mortem protection, including the difficulties of 'durational line-drawing' after death, and the increasing conflict between private rights and free speech the longer the right lasts.[49] The best policy argument in favour of a post mortem duration is, they conclude, the risk that the right could be suddenly cut off at any time as a result of the death of the individual, harming the economic interests of the individual and licensees.[50] Landes and Posner also advance an economic justification in favour of a post mortem right. Although the heir to an individual is unlikely to need post mortem protection to recoup the initial investment in that individual's persona, the heir could 'argue that, unless there is a property right in the public figure's name and likeness, there may be congestion, resulting in a loss of value'.[51]

Despite, or because of, the over-reliance on the property syllogism, post mortem rights are now firmly established in the United States. Of those states

---

[41] Beverley-Smith et al (2005) 126–27.
[42] ibid 128.
[43] Neethling, 'Personality Rights' (2005) 243.
[44] ibid 243.
[45] ibid 240.
[46] ibid 240.
[47] See chapter two, section II. and the US state legislation referred to therein.
[48] D Westfall and D Landau, 'Publicity Rights as Property Rights' (2005–2006) 23 *Cardozo Arts and Ent LJ* 71 83 *et seq.*
[49] ibid 86.
[50] ibid 87–88.
[51] WM Landes and R Posner, 'An Economic Analysis of Copyright Law' (1989) 18 *J Legal Stud* 325, 362–63.

that have judicially considered the matter, most 'have recognised that the right is descendible and has a limited post mortem duration of between 10 and 100 years'.[52] Statutory provision also allows a post mortem duration. In Florida, for example, the right expires 40 years after the death of the individual,[53] while Kentucky favours 50 years[54] and Indiana extends protection for 100 years post mortem.[55] Washington takes a slightly different approach, and offers post mortem protection for 10 or, in the case of a 'personality',[56] 75 years post mortem.[57]

Nonetheless, allowing the right of publicity to continue post mortem adversely impacts upon the use of persona by the public in general, conflicting with the principles of freedom of expression and cultural communication, identified in chapter seven. To prevent persona from falling into the public domain on death is a considerable extension of any publicity right. This is particularly the case since publicity rights are predicated in part on the personal nature of persona yet, after the death of the individual, persona can only ever be of interest to other parties, whether heirs or other users.

Although the publicity value does not necessarily cease on death, the personal interest in protecting it does. There is therefore a strong case for terminating a right of publicity on the death of the individual, not least because the subject of the right is so closely tied to the existence of the individual in question. This also has the practical advantage of ensuring the date of expiry of the right can be determined with clarity.

One further option is to find a 'middle way' for post mortem protection. In Nevada, for example, the commercial use of a deceased person's name, voice, signature, photograph or likeness does not require consent where the publicity right has not been conveyed by the person in life to another party and where that person has no surviving successor.[58] Thus, if there is no one with a direct interest, derived from the deceased, to enforce the publicity right, it will lapse on the death of the individual. Further, even where there is a surviving successor, the publicity right can only be asserted where the successor's claim has first been registered with the Office of the Secretary of State, on payment of a filing fee.[59] This mechanism ensures that the publicity right does not endure post mortem when

---

[52] Beverley-Smith, *The Commercial Appropriation of Personality* (2002) 184. See also Westfall and Landau (2005–2006) 83.

[53] The Florida Regulation of Trade, Commerce, Investments and Solicitations, ch 540 s 08 (5).

[54] Kentucky Acts 1984, 391.170(2).

[55] Indiana's Publicity law IC 32–36–1-8.

[56] Defined as an individual whose name and likeness has a *commercial* value.

[57] Chapter 63.60 RCW Personality Rights, s 040(1) and (2).

[58] The Nevada Right of Publicity, NRS 597.800(2).

[59] ibid NRS 597.800(3) and (4). The filing fee is $25: the relevant form is available at http://nvsos. gov/index.aspx?page=57.

there is no one with any interest or title to enforce it. Similar provisions have been adopted, minus the requirement to register, in Illinois,[60] Indiana,[61] and Oklahoma.[62]

A compromise would, therefore, be to allow a post mortem duration for the right where the individual has specifically sought such protection, for example, by specifically including it in a testamentary disposition. However, it is suggested that a more restrictive approach, providing greater certainty, would be to grant a post mortem right only on registration of the persona by the individual prior to death. Whereas registration was deemed to be undesirable for the exercise of the right during life, given the dual considerations of universal application and accessibility, these issues do not apply to a right which is to operate after the death of the individual. Individuals who have a track record of exploiting their persona or who desire to protect it post mortem would be able to ensure its limited continuity by registering indicative elements of their persona (for example, by specifying their name, any pseudonyms, and evidence of their image and indicia). One considerable advantage that registration would bring would be the increased ease with which it would allow tracing of rights-holders.[63] Further, the imposition of a registration fee, which would seem inappropriate for a right which in part protects dignitarian interests, is far less objectionable when the registered publicity right would be used primarily for commercial gain by the surviving relatives or beneficiaries.

The need for registration prior to death raises the question of what happens if the individual dies, perhaps unexpectedly, without registering but surviving relatives nevertheless wish to exercise the right post mortem.[64] Should a period of grace be recognised in which to allow for post mortem registration?[65] Although surviving relatives may understandably desire such a period, it is not clear that there is a pressing need for it. Those whose persona is likely to have an ongoing significance post mortem are likely to be well advised by their lawyers or brand managers (wide-ranging celebrity trade mark registrations provides evidence of this), and thus in a position to register for a post mortem right as soon as they feel the need for it. Where the individual has not seen fit to register his or her persona, thereby allowing it to lapse into the public domain on death, it is not clear why relatives should be able to override this position. Further, providing

---

[60]   The Illinois Right of Publicity Act (765 ILCS 1075) s 25.

[61]   Indiana's Publicity law IC 32–36–1-19.

[62]   Oklahoma Stat tit 12 para 1448E.

[63]   As noted above, although tracing costs are minimised during life, since the right-holder is the individual, this is not the case post mortem: requiring registration makes it considerably easier to trace the holder of the right post mortem.

[64]   This consideration also applies to individuals who die before any statutory right is introduced. For example, would the surviving relatives of Stephen Gately, of Boyzone, be entitled to register his name and image?

[65]   Similar to the period of grace in US patent law (but not in Europe), allowing inventions to be patented within a limited period of the invention being disclosed publicly. See Cornish and Llewelyn (n 4) para 5.10 *et seq.*

that only the individual is entitled to register his or her persona ensures that the individual can make the necessary testamentary provision for it, consequently avoiding the practical difficulties of determining which surviving relative is entitled to register and thereafter exercise the right post mortem.[66]

The only remaining question is how long this registered right should last. This is ultimately a question of policy,[67] but there seems no need for the lengthy protection offered in some US states. Given the greater emphasis on commercial interests following the death of the individual, it is not inappropriate to compare the duration post mortem with the industrial intellectual property rights: trade marks and patents. This would suggest a post mortem duration of between 10 and 20 years, with the option, if there is evidence of a need, for an extension of term through re-registration in the manner of trade marks, rather than through the initial grant of a right. Thus, if the right is exploited and enforced post mortem, it would be open for the beneficiaries to re-register the right: in the absence of this, the persona would lapse into the public domain. A shorter post mortem right based on these economic considerations also reflects the dignitarian approach reflected in the post mortem treatment of personality rights in Civilian systems.

IV. Transmission and Transferability

The review thus far has recognised that the publicity right is inherently connected to the individual, with the consequence that it should be exercised by the individual and last for his or her lifetime and potentially, subject to registration, for a fixed period thereafter. Two subsequent questions derive from this conclusion: can the right be transferred during life and can the right be transmitted after death?[68]

---

[66] Entitlement of surviving relatives to register persona is likely to be a particularly thorny problem post mortem.

[67] Davies refers to Macaulay's comment in the House of Commons in 1841, regarding the post mortem duration of copyright, and his observation applies equally here: 'this is a point which the legislature is free to determine in the way which may appear to be most conducive to the public good'. G Davies, *Copyright and the Public Interest*, 2nd edn (London, Sweet & Maxwell, 2002) para 10–006, citing Macaulay in Hansard HC vol 56 col 365 (5 February 1841).

[68] This section is concerned with the transmission of publicity as a right in its own right: for a detailed analysis of the transmissibility of secondary rights in personality, see N Whitty, 'Overview of Rights of Personality in Scots Law' in N Whitty and R Zimmermann (eds), *Rights of Personality in Scots Law, a Comparative Perspective* (Dundee, Dundee University Press, 2009) section 3.6.

A. Transfer of the Right in Life: Assignation and Licensing

Regardless of the post mortem extent of a publicity right, the individual will be faced with more immediate concerns regarding the transfer of the right during his or her lifetime. As MacQueen notes in relation to intellectual property:

> Although each of the rights confers on the owner an ability to stop activity using the property in question, *in most cases the owner will prefer that such activity take place.* A major purpose of the laws of intellectual property is to provide a legal framework under which the inventive, creative and entrepreneurial will be remunerated for their work.[69]

This juxtaposition of the right to prevent with the need to enable third party activity arises in the context of publicity rights, reflecting the positive and negative uses identified in chapter three. Individuals will be best able to exploit the value in their persona if they are able to share that with other parties, and control this external use of it. However, as per chapter eight, publicity is inalienable in life because it is inherently connected to the individual. The practical reality of commercial exploitation comes up against the theoretical analysis which confines publicity to the individual.

This is most evident in the Civilian tradition: '[n]one of the civil law systems seek to abandon the traditional doctrine of the inalienability of personality rights'.[70] Yet, the tension between theory and practice is well illustrated by Beverley-Smith et al's review of French and German law, where strong statements of principle are later modified by an awareness of the practice. Thus the statement that '[i]t is traditionally asserted in France that personality rights are inalienable, that is can neither be waived nor assigned'[71] is followed six pages later with the recognition that, in France, agreements are made 'daily' for the 'commercial exploitation of personal attributes'.[72] Although it is not clear whether consent to use of personality rights in France 'operates merely as an enforceable promise not to sue or as the transfer of a right, in the nature of a property right… enabling the licensee to sue third parties',[73] such commercial agreements are nonetheless concluded. Similarly, for German law, the authors discuss four different methods for allowing third party use of an allegedly inalienable right,[74] concluding that the 'attempt to reconcile the inalienability of personality rights with the demands of the advertising and merchandising business is hard to sustain doctrinally'.[75]

---

[69]   H MacQueen, 'Property', in *Stair Memorial Encyclopaedia* Vol 18, Pt II (1993) para 802, emphasis added.

[70]   Waelde and Whitty, 'A Rights of Personality Database' (2009) para 11.4.3(d).

[71]   Beverley-Smith et al (n 39) 191.

[72]   ibid 197.

[73]   Waelde and Whitty (n 38) para 11.4.3(d).

[74]   These are waiver, medical law consent, irrevocable consent and licensing: see Beverley-Smith et al (n 39) 130–37.

[75]   ibid 132.

This problem is not so evident in the United States, where publicity is treated as a property right, with all the consequences that entails. The pragmatism of the American 'publicity as property' approach is evident in the words of Judge Frank: 'Whether it be labelled a "property" right is immaterial; for here, as often elsewhere, the tag "property" simply symbolizes the fact that courts enforce a claim which has a pecuniary worth.'[76]

As Madow observes, it 'seemed natural and obvious to the court that celebrity personas should be treated as garden variety commodities, to be bought and sold in the market like any other... The court was simply giving legal form (and protection) to preexisting commercial practice.'[77]

Yet this approach, which reflects the commercial reality of transfer and exploitation of publicity rights, is not without its problems either. Whether or not one classes persona as property does not alter the fact that it is not separable from the individual in the sense that one's house, shares and patents are separable and capable of being permanently alienated.

Therefore, there is a risk that courts and academics become entrenched on one side or other of the debate, determined either to reflect the reality of exploitation by allowing transfer or to uphold the sanctity of legal taxonomy by refusing to countenance the transfer of a right so inherently bound to the individual.

However, a transfer of rights does not have to be outright, but could be constituted by the grant of a temporary right to use the persona by way of a licence. Whereas sale or, in intellectual property, assignation transfers full owner-ship, a licence ensures that control remains with the owner, subject to the terms of the licence. While an inalienable aspect of an individual, such as persona, could not be assigned, there is no reason why its use could not be licensed for a particular purpose.

Licensing offers a very flexible solution, where matters such as the duration, the territory, and the purposes for use can all be specified, subject to any necessary provisions for termination or revocation if required by the licensor.[78] In the words of Beverley-Smith et al, regarding German law,

> the personality right is regarded as one single right, which protects both economic and non-economic interests. A licence transfers one piece of this cake to the licensee. However, since the licence can be revoked under exceptional circumstances and since the licence usually expires after a certain time, the 'daughter right' granted to the licensee is not entirely separated from the 'mother right'.[79]

This split between 'mother' and 'daughter' rights is arguably what all licences seek to achieve, and conveys the duality of a grant of a right together with the retention of control by the licensor.

---

[76] *Haelan Laboratories v Topps Chewing Gum* 202 F.2d 866, 868 (Frank J).
[77] Madow (n 2) 174, but note he should not be taken to endorse this view.
[78] See, for example, Cornish and Llewelyn (n 4) para 7–25 regarding patents, but applicable to all licences.
[79] Beverley-Smith et al (n 39) 133. See also Waelde and Whitty (n 38) para 11.4.3(d).

The study of authorised exploitation in chapter three demonstrated that most contracts in Scotland and England for authorised exploitation of publicity are constituted by licence, rather than an attempt to assign the rights. Some of these licences, such as the *pro forma* licence between the sportsman and the Club or the agreement between Irvine and Ferrari, are drawn in such broad terms as to be close to a full assignation, but stop short of a full transfer. Indeed, a licence can be drafted in such a way that the *practical* outcome for the licensee is almost the same as if the licensee had taken a full assignation, but the distinction remains, since 'an assignment is in essence a transfer of ownership (however partial), while a licence is in essence permission to do what otherwise would be infringement'.[80]

Classification of publicity as a statutory monopoly right is capable of enabling some degree of transfer, which stops short of full assignation. The conclusion that can be drawn is that the monopoly right of publicity should be capable of being licensed but not assigned.

B.   Transmission of the Right Post Mortem

Whether or not the right can be transmitted to heirs, or transferred on thereafter, has largely been answered by the foregoing analysis. Where the persona has been registered, successors in title to the individual should benefit from a publicity right and, since the right is no longer tied to the individual upon whose persona it depends, there is no theoretical obstacle to recognising the right as fully transferable. This alters the attributes of the right in two ways.

In the first place, as was discussed above, it diminishes the justifications for the right, so that the right should continue in existence only if specific steps have been taken to that end, namely registering the persona. Further, the duration of the right becomes tied to the statutory period. The second consequence, however, is that the right can be transmitted on death in accordance with the individual's testamentary wishes, and thereafter becomes freely transferable, by assignation as well as licensing, for the duration of the right post mortem.

Thus, on death, the right of publicity becomes a more explicitly economic right, and falls to be treated with other economic monopoly rights, such as trade marks. Only by registering the mark in life can a post mortem right be created, to take effect on death, for the benefit of the beneficiaries according to the deceased's will.

---

[80]   Cornish and Llewelyn (n 4) para 13–11.

10

The Permitted Uses of Persona

I. Introduction

S INCE PUBLICITY IS not an absolute right, it is necessary to consider those uses of persona which will not infringe the individual's publicity right: in the words of copyright legislation, for example, these are the permitted uses. These would be relevant where the other elements of publicity right infringement can be proved, that is to say, where there has been unauthorised use of persona for the media information, promotion or merchandising purposes (all as defined in chapter three).

II. Private Use

A straightforward example of a permitted use is one which is entirely private. As discussed in chapter three, the focus of publicity rights is the public use of persona, and the definition of media information, promotion and merchandising uses reflects this element. Any use which involves making persona available to the public or any section of the public will constitute public use. Where the use made of persona is private, however, then there should be no breach of the individual's publicity right—although there may be other legal grounds upon which to challenge the use.[1]

III. Freedom of Expression

Where use is made of persona to receive and impart information and ideas, then it is prima facie protected under article 10 of the European Convention on

---

[1] Such as breach of the individual's article 8 right to private life, albeit not by dissemination. See the discussion on this point in chapter four.

Human Rights (ECHR). However, this right is not absolute either and must be balanced against the rights of others—specifically in this context the 'protection of the reputation or the rights of others, [or] for preventing the disclosure of information received in confidence'.[2] Subject to the need to achieve this balance, it would be open to a defender in a publicity action to claim that his use of persona was protected under his right to freedom of expression.

The scope of article 10 and its interaction with other rights was examined in chapter seven, and need not be reiterated here. It is sufficient to note that one of the most important limits on a right of publicity is likely to come from article 10—and indeed, that right to freedom of expression can be seen to underlie many of the other permitted uses considered in the rest of this chapter.

IV. Public Policy

Public policy can operate to deny legal protection to a claimed private right, thus ensuring that there can be no infringement of the so-called right. In the field of copyright, for example, public policy considerations may arise where it is determined that certain types of work 'are undeserving of the protection of copyright'.[3] Since no protection is granted to them, there can be no infringement by unauthorised use.[4] However, this exception to the grant of copyright depends on the nature or content[5] of the work in each case, whereas a publicity right protects only one type of 'work' —the persona. It is therefore difficult to see how public policy could apply to deny protection of persona in some circumstances but not in others. There is nothing inherent in any individual persona (that is name, image and reputation) which could in some cases give rise to a public policy objection over the grant of the right in the first place. There may, however, be good reason why unauthorised use of a persona should be permitted, but it is submitted that the right of publicity should always be recognised in that persona, even if it is subsequently curtailed on one of the grounds considered below.

---

² Article 10(2) of the ECHR.
³ H MacQueen et al, *Contemporary Intellectual Property* (Oxford, Oxford University Press, 2007) para 5.47. The authors give the examples of pornography and material published in breach of an obligation of secrecy. See also A Sims, 'The Denial of Copyright Protection on Public Policy Grounds' [2008] *EIPR* 189.
⁴ This is emphasised by Sims, where she also brings out the difference between public policy and public interest in copyright: Sims, 'The Denial of Copyright Protection' (2008) 190.
⁵ W Cornish and D Llewelyn, *Intellectual Property: Patents, Copyright, Trade Marks and Allied Rights*, 5th edn (London, Sweet & Maxwell, 2003) para 12–57.

V. Public Interest

The notion of the public interest often provides a catch-all defence, by permitting the infringement of a private right where this would benefit or advance the 'public interest'. In the case of publicity, it is suggested that unauthorised use of persona should be permitted where it is in the public interest.

Although there is no single definition of the public interest, it operates in a number of spheres: in privacy actions, by informing the article 10 right to freedom of expression;[6] in cases concerning confidential information, by operating to justify the breach of confidence,[7] with specific provision in cases of breach of confidence in medical circumstances[8] and employment relationships;[9] and in copyright where it exists in its own right and arguably underlies the permitted uses of copyright.[10] The public interest therefore plays a broad and vital role in allowing exceptions to the grant or enforcement of certain private rights—albeit these public interests must be balanced against counter-interests which the public have in securing an efficient market and upholding private rights.

While what qualifies as a matter in the public interest 'must be capable of being tested by objectively recognised criteria',[11] the precise nature of those criteria remains uncertain.[12] Crime and wrongdoing appear to be two fairly straightforward grounds on which to engage the public interest,[13] while morality is often cited, although more controversial since there is no single standard of morality in the twenty-first century. One case which neatly illustrates several categories of public interest, including morality, is *Mosley v News Group Newspapers Ltd*.[14] Eady J refers to a number of elements in *Mosley* which may have justified (but on the facts did not) the publication of Mosley's sexual activities by the *News of the World*. These included the allegedly criminal nature of the activity,[15] the alleged Nazi theme,[16] and the depravity of Mosley's actions and adultery.[17] In relation to this last category, Eady J stated:

> it is not for the state or for the media to expose sexual conduct which does not involve any significant breach of the criminal law. That is so whether the motive for such intrusion is merely prurience or a moral crusade. It is not for journalists to undermine

---

[6] See chapter four.
[7] See for example Cornish and Llewelyn, *Intellectual Property* (2003) paras 8–15 *et seq*; MacQueen et al, *Contemporary Intellectual Property* (2007) paras 18.58–18.61.
[8] See, for example, J Chalmers, *Legal Responses to HIV and AIDS* (Oxford, Hart, 2008) 64–65.
[9] The Public Interest Disclosure Act 1998 allows 'whistleblowing' if this is in the public interest.
[10] See G Davies, *Copyright and the Public Interest*, 2nd edn (London, Sweet & Maxwell, 2002).
[11] *Mosley v News Group Newspapers Ltd* [2008] EWHC 1777 [138].
[12] See for example, in copyright, MacQueen et al (n 3) para 5.47.
[13] *Mosley v News Group Newspapers Ltd* [2008] EWHC 1777 (QB) [234].
[14] *Mosley v News Group Newspapers Ltd* [2008] EWHC 1777 (QB).
[15] ibid [110]–[121].
[16] ibid [122]–[123].
[17] ibid [124]–[134].

human rights, or for judges to refuse to enforce them, merely on grounds of taste or moral disapproval. *Everyone is naturally entitled to espouse moral or religious beliefs to the effect that certain types of sexual behaviour are wrong or demeaning to those participating. That does not mean that they are entitled to hound those who practise them or to detract from their right to live life as they choose.* It is important, in this new rights-based jurisprudence, to ensure that where breaches occur remedies are not refused because an individual journalist or judge finds the conduct distasteful or contrary to moral or religious teaching. Where the law is not breached, as I said earlier, the private conduct of adults is essentially no-one else's business. The fact that a particular relationship happens to be adulterous, or that someone's tastes are unconventional or 'perverted', does not give the media *carte blanche.*[18]

Morally blameworthy conduct can be difficult to assess in a pluralist society, absent any criminal conduct, or a need to set the record straight.[19] In any event, while there may be a public interest in disclosing morally questionable conduct, this is of much greater relevance for an article 8 privacy action or for breach of confidence: it is less likely to have a role to play where the activity in question is the public use of persona.

Criminal activity is also a ground for employee disclosure in the public interest under the Public Interest Disclosure Act 1998, along with considerations such as whether a miscarriage of justice has occurred, whether the health or safety of any individual is endangered, whether the environment is being damaged, or indeed whether any of these events are likely to occur.[20] Similar considerations relating to the health and safety of individuals apply to the disclosure of patient details by the medical profession.[21]

In copyright cases, the public interest defence has arisen in respect of copyright-protected works.[22] Section 171(3) of the Copyright, Designs and Patents Act (CDPA) 1988 states that nothing in the Act regarding copyright 'affects any rule of law preventing or restricting the enforcement of copyright, on grounds of public interest or otherwise'. With reference to *Hyde Park Residence v Yelland*, Davies suggests that this affords the court's discretion to refuse to uphold an action for copyright infringement, 'but such jurisdiction is limited to cases

---

[18]   ibid [127]–[128], emphasis added. This is reminiscent of Lord Hope's comments on the idea that a shared notion of 'common sense' can resolve (the admittedly very different) issue of causation: 'As I survey my fellow passengers on my twice weekly journeys to and from Heathrow Airport on the Piccadilly Line – such a variety in age, race, nationality and languages – I find it increasingly hard to persuade myself that any one view on anything other than the most basic issues can be said to be typical of all of them.' *Chester v Afshar* [2004] UKHL 41 [83].

[19]   For the latter, see section VIII below.

[20]   The Employment Rights Act 1996 s 43B, as inserted by the Public Interest Disclosure Act 1998.

[21]   Chalmers, *Legal Responses to HIV and AIDS* (2008) para 61–68.

[22]   The public interest defence in copyright cases is complicated by the existence of specific statutory defences. For an analysis of the interaction between these and the public interest, see Davies, *Copyright and the Public Interest* (2002) paras 4–033–4–035.

where enforcement of the copyright would offend against the policy of the law. Public interest does not extend beyond misdeeds of a serious nature and importance to the country.'[23]

The Press Complaints Commission's Code of Practice provides a definition of the public interest as regards media publication, setting out when publication of otherwise unpublishable material will be justified:

1. The public interest includes, but is not confined to:
   — detecting or exposing crime or serious impropriety;
   — protecting public health and safety;
   — preventing the public from being misled by an action or statement of an individual or organisation.[24]

While such interests are unquestionably worthy of recognition, the courts have made clear in questions of media publication that catering to the public curiosity for gossip is not on a par with the above interests: 'what interests the public is not necessarily in the public interest'.[25]

The Press Complaints Commission's guidance is particularly helpful since the role of the media in publishing matters in furtherance of 'the public interest' is perhaps one of the most controversial elements of this defence. In *W v Edgell*, the public interest was found to justify the disclosure by the doctor in question of a psychiatric report to the medical officer at the plaintiff's secure hospital, but the judge suggested that disclosure to the press, especially for a price, would have breached the doctor's duty of confidence to his patient, the plaintiff.[26] Similarly, in the employment context, it has been observed of the Public Interest Disclosure Act 1998 that 'the stringency of these requirements [regarding disclosure to the media] is a clear signal that reporting to the media is intended to be a last resort'.[27] This suggests that even where *disclosure* can be justified in the public interest, publication in the media may be unjustified, if the public interest can be served by disclosing to the appropriate authority, such as the police, rather than to the world at large.[28] In some cases, however, where there are large numbers of

---

[23] ibid para 4–034, citing *Hyde Park Residence v Yelland* [2001] Ch 143. See also Cornish and Llewelyn (n 5) para 12–58; C Angelopoulos, 'Freedom of Expression and Copyright: the Double Balancing Act' [2008] *IPQ* 328, 335–336.

[24] Available at www.pcc.org.uk/cop/practice.html. The Code also notes that the interests of children under 16 are 'paramount' and that there must be an 'exceptional public interest' to override their private interests.

[25] *McKennitt v Ash* [2008] QB 73 [66]. See also *Mosley v News Group Newspapers Ltd* [2008] EWHC 1777 [114]; *Douglas v Hello!* [2006] QB 125 [254], where the public interest is contrasted with 'public curiosity'.

[26] *W v Edgell* [1990] Ch 359, as discussed by J Chalmers (n 8) 65.

[27] E Callahan, T Dworkin and D Lewis, 'Whistleblowing: Australian, UK and US Approaches to Disclosure in the Public Interest' (2003–2004) 44 *Va J Int'l Law* 879, 894.

[28] Although note Ouseley J's comment in *Theakston v MGN Ltd* [2002] EWHC 137 (QB) ([69]) that the 'free press is not confined to the role of a confidential police force; it is entitled to communicate directly with the public for the public to reach its own conclusion'.

entitled recipients, disclosure in the press may be appropriate in order to communicate that information to them.[29]

This distinction draws out one of the potential difficulties inherent in applying the public interest defence in publicity situations. Since many of these cases focus on preventing criminal or wrongful conduct, it is difficult to see the precise role to be played by the public interest in publicity cases where, as chapter three sought to show, most publicity use is intended to promote goods or services or enable media publication of aspects of celebrities' lives. A further distinction between the public interest situations discussed above and the right of publicity is that many of the above public interest disclosures were made in breach of a duty of confidence—yet not all (or indeed many) publicity infringements will be made in breach of such a duty.

The question for consideration here is whether there is any role for the public interest defence in a publicity right action, that is to say, separate from these existing grounds of action. It is certainly true, as Beverley-Smith et al observe, that '[u]sing the portrait of a celebrity in advertising, however, usually only serves the advertiser's interest'.[30] Where the use of persona is intended to benefit the interests of the party using it, rather than a wider public interest, then the defence should not be available.

However, it is submitted that there *is* a specific ground of public interest which should be recognised in the context of publicity rights: the cultural communication interest. Where use of persona is necessary to communicate cultural meaning, as advanced by Madow, Coombe, Carty and de Grandpre, amongst others,[31] then it should be permitted, on the basis of the public interest in allowing such use. Whereas the public interest is typically cited in the context of criminal behaviour or iniquity or public protection, this alternative ground would see it employed in a more creative and positive context. It is reliant on a broader concept of the 'public interest', but it is one which is very relevant to the publicity debate, as Coombe and others demonstrate.

Coombe gives an absorbing example of the extent of cultural communication through imagery—not all of it reliant on persona—in her depiction of a typical walk to work through downtown Toronto.[32] Where individuals make use of persona to communicate a cultural or sub-cultural meaning, such as the use of Nancy Sinatra's name by a lesbian band in Coombe's example, this use should be permitted—subject to other existing (non-publicity) rights, such as defamation or privacy. Thus, where the use of an individual's persona would not breach existing legal protection and where it contributes to cultural (and typically

---

[29] See *Lord Browne of Madingley v Associated Newspapers Ltd* [2008] 1 QB 103 [55].

[30] H Beverley-Smith et al, *Privacy, Property and Personality* (Cambridge, Cambridge University Press, 2005 107, in the context of German law.

[31] See chapter seven.

[32] R Coombe, *The Cultural Life of Intellectual Properties: Authorship Appropriation, and the Law* (Durham and London, Duke University Press, 1998) 1–6.

non-commercial) communication of ideas or criticisms, it should not constitute an infringement of the individual's publicity right, by virtue of being in the public interest. This would cover, for example, Lord Rodger's reference to Kylie Minogue in one of his judgments, to illustrate a social and cultural point.[33]

As with all public interest defences, the extent to which the use in question amounts to a genuine cultural communication will depend on the facts of each individual case, and it is, unfortunately, difficult to generalise. Overtly commercial use, such as advertising, may be less likely to constitute cultural communication—there is nothing apparently social or political in Talksport's use of Irvine to attract business. It is also likely that there will be an overlap between genuine cultural communication and the permitted uses of fair dealing and parody. Nonetheless, it is submitted that a genuine cultural communicative use of persona is in the public interest and should be recognised as a permitted use in its own right.

VI. Fair Dealing

The CDPA 1988[34] provides for certain permitted uses to be made of copyright work where such uses constitute 'fair dealing'.[35] Sections 29 and 30 of the CDPA 1988 allow fair dealing for the purposes of research and private study, criticism, review and news reporting, provided that the use is 'accompanied by a sufficient acknowledgement and provided that the work has been made available to the public'.[36] Where a use falls within one of these categories, has been acknowledged and is also 'fair',[37] it will be an excepted use, and will not constitute copyright infringement. There is a great deal of merit in ensuring that similar permitted uses are available in cases of publicity rights.

Section 31 of the CDPA 1988 also provides an exception for 'incidental inclusion' of the copyright work in an artistic work, sound recording, film or broadcast. As the authors of *Copinger and Skone James on Copyright* note, the provisions on incidental inclusion 'have a great deal of importance for photographers, advertisers, film makers and broadcasters'[38] since they allow, for example, a report to be filmed in front of a work of art, play, or even a building, all of which

---

[33] *HJ (Iran) v Secretary of State for the Home Department* [2010] UKSC 31 [78].

[34] As amended by the Copyright and Related Rights Regulations 2003 SI 2003/2498.

[35] A detailed analysis of the 'fair dealing' exceptions in copyright is beyond the scope of this work. See further MacQueen et al (n 3) paras 5.19–5.36; Cornish and Llewelyn (n 5) paras 12–36–12–55; K Garnett, G Davies and G Harbottle, *Copinger and Skone James on Copyright*, 15th edn (London, Sweet & Maxwell, 2005) paras 9–19–9–63; C Angelopoulos, 'Freedom of Expression and Copyright: the Double Balancing Act' [2008] IPQ 328, 336–41.

[36] CDPA 1988 s 30(1).

[37] For details of the sort of considerations that are relevant to determining fairness, see Garnett et al, *Copinger and Skone James on Copyright* (2005) para 9–55.

[38] ibid para 9–56.

would otherwise benefit from copyright protection as regards the film or broadcast. Where a camera crew captures celebrities spectating at a sporting or charity event as part of a wider report on the event, for example, the dissemination of those images should be permitted as constituting incidental inclusion.[39]

These grounds would also allow more generally for the use of persona which constitutes 'incidental inclusion' or in social commentary.[40] Unlike copyright, there is also no need for 'sufficient acknowledgement', since there is no creative content to be acknowledged, only persona. Where a newspaper runs a commentary piece (not simply a news report) on the morality of leading sportsmen and illustrates it with a photograph of a golfer, for example, who has been found to have had numerous extra-marital affairs, this (truthful) critical use should be permitted—as indeed should factual news reporting.[41] However, a manufacturer of herbal Viagra, for example, could have no 'fair dealing' grounds for promoting its goods by using the name or image of that individual, since there is no (genuine) element of criticism or review involved.

Reference to individuals, their image and reputation for the purposes of private study or non-commercial research should similarly be permitted, unless there is a breach of their article 8 right to privacy. Finally, individuals should accept that there is a legitimate need for criticism or review of their persona, whether that is academic, artistic or political. Where the criticism or review is untrue, existing doctrines such as defamation are capable of supplying a remedy.

Fair dealing as delineated in the CDPA 1988 therefore provides a carefully drawn set of exceptions to copyright, which could usefully be replicated to act as defences to a claim for infringement of publicity rights. As with fair dealing in copyright, the court should be able to consider the motives of the alleged infringer: 'was the use merely dressed up in the guise of criticism or review?'[42] Where there is genuine fair dealing use of persona, that should be accepted as a necessary exception to the publicity right.

VII. Parody

A further possible acceptable use of persona is provided by parody. Although there is no fixed definition of parody, a comprehensive overview is provided by Maniatis and Gredley. For them, parody can be defined as follows:

---

[39] A similar exemption exists in German law regarding privacy to allow photographs of assemblies and crowd scenes to be publicly exhibited: A Vahrenwald, 'Photographs and Privacy in Germany' [1994] *Ent LR* 205, 215.

[40] A use which is supported by Frazer, 'Appropriation of Personality – a New Tort?' (1983) 99 *LQR* 281, 313.

[41] ibid 312. While this would appear to allow publication of the Douglases's wedding picture, since it constituted factual news reporting, Hello! would still have had to overcome other existing legal rights, including confidence and privacy (since the pictures were taken in a private setting).

[42] Garnett et al (n 35) para 9–55.

Unlike other forms such as satire, parody uses the preformed material of its source 'as a constituent part of its own structure'. It involves at first an imitation and then a change of the style, subject-matter or vocabulary of another work, achieving its effect through comic incongruity between the original and the parody work.[43]

It is this comic incongruity which is at the heart of parody: 'the parodist relies on the audience's awareness of the target work or genre; in turn, the complicity of the audience is the *sine qua non* of its enjoyment'.[44] Critically, if 'parody does not prickle it does not work'[45] but, when it does work, it is 'for the most part a form of healthy social and artistic criticism'.[46]

The importance of parody is well recognised[47] as it potentially impacts upon a range of intellectual property rights, including copyright, moral rights, passing off and trade marks. Opinion is divided, however, as to whether it ought to be afforded special treatment as a distinct genre or defence.[48] This wider question can however be left aside in the present discussion, to focus instead on the role that could be played by parody as a defence to publicity rights infringement.

Perhaps the leading judgment on parody in any jurisdiction is that of Sachs J in the Constitutional Court of South Africa, in the trade mark infringement case of *Laugh it Off Promotions CC v South African Breweries International (Finance) BV*[49] when the appellant company printed t-shirts featuring parodies of well known trade marks. In a comprehensive legal, social and political review of trade mark law and social commentary, Sachs J reflected on the vital role that parody can play in society. Specifically, branding can operate to level the playing field between the corporations on the one hand and the cultural communicators on the other:

[i]n our consumerist society where branding occupies a prominent space in public culture, one does not have to be a 'cultural jammer' to recognise that there is a legitimate place for criticism of a particular trademark, or of the influence of branding in general or of the overzealous use of trademark law to stifle public debate.[50]

---

[43] S Maniatis and E Gredley, 'Parody: A Fatal Attraction? Part 1: The Nature of Parody and its Treatment in Copyright' [1997] *EIPR* 339, 339, fn omitted.

[44] ibid 340.

[45] *Laugh it Off v SAB* 2006 (1) SA 144 [75].

[46] C Rutz, 'Parody: a Missed Opportunity?' [2004] *IPQ* 284, 314, fn omitted.

[47] Recent articles include: ibid; M Spence, 'Intellectual Property and the Problem of Parody' (1998) 114 *LQR* 594; and Maniatis and Gredley, 'Parody: A Fatal Attraction? Part 1 (1997) and 'Parody: A Fatal Attraction? Part 2: Trade Mark Parodies' [1997] *EIPR* 412; C Angelopoulos, 'Freedom of Expression and Copyright: the Double Balancing Act' [2008] *IPQ* 328. In particular, the distinction between weapon parody (where the original work is parodied to comment on other aspects of culture) and target parody (where the parody comments upon the original work), which is drawn in several of these commentaries, is not made here in relation to publicity, since both may be equally valid in a publicity context, especially in light of the 'cultural communication' use of persona.

[48] Contrast Spence, 'Intellectual Property and the Problem of Parody' (1998) 601 and 615–617, who does not think so, with Maniatis and Gredley (n 43) 344, who do.

[49] *Laugh it Off Promotions CC v South African Breweries International (Finance) BV* 2006 (1) SA 144.

[50] *Laugh it Off v SAB* 2006 (1) SA 144 [86].

This comment applies equally to publicity, whereby overzealous use of publicity rights could stifle public debate and criticism, in the way Madow feared. Where the genuinely parodic use of a trade mark was prevented by the trade mark owner's intellectual property rights, then the 'result was inappropriately to allow what were tenuous property interests to outweigh substantial expression rights'.[51] It is critical that the same cannot be said of publicity rights.[52]

However, the existing 'publicity cases' do not provide much evidence of parodic use to date: neither Hello! or Talksport could have claimed that their use of the persona of the Douglases or Irvine respectively had any element of parody. Although the majority of instances of publicity use may involve the straightforward use of persona, it is important that the possibility of parody is not excluded or restricted by granting a publicity right.

Parody is necessary to provide a vent for society and a method of enabling discussion: 'A society that takes itself too seriously risks bottling up its tensions and treating every example of irreverence as a threat to its existence. Humour is one of the great solvents of democracy.'[53]

Where there is genuine parody of an individual's image or identity—'a take-off, not a rip-off'[54]—then the right of the parody artist must outweigh that of the individual. It may be that the individual has a claim under defamation, for example, or through article 8 privacy rights, but these are separate actions and do not affect the conclusion reached here: genuine parody should not be capable of being struck down through a *sui generis* publicity right.

VIII. Other Possible Permitted Uses

To finish this review of permitted uses of persona, it is helpful to touch upon two uses which are, it is submitted, largely protected by the foregoing exceptions to the right.

The first is the need to use persona to 'set the record straight'—a factor which played a key role in MGN's defence in *Campbell v MGN*.[55] Such a claim would allow use of an individual's persona where it was necessary to correct a lie or hypocritical stance adopted by the individual in question. In fact, insofar as such

---

[51] ibid [76].
[52] The brief and largely dismissive treatment of the parody defence by the Ninth Circuit in *White v Samsung Electronic America Inc* 971 F.2d 1395, 1401 suggests that parody is given insufficient consideration in American courts.
[53] *Laugh it Off v SAB* 2006 (1) SA 144 [109].
[54] ibid [102].
[55] *Campbell v MGN* [2004] 2 AC 457. Similar observations have been made about John Terry's adultery, coming shortly after his recognition as a 'Dad of the Year': see Craig Callery, 'John Terry: Reflections on Public Image, Sponsorship, and Employment' [2010] *ISLR* 48, 49; and also about Tiger Woods: Matthew Syed, 'Tiger Woods has Forfeited his Right to Privacy' *The Times* (9 December 2009).

a use is necessary,[56] this is likely to be covered by the general 'public interest' ground, since disclosure of lies and the need to ensure the public knows the truth certainly falls within this category. Further, such use is likely to be protected by the article 10 right to freedom of expression, as indeed was the case in *Campbell v MGN*.

The second possible use which could be permitted is where there is 'fair comment'.[57] This is one of the available defences to an action for defamation, and arises where the allegedly defamatory comment is in fact a statement of opinion. Liability will not attach in defamation where the defender can demonstrate that his opinion was based upon true facts and concerned a matter of public interest, and that there was no intention to harm the pursuer. It is submitted that non-defamatory[58] use of persona to express an opinion is likely to be protected, where necessary, by article 10 and should, to this extent, be permitted.

›

---

[56] And there are those such as Gordley who suggest it is not a beneficial defence, at least in the case of privacy, on the basis that hypocrisy is preferable to the disclosure of vice: J Gordley, *Foundations of Private Law: Property, Tort, Contract, Unjust Enrichment* (Oxford, Oxford University Press, 2006) 236. See also Mosley's comments to the House of Commons Culture, Media and Sport Committee (HC275-ii, 10 March 2009, in answer to Q145).

[57] This is supported, for example, by Frazer, 'Appropriation of Personality – a New Tort?' (1983) 99 *LQR* 281, 313.

[58] If the opinion *was* defamatory, the individual would have a claim under the action of defamation instead of, or as well as, the publicity rights claim.

11

Remedies for Breach of Publicity Rights

I. Introduction

IF AN INDIVIDUAL successfully establishes that his or her persona has been used for the media information, promotion or merchandising use without his or her consent and without the benefit of any of the countervailing rights or limits examined in chapter 10, then he or she will be entitled to a remedy for this infringement. Remedies for unauthorised exploitation fall into two camps, being those directed at preventing the unauthorised use and those intended to provide redress for it. An authorised exploiter, whose rights under an exclusive licence have been jeopardised, may also wish to seek a remedy from the unauthorised exploiter. This chapter considers these issues.

II. Preventing Unauthorised Use

Under the heading of prevention, the two appropriate remedies are interdict/injunction and interim interdict/injunction.

Where the use is to be made by an authorised licensee, in breach of its licence agreement, then the individual should be entitled to seek an interdict or injunction to prevent the anticipated or ongoing breach of contract.[1]

In other cases of unauthorised use, if an individual is able to prove a proposed unauthorised use of his or her persona would breach his or her publicity right and cannot be defended, then he should be entitled to seek an interim or permanent interdict. The test for these remedies in Scotland requires a prima facie case and satisfaction of a test of balance of convenience, in the case of the former, or proof of a continuing or apprehended wrong for the latter. In England, an interim injunction (to preserve matters pending trial) will be granted where the injury is certain

---

[1] Lord Mackay of Clashfern (ed), *Halsbury's Laws of England*, 'Civil Procedure', 5th edn (Lexis-Nexis, 2009) vol 11 para 453.

or imminent and the court is satisfied that there is a serious question to be tried. Moreover, the claimant must also satisfy the balance of convenience test. An interim injunction will be refused if a doubt exists as to the right, especially if the grant would cause great hardship to the defendant.[2] A permanent restrictive injunction will be granted if the injury is continuous or irreparable.

The courts in England have discretion to refuse an interdict if damages would be an appropriate remedy.[3] However, given the nature of unauthorised publicity use—which, by definition, involves use of persona—it is suggested that damages would not be an appropriate remedy where the individual seeks an injunction. The right is based in part on the importance of autonomy and dignity and the individual's right to control use of something so inherently personal to him. Damages cannot compensate for this dignitarian invasion, even if they could adequately reimburse his economic interest. If one asked the Douglases and Eddie Irvine whether they would rather have had the financial awards made (£15,000 and £25,000 respectively) or no publication at all, it seems safe to speculate that they would all have chosen no publication at all. The fact that the Douglases (unsuccessfully) sought an interdict demonstrates that their primary concern was to prevent publication, not to be compensated for it. Similarly, Irvine was concerned at the long-term negative impact on his image and reputation which would arise from Talksport's use.

Balancing the interests between restraining use and permitting it will always be difficult, especially when faced with the option of allowing publication followed by financial compensation. It is true that in some cases (perhaps the majority) the persona sought to be protected may not be particularly private or sensitive, but it is also true that in an equal number of cases the use may not be particularly worthy—especially in cases of commercial (promotion or merchandising) speech, rather than social or political commentary. In cases such as these, the individual's dignitarian interests must be preferred to the third party's commercial interests.

Super-injunctions merit special consideration. A super-injunction[4] is one which prevents the media reporting a particular story and, critically, from even reporting the existence of the proceedings and injunction—the court file is sealed in what is effectively a media blackout.[5] Because they are typically used in controversial circumstances (Trafigura[6] and John Terry[7] being two examples),

---

[2] Although the defendant must undertake to keep an account, pending the outcome of the trial: ibid para 336.

[3] ibid paras 337, 356 and 364 *et seq*. This is a rule of equity and was originally found in Lord Cairns's Act: for the historical background see para 364, fn 3.

[4] 'Super-injunction' is the media term for these orders: officially they are injunctions with an order to seal the file made under Civil Procedure Rule 5.4C, which regulates the supply of documents to non-parties.

[5] And described as 'Kafkaesque' by Lord Neuberger MR, 'Privacy and Freedom of Expression: A Delicate Balance', speech delivered at Eton on 28 April 2010, and available at www.judiciary.gov.uk.

[6] See for example the BBC report on Trafigura's super-injunction: http://news.bbc.co.uk/1/hi/uk_politics/8311885.stm.

[7] *Terry v Persons Unknown* [2010] EWHC 119 (QB).

they are themselves controversial.[8] It is submitted that they can have no role to play in publicity cases. Even where the individual is entitled to an injunction to prevent use of his persona by a third party, there can be no reason to stop the fact of that injunction being reported. If there are also privacy issues or other reasons which would justify it, then the individual would be entitled to seek a super-injunction on that basis: but on 'pure' publicity grounds, there can be no justification for a media gag of this nature.

III. Redressing Unauthorised Use: Damages

A. Introduction

Infringements of private rights are frequently remedied by an award of damages and it is well established that damages are intended to compensate the pursuer for his or her loss, by putting him or her in the position he or she would have been in but for the breach, rather than to punish the defender for her wrongful action or breach.[9]

In addition to this compensatory function, there may be an amount of damages awarded to vindicate the right infringed. This is supported by evidence from a number of English tort law cases, most notably those which also protect human rights under the European Convention on Human Rights (ECHR). Lord Hope of Craighead, for example, explained that the 'function of the law is to enable rights to be vindicated and to provide remedies when duties have been breached. Unless this is done the duty [to warn in medical cases] is a hollow one, stripped of all practical force and devoid of all content.'[10] Eady J has applied this principle in a privacy case, by acknowledging that an award can be necessary 'to

---

[8] See the House of Commons Culture, Media and Sport Committee, Second Report of Session 2009–10, Volume 1, 31. Since then, a committee has been set up by the Master of the Rolls (in April 2010) to examine the use of super-injunctions (Judicial Communications Office news release 15/10 of 6 April 2010), so future changes may be forthcoming.

[9] In the context of remedies for intellectual property rights, see H MacQueen et al, *Contemporary Intellectual Property* (Oxford, Oxford University Press, 2007) para 21.97; W Cornish and D Llewelyn, *Intellectual Property: Patents, Copyright, Trade Marks and Allied Rights*, 5th edn (London, Sweet & Maxwell, 2003) para 2–39. Eady J considered and rejected an award of exemplary (or punitive) damages in *Mosley v News Group Newspapers Ltd* [2008] EWHC 1777 (QB) [172]–[211], for example. For further analysis of the possible role of exemplary damages, see J Edelman, 'In Defence of Exemplary Damages' in C Rickett (ed), *Justifying Private Law Remedies*, (Oxford, Hart, 2008), but note that punitive damages for personality rights are exceptional in Civilian systems: C Waelde and N Whitty, 'A Rights of Personality Database' in Niall Whitty and Reinhard Zimmermann (eds), *Rights of Personality in Scots Law, a Comparative Perspective*, (Dundee, Dundee University Press, 2009) para 11.6.

[10] *Chester v Afshar* [2005] 1 AC 134 [87].

mark the fact that either the state or a relevant individual has taken away or undermined the right of another – in this case taken away a person's dignity and struck at the core of his personality'.[11]

Where there is a dignitarian loss, compensation could be granted by an award of *solatium* to compensate for distress, anxiety and mental suffering of the pursuer resulting from the unauthorised use of his image or identity.[12] *Solatium* recognises a personal loss rather than a patrimonial loss and, according to the Court of Session, the 'proper course is to quantify *solatium* as being such sum of money as will reasonably mark the jury's (or the judge's) sense of the seriousness of the suffering, or as a reasonable recognition of its seriousness'.[13]

Compensating the economic loss is likely to prove more troublesome, however, since it will require to be calculated according to some quantifiable loss. Where the pursuer can show that he or she has lost some or all of his or her licence fee with an *authorised* exploiter as a result of the *unauthorised* use, as per examples given by Lord Brown in *Douglas v Hello!*,[14] this lost fee could be recoverable from the unauthorised user. However, in some cases there may be no obvious financial loss, yet the defender will still have had the benefit of the pursuer's publicity right, for which he or she would otherwise have had to pay. In order to address this problem, a remedy which looks to the defender's gain (in an unjustified enrichment, or quasi-enrichment, action) may be appropriate.

B. The Notional Licence Fee

A 'notional licence fee' award is based on enrichment or restitutionary principles, and is calculated by reference to what would be a 'reasonable sum' for the use of the thing or right used without consent. A good example of such a measure is the 'notional licence fee' award, known variously as the hypothetical release measure,[15] the *quid pro quo* measure[16] or, as a wider category, gain-based damages.[17] It is calculated according to the fee that the defender would have had to pay for the

---

[11] *Mosley v News Group Newspapers Ltd* [2008] EWHC 1777 (QB) [216]. In October 2008, Mosley announced he would be appealing to the European Court of Human Rights (ECtHR) on the basis that the award of damages in this case was not a satisfactory remedy—further updates are awaited: www.guardian.co.uk/world/2008/oct/04/humanrights.pressandpublishing.

[12] See N Whitty, 'Overview of Rights of Personality in Scots Law' in N Whitty and R Zimmermann (eds), *Rights of Personality in Scots Law, a Comparative Perspective* (Dundee, Dundee University Press, 2009) para 3.7.6.

[13] *M'Callum v Paterson* 1968 SC 280, 284, per Lord Walker.

[14] *Douglas v Hello!* [2008] 1 AC 1 [328].

[15] *Wrotham Park Estate Co v Parkside Homes Ltd* [1974] 1 WLR 798; *Experience Hendrix v PPX Enterprises* [2003] 1 Comm All ER 830. See also Whitty, 'Overview of Rights of Personality in Scots Law' (2009) para 3.7.7, especially fn 585

[16] *Wrotham Park Estate Co v Parkside Homes Ltd* [1974] 1 WLR 798.

[17] J Edelman, *Gain-Based Damages: Contract, Tort, Equity and Intellectual Property* (Oxford, Hart, 2002), especially chapter 3.

unauthorised use made, and has been the subject of much academic debate.[18] The remedy has been pressed into service in relation to patent infringement[19] or breach of contract[20] where there has been no quantifiable loss suffered by the claimant as a result of the defendant's breach of contract.

In wider circumstances, the notional licence fee is often sought where the contract creates an effective monopoly in favour of the claimant, which is destroyed by the defendant's action in breach of contract with no hope of restoring the *status quo ante*. For example, where the breach arises from building additional houses[21] or producing recordings[22] in breach of a contractual covenant, that breach cannot be reversed, that is, the newly built houses cannot (for reasons of public policy) be torn down, nor can the records sold to the public be unsold. Similarly, where the unlawful use has infringed a patent, it is not possible to reverse the infringement after the goods have been distributed.[23] These situations are equivalent to the position with publicity rights, where any breach of the right cannot easily be reversed: once Hello! had published the unauthorised wedding pictures of the Douglases, there was no way to undo the publication; once Talksport had circulated brochures featuring Irvine, there was no way to reverse the circulation. In the words of Eady J, in cases such as these involving publication, the 'dam has effectively burst'.[24]

Although not a breach of contract, infringement of a monopoly right of publicity would likely be, by its very nature, irreversible in this way. The notional licence fee therefore has a role to play in providing financial compensation for breaches which cannot otherwise be undone. It allows the pursuer to recover damages, calculated according to the notional fee that the defender would have had to pay to make authorised use of the persona, under licence.

The notional licence fee award has been recognised in personality cases in the Civilian jurisdictions of France and Germany. French courts will award compensation 'in the amount which would have been paid if the person concerned had asked for permission'.[25] German law recognises this measure as a head of damages, where there has been fault,[26] and under unjust enrichment.[27]

---

[18] ibid; also D Campbell and P Wylie, 'Ain't no Telling (Which Circumstances are Exceptional)' (2003) 62 CLJ 605. For a Scottish perspective on this debate, see G Black, 'A New Experience in Contract Damages? Reflections on *Experience Hendrix v PPX Enterprises Ltd*' [2005] *JR* 31.

[19] *General Tire and Rubber Company v Firestone Tyre and Rubber Company Ltd* [1975] FSR 273.

[20] See, for example, *Wrotham Park Estate Co v Parkside Homes Ltd* [1974] 1 WLR 798; *Attorney General v Blake* [2001] 1 AC 268; *Experience Hendrix v PPX Enterprises* [2003] 1 Comm All ER 830.

[21] *Wrotham Park Estate Co v Parkside Homes Ltd* [1974] 1 WLR 798.

[22] *Experience Hendrix v PPX Enterprises* [2003] 1 Comm All ER 830.

[23] *General Tire and Rubber Company v Firestone Tyre and Rubber Company Ltd* [1975] FSR 273.

[24] *Mosley v News Group Newspapers Ltd* [2008] EWHC 687 (QB) [36].

[25] H Beverley-Smith et al, *Privacy, Property and Personality* (Cambridge, Cambridge University Press, 2005) 191.

[26] ibid 142–43.

[27] ibid 141–42.

It has also been the subject of judicial consideration in England, in the two leading cases, *Irvine v Talksport* and *Douglas v Hello!*. In fact, the award of damages to Irvine was exactly this measure. The Court of Appeal overturned the *amount* of Laddie J's original award, but endorsed the *basis* of it, which was stated to be the 'fee which would have been arrived at as between a willing endorser and a willing endorsee'.[28] Laddie J's award of £2,000, calculated on the somewhat curious basis of £2 per brochure,[29] was replaced with an award of £25,000 which was explicitly based on Irvine's current fee for endorsing products at the time that Talksport used his image.[30] Further, the Court of Appeal emphasised that the award should be based on what the defendant *'would have had to pay... It is not the fee which* [Talksport] *could have afforded to pay'.*[31] The end result was that

> the unchallenged evidence leads ineluctably to the conclusion that [Talksport] would in all probability have had to pay at least £25,000 in order to enable it to do lawfully that which it did unlawfully, that is to say represent by means of the image appearing on the front of the leaflet that Mr Irvine had endorsed Talk Radio.[32]

Although the Court of Appeal's assessment of the amount of the notional licence fee differed from Laddie J's, the underlying principles were approved. Importantly, both courts noted the difficulties inherent in attempting to calculate a licence fee when neither party would have reached agreement in reality. It was acknowledged that Irvine would never have agreed to permit his image to be used in such a non-prestigious context, compared with his existing portfolio of glamorous high-profile endorsements and deals.[33] Talksport would equally have refused to enter into an agreement with Irvine based on his standard fee, when it could have achieved a similar result by using a different photograph,[34] such as one posed by a model. Despite these difficulties, both the High Court and the Court of Appeal adopted the reasonable endorsement fee approach. The Court of Appeal affirmed that this was to be calculated according to the fee that the defendant would have had to pay, as demonstrated by the claimant's evidence, for use of that image.[35]

---

[28]   *Irvine v Talksport Ltd* [2003] 2 All ER 881 [70], citing [2002] EWHC 539 [9]. This of course reflects the concept of the willing licensor and willing licensee applied by the House of Lords in *General Tire and Rubber Company v Firestone Tyre and Rubber Company Ltd* [1975] FSR 273.

[29]   The Court of Appeal noted that this result 'bears no relation at all to the evidence before him [Laddie J] as to what [Talksport] would have had to pay'. See *Irvine v Talksport Ltd* [2003] 2 All ER 881 [115].

[30]   ibid [111]–[116].

[31]   ibid [106], their emphasis.

[32]   ibid [114].

[33]   ibid [111].

[34]   ibid [70], approving Laddie J's comments at [2002] EWHC 539 [9].

[35]   Lord Wilberforce has indicated that, although this is a hypothetical exercise, it is possible to take into account factors relevant to the actual parties of which 'either side, or both sides, would necessarily and relevantly take account when seeking agreement'. *General Tire and Rubber Company v Firestone Tyre and Rubber Company Ltd* [1975] FSR 273, 288.

The claim for a notional licence fee or reasonable royalty had less success in *Douglas*. Since the Douglases had committed themselves to an exclusive licence with OK!, then any grant of a licence by them to Hello! would have left them in breach of contract as regards OK!. Accordingly, there was no notional licence fee to be calculated here: the Douglases could not have granted rights to Hello! without breaching their prior contract with OK!. It is therefore arguable that had the Douglases chosen not to exploit their wedding photographs though OK!, they would have been able to claim a lost licence fee against Hello!.

The Court of Appeal raised a further objection to the award of a notional licence fee to the Douglases, by observing that 'the Douglases would never have agreed to any of the unauthorised photographs being published. The licence fee approach will normally involve a fictional negotiation, but the unreality of the fictional negotiation in this case is palpable.'[36] However, it is not obvious that the Douglases were any less likely to grant consent than Irvine was, or, perhaps more accurately, evidence from the case reports seems to indicate that both Irvine and the Douglases would have been equally adamant in refusing consent. As Laddie J observed when applying this measure at first instance in *Irvine v Talksport*, 'Neither side has a power of veto.'[37] If the Court of Appeal was then able to deal with the fiction of a negotiation between Irvine and Talksport, it is not clear why it was unable to deal with it as between the Douglases and Hello!.

A further obstacle identified by the Court of Appeal was that 'while it is not a sufficient reason for rejecting the notional licence fee approach, there is the difficulty of assessing a fee'.[38] Again, the Court of Appeal arguably overstated this difficulty. Evidence from *Irvine*, together with other commercial cases which endorse the notional licence fee approach, can be referred to in order to provide guidance as to this assessment. As with *Irvine*, there was direct evidence available of the sort of fees that the Douglases would charge or that magazines such as Hello! and OK! would be prepared to pay for the exclusive right to publish celebrity wedding photographs. The complicating factor here, that Hello! would have needed to negotiate a fee to publish *unauthorised* photographs, is not dissimilar from *Irvine*, where the Court of Appeal accepted that Irvine would never have agreed to endorse a company such as Talksport, yet was still able to assess a notional licence fee for the purposes of damages.

The notional licence fee approach is fraught with obstacles if one takes it literally and looks at what the two warring parties would have tried to agree, pre-breach. However, if one treats it as a method of calculating damages where no other quantifiable financial loss is demonstrable, then it is a valuable tool for dealing with unauthorised use of intangibles, whether that unauthorised use breaches a contract or amounts to an unjustified taking of a monopoly right. Attempting to quantify the licence fee is no more of a fiction than attributing a

---

[36] *Douglas v Hello!* [2006] QB 125 [246].
[37] *Irvine v Talksport* [2003] EMLR 6 [11].
[38] *Douglas v Hello!* [2006] QB 125 [248].

specific value to lost or damaged body parts, as the courts frequently do in personal injury actions.[39] Criticisms of the approach as being too subjective can also be dismissed for this reason. All breaches giving rise to litigation will have a subjective value for the pursuer, yet the courts are prepared to impose a 'reasonable' or objective sum, determined by accepted rules on quantification. There is no reason why the courts should be reticent about what is in effect another exercise in calculating loss, based on a notional licence fee, using the best evidence available.[40]

It is submitted that this measure should, however, be subject to a defence where the individual could never have granted a licence to the unauthorised user because of a prior grant of an exclusive licence to an authorised user. This was, of course, the outcome of *Douglas v Hello!*, where the Douglases' claim against Hello! was limited to their dignitarian interest in the personal information, while the commercial claim was brought by OK!, to whom the Douglases had effectively licensed the economic value. The Court of Appeal rejected the notional licence fee claim because

> having sold the exclusive right to publish photographs of the reception to OK!, the Douglases would not have been in a position to grant a licence to Hello! . . . Accordingly, an award of a notional licence fee would involve the Douglases being unjustly enriched: they have already been paid £1m for the exclusive right to publish photographs of the reception. As was said in argument, they have thereby exhausted their relevant commercial interest.[41]

By exercising the positive power to exploit the information, via their contract with OK!, the Douglases had exploited, and exhausted, their commercial interest in the information. Their claim against Hello! could only be for the loss sustained, and no loss of a licence fee was sustained, because OK! still paid the agreed fee for the exclusive. Accordingly, in this situation, the claim against the unauthorised user for the economic interests will come from the exclusive licensee, as considered in section V below.

---

[39] See The Hon Lady Paton, *McEwan and Paton on Damages for Personal Injuries in Scotland,* 2nd edn (Edinburgh, W Green/ Sweet and Maxwell, 1989). This lists current awards of damages for bodily injuries and can be used as a basis for future claims.

[40] This 'hypothetical release' calculation has being used in other circumstances and seems to be increasingly accepted: see for example *Wrotham Park v Parkside Homes* [1974] 1 WLR 798; *Experience Hendrix* [2003] EMLR 25; and a recent Privy Council decision, *Pell Frischmann Engineering Ltd v Bow Valley Iran Ltd* [2009] UKPC 45. The measure has previously been approved (although not awarded in that case) by the House of Lords in *Attorney-General v Blake* [2001] 1 AC 268.

[41] *Douglas v Hello!* [2006] QB 125 [247]. The Court also had concerns that the Douglases' action was founded upon 'upset and affront at invasion of privacy, not loss of the opportunity to earn money' ([246]) and that the practicalities of assessing a notional licence fee would have involved an element of 'unreality' ([246]). The former difficulty has been acknowledged already, not least in relation to the dangers of 'shoehorning' a publicity foot into another boot, while the latter has been addressed and, it is submitted, overcome in this section.

C. Additional Damages

There is specific provision in the Copyright, Designs and Patents Act (CDPA) 1988 entitling the court to take into account all the circumstances of the breach of copyright, particularly the flagrancy of the infringement, and to award additional damages for these circumstances 'as the justice of the case may require'.[42] A non-statutory equivalent of this can be detected in Eady J's decision in *Mosley v News Group Newspapers Ltd*, where he referred to similar awards in defamation actions and stated '[i]t must be recognised that it may be appropriate to take into account any aggravating conduct in privacy cases on the part of the defendant which increases the hurt to the claimant's feelings or "rubs salt in the wound"'.[43] It is submitted that the possibility of awarding additional damages should be recognised in publicity cases, to reflect any unauthorised use which is particularly flagrant or offensive to the claimant. An example might be the unauthorised use of an anti-fur trade campaigner's image to promote furs.

D. Account of Profits

English law recognises a further remedy which is particularly prevalent in intellectual property cases.[44] An account of profits is an equitable remedy 'based on the principle that the infringer has carried out the infringing act on behalf of the right owner'.[45] Cornish and Llewelyn note that this remedy 'is not a notional computation as with damages, but an investigation of actual accounts'.[46] Where the investigation of the accounts reveals that no profit was made by the defendant from his infringing act, then there can be no claim of an account of profits. Since an account looks to strip the defendant of his gains, it is very different in nature from the notional licence fee, which looks to the cost of doing lawfully that which was done unlawfully, regardless of whether a profit or loss was made.

Support for awarding an account of profits in publicity cases can be derived from the judgment of the Court of Appeal in *Douglas v Hello!*. The Court stated:

> If, however, Hello! had made a profit on the publication, we would have had no hesitation in accepting that the Douglases would have been entitled to seek an account of that profit. Such an approach would not run into the difficulties of principle which

---

[42] CDPA 1988 s 97(2). See also MacQueen et al, *Contemporary Intellectual Property* (2007) paras 21.100–21.101.

[43] *Mosley v News Group Newspapers Ltd* [2008] EWHC 1777 (QB) [222].

[44] A similar measure will be introduced by Part 7 of the Coroners and Justice Act 2009 (when it comes into force), which makes provision for 'exploitation proceeds orders' to strip offenders of gains made from criminal memoirs, etc and hand the money over to the state.

[45] MacQueen et al (n 9) para 21.102. In Scots law, it is sometimes referred to as 'count, reckoning and payment': M Hogg, *Obligations*, 2nd edn (Edinburgh, Avizandum, 2006) para 6.16, and references therein.

[46] Cornish and Llewelyn, *Intellectual Property* (2003) para 2–43.

' their notional licence fee argument faces. Such an approach may also serve to discourage any wrongful publication, at least where it is motivated by money.[47]

An account of profits is likely to be particularly relevant in respect of the merchandising use, where there is frequently a direct correlation between the use of an individual's image on t-shirts, for example, and the profits made from selling those t-shirts.

Where the claimant successfully establishes an infringement of intellectual property rights, he must claim either damages (including, where appropriate, additional damages) or an account of profits, since he cannot seek to be reimbursed both through an account and compensated through damages for the same infringement.[48]

Given the potential for profit through the unauthorised use of persona, an account of profits would seem an apt remedy for the claimant. As with intellectual property claims, however, there would need to be a choice between damages and an account of profits: and of course in some cases, such as *Douglas* and *Irvine*, there may be no profits to be disgorged under this remedy.

E. The Calculation of the Award

One final point is the calculation of the award, where the claimant seeks damages. Although the same right and remedy(ies) should be available to all, this does not lead to the conclusion that the amount of damages awarded will be the same for all. Whether compensatory damages or a notional licence fee is awarded, there can be a presumption that an individual with celebrity status is likely to suffer more economic loss than unknown claimants.[49] In turn, 'A-list' celebrities may well be able to demonstrate a greater loss or a higher notional licence fee than 'C-listers'. As McCarthy notes of publicity '[l]ike all other property, that value may be great or small, as the marketplace determines'.[50] The value of persona, and the loss suffered, is likely to depend on the status of the individual—as determined by the marketplace.

This is hardly a novel concept, nor is it restricted to publicity. Anything which can be traded on the open market will typically have its price set by market conditions: supply and demand creates a price differential which is not reflective of the use value of the thing or any value other than market value.[51] Thus, although made in the context of publicity as property, Nimmer's assessment of

---

[47] *Douglas v Hello!* [2006] QB 125 [249].

[48] Cornish and Llewelyn (n 9) para 2–43.

[49] It should be noted that this would not apply where the award is an account of profits, since this looks to the profit made by the party in breach, and not the loss suffered by the pursuer. However, it is likely that the profit in question would be greater in the case of a higher-profile individual.

[50] T McCarthy, *The Rights of Publicity and Privacy*, 2nd edn (United States, West Group, 2001) para 1:39.

[51] See, for example, the discussion of the role of the market and persona in G Armstrong, 'The Reification of Celebrity: Persona as Property' (1990–1991) 51 *La L Rev* 443.

the situation applies to the calculation of the award here: 'the damages which a person may claim for infringement of the right will depend upon the value of the publicity appropriated which in turn will depend in great measure upon the degree of fame attained by the plaintiff'.[52]

In summary, financial compensation should be available to individuals where there has been unauthorised use of their persona. This could take the form of an award to vindicate the right, an award of *solatium* to compensate for the damage to dignitarian interests, and/or a sum to compensate for the economic loss suffered. Where there is no quantifiable financial loss, the pursuer may choose to seek a measure based on the notional licence fee or, in cases where the defender has made a profit from his unauthorised use, an account of profits.

F. Windfalls

One reservation which is sometimes expressed about awarding financial compensation is that it may appear to award the individual (especially already wealthy celebrities) a lucky windfall—something for nothing. It is possibly for this reason, and to avoid claims that they are motivated by money, that some celebrities choose to give any award or out of court settlement (particularly in privacy or defamation cases) to charity.[53] In this way they have vindicated their rights without personally profiting. However, if the award is calculated according to one of the three measures discussed above, then the damages should be no greater or less than damages in any commercial or personal situation, reflecting the economic and dignitarian interests involved. Only where the measure of damages exceeds one of these accepted bases is there a risk that the individual profits from the unauthorised exploitation—and there is no suggestion that exemplary damages would be merited or necessary here.[54] A more creative solution, which would enable a punitive and deterrent element to be introduced without awarding exemplary damages, was raised by Max Mosley in his oral evidence to the House of Commons Culture Media and Sport Committee, in the context of privacy invasion:

> [exemplary damages are] like a windfall and there is something wrong about that. If there is going to be enough money to make any difference at all to News Group Newspapers and News Corp it has to go into the public purse and then nobody feels

---

[52] M Nimmer, 'The Right of Publicity' (1954) 19 *Law and Contemporary Problems* 203, 217. See also chapter eight, section II.

[53] A recent example being the undisclosed sum paid to Angelina Jolie and Brad Pitt by the *News of the World* in an out of court settlement of the Jolie-Pitt privacy claim, which (together with their costs) will be donated to their charity, the Jolie-Pitt Foundation: www.bbc.co.uk/news/entertainment-arts-10725480.

[54] See n 7 above.

bad about that at all. I would not mind seeing them fined, rather like in competition law cases in Brussels, up to 10 per cent of their turnover.[55]

While that may be a relevant proposal for privacy cases, it is suggested that there is no particular need for it here, especially where an account of profits is available to strip the defendant of his gain.

IV. Other Disposals

A practical response for a pursuer would be to seek an order *ad factum praestandum* to seek, for example, the delivery up or destruction of documents or merchandise which infringe, or are likely to if made public, his publicity right.[56]

Continental jurisdictions typically offer a wider range of remedies for infringement of personality rights, which reflect the greater emphasis placed on protection of dignitarian interests than economic interests. Thus, in France, damages are not necessarily widely available but a range of other remedies are designed to restore the dignity of the individual.[57] Such remedies include the award of the *franc symbolique*,[58] designed to indicate the liability of the defendant and condemn his conduct, while recognising the lack of identifiable harm caused to the claimant.[59] Other remedies include destruction of the infringing material, undertakings not to publish it, anonymisation of the individual's features/ identity, and rectification of an untruthful passage or the addition of a statement to avoid public confusion.[60] Similar options are available under German law, including destruction, correction, the award of *solatium*, and the publication of a counter-statement by the individual.[61]

---

[55] House of Commons Culture Media and Sport Committee, HC 275-ii, Minutes of evidence of 10 March 2009, in answer to Q152.

[56] Whitty (n 12) para 3.7.4.

[57] Beverley-Smith et al, *Privacy, Property and Personality* (2005) 188. The authors also observe that even where monetary remedies are awarded, the level of compensation tends to be lower than in Germany or England.

[58] This is of course now a symbolic euro instead, and was awarded to French President Nicolas Sarkozy following an advert run by Ryanair which used a photograph of Sarkozy and his wife Carla Bruni. Note that Bruni was awarded €60,000, being a notional licence fee calculated according to what she would usually seek, as a model, for appearing in such an advert, albeit this was a considerable reduction from the €500,000 she claimed: http://news.bbc.co.uk/1/hi/world/europe/7228457.stm.

[59] Beverley-Smith et al (n 25) 187. The authors cast doubt on its efficacy, since such a minimal award suggests that the harm itself was minimal or even of dubious standing, and there is not necessarily any public awareness of the award once made.

[60] ibid 181–85.

[61] ibid 138–46. *Solatium* will be awarded in Germany where the court refuses to award the notional licence fee on the grounds that the individual would never have granted a licence because of the degrading use made of the individual, for example the use of someone in an advertisement for a sexual stimulant (at 145). See also Whitty (n 12) para 3.7.6.

A final remedy which is worth consideration, particularly to address dignitarian damage caused, is derived from the remedy of the palinode.[62] This remedy 'required a person who had defamed another to apologise and to retract the defamatory imputation'.[63] Although it was never abolished in Scotland, Whitty notes that it had 'withered away' by the middle of the nineteenth century.[64] There is a statutory form of palinode in section 2 of the Defamation Act 1996, which provides for an 'offer to make amends'.[65] This could operate as a useful template for a similar remedy in respect of a statutory publicity right. Further, published retractions have also been endorsed recently by the Council of Europe in Resolution 1165. Paragraph 14 of that Resolution obliges governments to ensure that a number of legal measures are in place, including that 'when editors have published information that proves to be false, they should be required to publish equally prominent corrections at the request of those concerned'.[66] The use of a published apology or retraction may help to address dignitarian concerns in publicity rights—although it may of course work to generate further publicity for the defender and keep the infringement fresh in the public eye, contrary to the individual's wishes. For this reason, any such retraction should be awarded, where appropriate, only with the consent of the individual concerned.

The advantage of these disposals is that they reflect the dignitarian or moral interests protected by such rights, which are a key part of the proposed publicity right. While an award of damages may address the economic loss suffered, a sum of money may be less appropriate to resolve damage to the individual's right to control use of persona. It is not unreasonable to suppose that the Douglases, who spent £60,000 on the pre-wedding party alone,[67] were more comforted by the vindication of their rights by the Court of Appeal than with the award of less than £15,000 in compensation. In this situation, a non-monetary remedy may well be appropriate in reversing some of the harm caused to the claimant's personal interests. An order compelling the defendant to publish an apology or retraction may therefore serve the interests of the claimant more effectively than a financial award.

V. Remedies for Authorised Users

In brief, it is worth noting that an exclusive licensee, as authorised user, may have two different claims, against: (i) the individual, for breach of the licence terms;

---

[62] This can be equated to remedies such as retraction and apology, which are often available: see Waelde and Whitty, 'A Rights of Personality Database' (2009) para 11.6.

[63] Whitty (n 12) para 3.7.2.

[64] ibid.

[65] Section 2 of the Compensation Act 2006 enables an apology to be made by the defendant without this constituting an admission of liability.

[66] Council of Europe Resolution 1165 of 1998 para 14(iii).

[67] Hello! Number 639, November 28, 2000, 87–91.

and (ii) an unauthorised user where that unauthorised use breaches the grant in the licence. In the case of an action against the individual for breach of the licence, this will be a fairly straightforward action for breach of contract, and may be limited by the terms of the licence itself.

However, a statutory right for authorised users against unauthorised users is a more complex matter. It would allow these issues to be redressed directly, and would provide a clear legal basis for this redress, thus avoiding the rather dubious (if commercially understandable) decision of the House of Lords in *Douglas v Hello!*.[68] In doing so, guidance can be drawn from the comparable rights of an exclusive licensee under the CDPA 1988. This provides that the exclusive licensee shall have the same rights and remedies as if the licence had been an assignment,[69] and that these rights and remedies are concurrent with the copyright owner's rights.[70] Any remedies exercisable by the defender against the copyright owner will also be applicable against the exclusive licensee.[71] A statutory grant to an exclusive licensee, that is to say an authorised user, against an unauthorised user, is therefore a natural consequence of the right to grant an exclusive licence.

Further, there should be no danger of a double award against the unauthorised user. As *Douglas v Hello!* demonstrates,[72] and as discussed above, it is not possible for both the individual and the authorised user to have the same claim against the unauthorised user in a privacy action, and it is submitted that the same should apply in publicity actions. Instead, the effect of an exclusive licence should be that the commercial element of the individual's claim is transferred to the exclusive licensee. The net extent of the defender's liability remains unchanged: the grant of a remedy to the authorised user simply reallocates the distribution of it. A statutory provision for exclusive licensees in publicity would provide some much needed clarity and certainty in this area.

---

[68] For commentary on this see C Michalos, '*Douglas v Hello*: The Final Frontier' [2007] *Ent LR* 241; G Black, 'OK! For Some: *Douglas v Hello!* in the House of Lords' (2007) 11 *Edin LR* 402; and H Carty, 'An Analysis of the Modern Action for Breach of Commercial Confidence: When is Protection Merited?' [2008] *IPQ* 416.

[69] CDPA 1988 s 101(1).

[70] ibid s 101(2).

[71] ibid s 101(3).

[72] *Douglas v Hello!* [2006] QB 125.

12

Conclusion

T HE FOREGOING ANALYSIS of publicity rights has attempted to assess the practice and review the ensuing judicial and academic responses. Whether one is for or against legal protection for publicity, most observers would agree that the current legal regulation is unsatisfactory and in need of substantial review. This is especially the case in the United Kingdom, where the absence of a specific right means that publicity interests are shoe-horned into other legal doctrines by claimants attempting to protect or vindicate their interests. At the other end of the spectrum, the myriad common law and statutory protection in the United States, based on property and commercial interests and on tortious and dignitarian interests, also draws criticism, not least for the very volume of rights. Civilian jurisdictions appear to provide the most principled solution, but even then the focus on personality rights has struggled to accommodate the undeniable economic dimension to publicity exploitation. Rather than seeking to find a best fit amongst existing approaches, the present analysis has opted out of a jurisdiction-specific approach. By going back to first principles and building up a picture of the practice as a whole, the aim has been to provide a comprehensive picture of what publicity rights *should* look like, rather than what they *do* look like in any one jurisdiction.

A review of the main analytical approaches to legal protection reveals that, while property, personality and appropriation doctrines all identify certain key elements of the right, no single approach is comprehensive— and certainly none produces any widely accepted terminology. Assessing what happens in practice helps us address this point, by providing a clearer understanding of the use and subject matter at the heart of publicity exploitation. Thus, publicity involves the use of persona for media information, promotion or merchandising purposes. Publicity exploitation can be authorised or unauthorised, and any right must recognise both elements of the practice. Importantly, it must be a right and not only a remedy. Establishing a clear (and neutral) terminology helps to ensure that confusion is minimised, especially where the same practice is discussed across different legal systems, with very different doctrinal bases.

This understanding of publicity practice, reflecting common practice in Western jurisdictions, also enables privacy to be rejected as a home for publicity.

Despite certain shared themes relating to information and image, privacy is both too wide and too narrow to provide a principled basis for publicity rights.

Although there is a need to start by establishing clear parameters and uniform terminology, the question which lies at the heart of publicity in law is whether or not legal protection is justified. It is this element which typically provokes most discussion and, inevitably, disagreement. As well as advancing justifications in favour of publicity, it is of course necessary to respond to the many arguments advanced against publicity rights. Three counter-arguments in particular can be accepted as entirely warranted, namely the arguments against the incentive, labour-desert and consumer protection justifications.

Recognising the twin elements of dignitarian and economic interests inherent in publicity exploitation provides a basis for advancing justifications which reflect these interests and demonstrate that a legal right is warranted. Three justifications are proposed, the first of which is based on the pragmatic need to recognise the flaws with current responses and provide certainty and order in law. The second looks to the fundamental need to protect autonomy and dignity through control of publicity use of persona—an individual's name, image, indicia, information and reputation—all of which are inherently personal and worthy of protection. The third justification turns from dignitarian considerations to economic efficiency, both for individuals and for the market as a whole, and the need to balance private rights and public interests. Together, these three justifications operate to justify a publicity right to protect the dignitarian and economic interests at stake, whether exploited through authorised or unauthorised use. They also enable further criticisms of publicity justifications to be countered. Thus, the final conclusion is that publicity rights are necessary and justified. This conclusion holds good whether one asks the moral question 'is a right deserved?', or the alternative factual question 'who should benefit?'.

As well as justifying the right, the rationales examined provide a further benefit: they start to shape the right itself. Thus, some of the primary features of a legal right, including the holder of the right, its inalienability and consequently the difficulties in classing it as a property right, can be deduced from the fact that the right must protect personal interests inherent to each individual. Similarly, the acknowledged competing interests play a role not in defeating the claim for publicity, but in further shaping the right. The permitted uses of persona, the defences that must be recognised, and the remedies that should be available where breach is proved all emerge from this analysis of the interests in freedom of expression and cultural communication. These interests do not constitute reasons for dismissing publicity, but for considering limitations on the right for the benefit of the wider public. A balance can therefore be achieved between a private right of publicity and the public interests. The question of justifying a right is not an all-or-nothing quest for an unanswerable case for or against publicity. Rather, it is an opportunity to admit interests on both sides of the equation, and search for a balance through the initial recognition of the right and corresponding permitted uses.

In carrying out this examination, I have sought to recognise and reconcile the tensions inherent in publicity rights and to reflect the essential characteristics of publicity exploitation in practice. My final conclusion is that a monopoly right of publicity would meet these objectives, by reflecting the economic and dignitarian interests of each individual through the right to control the use of persona, and recognising the legitimate interests of other parties in using that persona in public to communicate and to share cultural meaning. This right would be balanced and coherent, thereby protecting the interests of all parties involved and providing much needed clarity and certainty in the field of publicity.

While the political reality is such that a statutory monopoly right of publicity is unlikely to be embraced by the legislatures in the United Kingdom in the near future, nevertheless these conclusions remain valid. Whatever legal developments may arise, however, it is safe to predict that publicity as a practice will persist undiminished: celebrities will continue to operate as 'cultural lodes of multiple meanings' and to feature prominently in our daily lives, whether we are reading magazines, buying shampoo, or choosing a calendar for the coming year.

Appendix 1

T HE TEXT ABOVE the photograph of Miss Shaw (a 'Picture of Health') reads: 'Photo of Miss SHAW, nourished to complete health on MACLEANS' REVALENTA FOOD, although suffering from intense weakness of digestive organs.'

Photograph © Callum Black, September 2008

Bibliography

Monographs/ Textbooks

ADENEY, ELIZABETH, *The Moral Rights of Authors and Performers* (Oxford, Oxford University Press, 2006).

ANDERSON, ROSS G, *Assignation* (Edinburgh, Edinburgh Legal Education Trust, 2008).

BEALE, HUGH G (ed), *Chitty on Contracts, Volume 1 General Principles*, 29th edn (London, Sweet and Maxwell, 2004).

BELL, GEORGE JOSEPH, *Commentaries on the Law of Scotland* edited by John McLaren, 7th edn (Edinburgh, T&T Clark, 1878; reprinted The Law Society of Scotland/ Butterworths, 1990).

BENTLY, LIONEL and SHERMAN, BRAD, *Intellectual Property Law*, 2nd edn (Oxford, Oxford University Press, 2004).

——, *Intellectual Property Law*, 3rd edn (Oxford, Oxford University Press, 2008).

BEVERLEY-SMITH, HUW, *The Commercial Appropriation of Personality* (Cambridge, Cambridge University Press, 2002).

BEVERLEY-SMITH, HUW, OHLY, ANSGAR and LUCAS-SCHLOETTER, AGNES, *Privacy, Property and Personality* (Cambridge, Cambridge University Press, 2005).

BLACK, GILLIAN, 'Data Protection', in *The Laws of Scotland: Stair Memorial Encyclopaedia Reissue* (Edinburgh, The Law Society of Scotland/LexisNexis, 2010)

BLACK, ROBERT (ed), *The Laws of Scotland: Stair Memorial Encyclopaedia vol XIII* (Edinburgh, The Law Society of Scotland/Butterworths, 1992).

——, *The Laws of Scotland: Stair Memorial Encyclopaedia vol XV* 'Obligations' (Edinburgh, The Law Society of Scotland/Butterworths, 1996).

BURCHELL, JONATHAN, *Personality Rights and Freedom of Expression: The Modern Actio Injuriarum* (Kenwyn, JUTA, 1998).

CARRUTHERS, JANEEN M, *The Transfer of Property in the Conflict of Laws* (Oxford, Oxford University Press, 2005).

CHALMERS, JAMES, *Legal Responses to HIV and AIDS* (Oxford, Hart, 2008).

COLLINS, HUGH, *Marxism and Law* (Oxford, Oxford University Press, 1984).

COLSTON, CATHERINE and MIDDLETON, KIRSTY, *Modern Intellectual Property Law*, 2nd edn (London, Cavendish, 2005).

COOMBE, ROSEMARY J, *The Cultural Life of Intellectual Properties: Authorship Appropriation, and the Law* (Durham and London, Duke University Press, 1998).

CORNISH, WILLIAM and LLEWELYN, DAVID, *Intellectual Property: Patents, Copyright, Trade Marks and Allied Rights*, 5th edn (London, Sweet & Maxwell, 2003).

——, *Intellectual Property: Patents, Copyright, Trade Marks and Allied Rights*, 6th edn (London, Sweet & Maxwell, 2007).

DALRYMPLE, JAMES, VISCOUNT STAIR, *The Institutions of the Law of Scotland*, edited by DM Walker (Edinburgh, Edinburgh and Glasgow University Presses, 1981).

DAVIES, GILLIAN, *Copyright and the Public Interest*, 2nd edn (London, Sweet & Maxwell, 2002).

DAVIES, HOWARD and HOLDCROFT, DAVID, *Jurisprudence: Texts and Commentary* (London, Butterworths, 1991).

DEAZLEY, RONAN, *On the Origin of the Right to Copy* (Oxford, Hart, 2004).

——, *Rethinking Copyright: History, Theory, Language* (Cheltenham, Edward Elgar, 2006).

DE VAUS, DAVID, *Surveys in Social Research* (London, Routledge, 2002).

DWORKIN, RONALD, *Law's Empire* (London, Fontana Press, 1986).

EDELMAN, JAMES, *Gain-Based Damages: Contract, Tort, Equity and Intellectual Property* (Oxford, Hart, 2002).

ENDICOTT, TIMOTHY, GETZLER, JOSHUA and PEEL, EDWIN(eds), *Properties of Law: Essays in Honour of Jim Harris* (Oxford, Oxford University Press, 2006).

ERSKINE, JOHN, *An Institute of the Law of Scotland* edited by JB Nicolson, 8th edn (Edinburgh, The Law Society of Scotland/ Butterworths, 1871, reprinted 1989).

EVANS-JONES, ROBIN, *Unjustified Enrichment: Enrichment by Deliberate Conferral: Condictio, Volume 1* (Edinburgh, Scottish Universities Law Institute, Thomson/W Green, 2003).

FENWICK, HELEN and PHILLIPSON, GAVIN, *Media Freedom under the Human Rights Act* (Oxford, Oxford University Press, 2006).

FLANDERS, JUDITH, *Consuming Passions: Leisure and Pleasure in Victorian Britain* (London, Harper Press, 2006).

GARNETT, KEVIN, DAVIES, GILLIAN and HARBOTTLE, GWILYM, *Copinger and Skone James on Copyright*, 15th edn (London, Sweet & Maxwell, 2005).

GLOAG, WILLIAM M, *Gloag on Contract*, 2nd edn (Edinburgh, W Green & Son, 1929).

GLOAG, WILLIAM M and HENDERSON, R CANDLISH, *The Law of Scotland* edited by Lord Coulsfield and Hector MacQueen, 12th edn (Edinburgh, W Green/Sweet & Maxwell, 2007).

GORDLEY, JAMES, *Foundations of Private Law: Property, Tort, Contract, Unjust Enrichment* (Oxford, Oxford University Press, 2006).

HARRIS, JAMES W, *Property and Justice* (Oxford, Clarendon Press, 1996).

——, *Property Problems From Genes to Pension Funds*, (London, Kluwer Law International, 1997).

HOBSBAWM, ERIC, *The Age of Revolution 1789–1848* (London, Abacus 1977, reprinted 2002).

——, *The Age of Empire 1875–1914* (London, Abacus, 1994, reprinted 2002).

——, *The Age of Capital 1848–1875* (London, Abacus, 1997, reprinted 2006).

HOGG, MARTIN, *Obligations*, 2nd edn (Edinburgh, Avizandum, 2006).

HOLDSWORTH, WILLIAM, *A History of English Law*, 7th edn (London, Methuen, 1956).

HUME, DAVID, *Baron David Hume's Lectures 1786–1822 vol IV* edited by G Campbell H Paton (Edinburgh, Stair Society, Vol 17, 1955).

JAY, ROSEMARY, *Data Protection: Law and Practice*, 3rd edn (London, Sweet & Maxwell, 2007).

KAMPERMAN SANDERS, ANSELM, *Unfair Competition Law: The Protection of Intellectual and Industrial Creativity* (Oxford, Clarendon Press, 1997).

KANT, IMMANUEL, *The Moral Law* translated by HJ Paton, 2nd edn (London, Routledge, 2005, reprinted 2007).

LANDO, OLE and BEALE, HUGH G (eds), *Principles of European Contract Law* (The Hague/ London, Kluwer Law International, 2000).

LORD MACKAY OF CLASHFERN (ed), *Halsbury's Laws of England*, Volume 11 'Civil Procedure', 5th edn (London, LexisNexis, 2009).

MACCORMICK, NEIL, *Legal Right and Social Democracy* (Oxford, Clarendon Press, 1982, reprinted 1986).

——, 'General Legal Concepts', in *The Laws of Scotland: Stair Memorial Encyclopaedia* Vol 11 (Edinburgh, The Law Society of Scotland/Butterworths, 1990).

——, *Institutions of Law: An Essay in Legal Theory* (Oxford, Oxford University Press, 2007).

——, 'General Legal Concepts', in *The Laws of Scotland: Stair Memorial Encyclopaedia Reissue* (Edinburgh, The Law Society of Scotland/LexisNexis, 2008).

MACPHERSON, CRAWFORD B, *Property – Mainstream and Critical Positions* (Oxford, Basil Blackwell, 1978).

MACQUEEN, HECTOR, 'Property', in *The Laws of Scotland: Stair Memorial Encyclopaedia* Vol 18, Pt II (Edinburgh, The Law Society of Scotland/Butterworths, 1993).

——, *Copyright, Competition and Industrial Design*, Hume Papers on Public Policy, 2nd edn (Edinburgh, Edinburgh University Press, 1995) vol 3, no 2.

——, *Unjustified Enrichment Law Basics* (Edinburgh, W Green, 2004).

MACQUEEN, HECTOR and THOMSON, JOE, *Contract Law in Scotland*, 2nd edn (Edinburgh, Tottel, 2007).

MACQUEEN, HECTOR, WAELDE, CHARLOTTE and LAURIE, GRAEME, *Contemporary Intellectual Property* (Oxford, Oxford University Press, 2007).

MARKESINIS, BASIL S and DEAKIN, SIMON, *Tort Law*, 5th edn (Oxford, Clarendon, 2003).

MARKESINIS, BASIL S, Unberath, Hannas and Johnston, Angus, *The German Law of Contract a Comparative Treatise*, 2nd edn (Oxford, Hart, 2006).

MATTEI, UGO, *Basic Principles of Property Law – A Comparative Legal and Economic Introduction* (Connecticut, Greenwood Press, 2000).

MCBRYDE, WILLIAM M, *The Law of Contract in Scotland*, 3rd edn (Edinburgh, Scottish Universities Law Institute, Thomson/W Green, 2007).

MCCARTHY, J THOMAS, *The Rights of Publicity and Privacy*, 2nd edn (United States, West Group, 2001).

MEEK, RONALD L, Raphael, David D and Stein, Peter G, *Adam Smith, Lectures on Jurisprudence* (Oxford, Clarendon Press, 1978, reprinted 1987).

MERRYMAN, JOHN HENRY, *The Civil Law Tradition*, 2nd edn (Stanford, Stanford University Press, 1985).

MILLER, FRED D, *Nature, Justice and Rights in Aristotle's Politics* (Oxford, Oxford University Press, 1997).

MILLIGAN, ANDY, *Brand it Like Beckham* (London, Cyan, 2004).

PENNER, JAMES E, *The Idea of Property in Law* (Oxford, Clarendon, 1997).

PHILLIPS, JEREMY and FIRTH, ALISON, *Introduction to Intellectual Property Law*, 4th edn (London, Butterworths LexisNexis, 2001).

POSNER, RICHARD A, *Economic Analysis of Law*, 7th edn (New York, Aspen Publishers/Wolters Kluwer, 2007).

RADIN, MARGARET JANE, *Contested Commodities* (London, Harvard University Press, 1996).

REED, ROBERT and MURDOCH, JAMES, *A Guide to Human Rights Law in Scotland*, 2nd edn (Edinburgh, Tottel, 2008).

REID, ELSPETH CHRISTIE and BLACKIE, JOHN WG, *Personal Bar* (Edinburgh, Scottish Universities Law Institute, Thomson/W Green, 2006).

REID, KENNETH, 'Property', in *The Laws of Scotland: Stair Memorial Encyclopaedia* Vol 18, Pt I (Edinburgh, The Law Society of Scotland/Butterworths, 1993).

REID, KENNETH and ZIMMERMANN, REINHARD (eds), *A History of Private Law in Scotland, Vol I. Property* (Oxford, Oxford University Press, 2000).

——, *A History of Private Law in Scotland, Vol II. Obligations* (Oxford, Oxford University Press, 2000).

ROSE, CAROL M, *Property and Persuasion* (Colorado, Westview, 1994).

ROTHSCHILD, EMMA, *Economic Sentiments: Adam Smith, Condorcet, and the Enlightenment* (Cambridge, Mass, Harvard University Press, 2002).

SHERMAN, BRAD and BENTLY, LIONEL, *The Making of Modern Intellectual Property Law: the British Experience 1760–1911* (Cambridge, Cambridge University Press, 1999).

SINGER, JOSEPH W, *The Edges of the Field: Lessons on the Obligations of Ownership* (Boston, Beacon Press, 2000).

SMITH, ADAM, *An Inquiry into the Nature and Causes of the Wealth of Nations* edited by K Sutherland (Oxford, Oxford University Press, 1993, reissued 1998).

THE HONOURABLE LADY PATON, *McEwan and Paton on Damages for Personal Injuries in Scotland,* 2nd edn (Edinburgh, W Green/Sweet and Maxwell, 1989).

THOMSON, JOE, *Delictual Liability*, 3rd edn (Edinburgh, Lexis Nexis, 2004).

TORREMANS, PAUL LC (ed), *Copyright and Human Rights: Freedom of Expression – Intellectual Property – Privacy* (The Hague, Kluwer Law International, 2004).

TURNER, GRAEME, *Understanding Celebrity* (London, SAGE, 2004).

UNDERKUFFLER, LAURA, *The Idea of Property – Its Meaning and Power* (Oxford, Oxford University Press, 2003).

VAN DER MERWE, CG, *The Law of Things* (Durban, Butterworths, 1987).

VAN DER MERWE, SCHALK, VAN HUYSSTEEN, LF, REINECKE, MFB and LUBBE, GERHARD F, *Contract General Principles*, 3rd edn (Cape Town, JUTA, 2007).

VON BAR, CHRISTIAN, CLIVE, ERIC and SCHULTE-NOLKE, HANS, *Draft Common Frame of Reference: Principles, Definitions and Model Rules of European Private Law* (Munich, Sellier, 2008).

WALDRON, J, *The Right to Private Property* (Oxford, Clarendon, 1988).

WALKER, DAVID M, *The Law of Delict in Scotland*, 2nd edn (Edinburgh, Scottish Universities Law Institute, Thomson/W Green, 1981).

——, *A Legal History of Scotland, Volume II, The Later Middle Ages* (Edinburgh, W Green, 1990).

——, *A Legal History of Scotland, Volume III, The Sixteenth Century* (Edinburgh, T&T Clark, 1995).

——, *The Scottish Legal System: an Introduction to the Study of Scots Law*, 8th edn (Edinburgh, W Green/ Sweet and Maxwell, 2001).

WATSON, ALAN, *Society and Legal Change,* 2nd edn (Philadelphia, Temple University Press, 2001).

WEINRIB, ERNEST, *The Idea of Private Law* (Cambridge, Mass, Harvard University Press, 1995).

WHITTY, NIALL R (ed), 'Medical Law', *The Laws of Scotland: Stair Memorial Encyclopaedia Reissue* (Edinburgh, The Law Society of Scotland/LexisNexis, 2006).

WHITTY, NIALL R and ZIMMERMANN, REINHARD (eds), *Rights of Personality in Scots Law: A Comparative Perspective* (Dundee, Dundee University Press, 2009).

WODEHOUSE, PG, *Carry On, Jeeves* (London, Penguin Books, 1999).

ZIMMERMANN, REINHARD, VISSER, DANIEL and REID, KENNETH (eds), *Mixed Legal Systems in Comparative Perspective: Property and Obligations in Scotland and South Africa* (Oxford, Oxford University Press, 2004).

Chapters from Books

BLACKIE, JOHN and FARLAM, IAN, 'Enrichment by Act of the Party Enriched' in Reinhard Zimmermann, Daniel Visser and Kenneth Reid (eds), Mixed Legal Systems in Comparative Perspective: Property and Obligations in Scotland and South Africa (Oxford, Oxford University Press, 2004).

BURCHELL, JONATHAN and McK NORRIE, KENNETH, 'Impairment of Reputation, Dignity and Privacy' in Reinhard Zimmermann, Daniel Visser and Kenneth Reid (eds), Mixed Legal Systems in Comparative Perspective: Property and Obligations in Scotland and South Africa (Oxford, Oxford University Press, 2004).

DANNEMANN, GERHARD, 'Unjust Enrichment as Absence of Basis: Can English Law Cope?' in Andrew Burrows and Lord Rodger of Earlsferry (eds), Mapping the Law: Essays in Memory of Peter Birks (Oxford, Oxford University Press, 2004).

EASTERBROOK, FRANK H, 'Intellectual Property is Still Property' in Adam Moore (ed), Information Ethics Privacy, Property, and Power (Seattle, University of Washington Press, 2005).

EDELMAN, JAMES, 'In Defence of Exemplary Damages' in Charles EF Rickett (ed), Justifying Private Law Remedies (Oxford, Hart, 2008).

FAGAN, ANTON, 'Negligence' in Reinhard Zimmermann, Daniel Visser and Kenneth Reid (eds), Mixed Legal Systems in Comparative Perspective: Property and Obligations in Scotland and South Africa (Oxford, Oxford University Press, 2004).

GIBSON, JOHANNA, 'A Right to My Public: Copyright, Human Right or Privacy?' in Fiona MacMillan and Kathy Bowrey (eds), New Directions in Copyright Law Volume 3 (Cheltenham, Edward Elgar, 2006).

HONORÉ, A, 'Ownership' in AG Guest (ed), Oxford Essays in Jurisprudence (Oxford, Oxford University Press, 1961).

HOWKINS, JOHN, 'Is it Possible to Balance Creativity and Commerce?' in Fiona MacMillan (ed), New Directions in Copyright Law Volume 2 (Cheltenham, Edward Elgar, 2006).

KREBS, THOMAS, 'The Fallacy of "Restitution for Wrongs"' in Andrew Burrows and Lord Rodger of Earlsferry (eds), Mapping the Law: Essays in Memory of Peter Birks (Oxford, Oxford University Press, 2004).

MACQUEEN, HECTOR and WDH SELLAR, 'Negligence' in Kenneth Reid and Reinhard Zimmermann (eds), A History of Private Law in Scotland, Vol II. Obligations (Oxford, Oxford University Press, 2000).

MACQUEEN, HECTOR, 'Peter Birks and Scots Enrichment Law' in Andrew Burrows and Lord Rodger of Earlsferry (eds), Mapping the Law: Essays in Memory of Peter Birks (Oxford, Oxford University Press, 2004).

NEETHLING, JOHANN, 'Personality Rights' in Jan M Smits (ed), Elgar Encyclopaedia of Comparative Law (Cheltenham, Edward Elgar, 2006).

NORRIE, KENNETH MCK, 'The Intentional Delicts' in Kenneth Reid and Reinhard Zimmermann (eds), A History of Private Law in Scotland, Vol II. Obligations (Oxford, Oxford University Press, 2000).

O'CINNEDE, COLM, HUNTER-HENIN, MYRIAM and FEDTKE, JORG, 'Privacy' in Jan M Smits (ed), Elgar Encyclopaedia of Comparative Law (Cheltenham, Edward Elgar, 2006).

OLIVER, DAWN, 'The Underlying Values of Public and Private Law' in Michael Taggart (ed), The Province of Administrative Law (Oxford, Hart, 1997).

PALMER, TOM G, 'Are Patents and Copyright Morally Justified?' in Adam Moore (ed), Information Ethics Privacy, Property, and Power (Seattle, University of Washington Press, 2005).

RICHARDSON, MEGAN and HITCHENS, LESLEY, 'Celebrity Privacy and Benefits of Simple History' in Andrew Kenyon and Megan Richardson (eds), New Dimensions in Privacy Law (Cambridge, Cambridge University Press, 2006).

VISSER, DANIEL and WHITTY, NIALL R, 'The Structure of the Law of Delict in Historical Perspective' in Kenneth Reid and Reinhard Zimmermann (eds), A History of Private Law in Scotland, Vol II. Obligations (Oxford, Oxford University Press, 2000).

WACKS, RAYMOND, 'Why There Will Never be an English Common Law Privacy Tort' in Andrew Kenyon and Megan Richardson (eds), New Dimensions in Privacy Law (Cambridge, Cambridge University Press, 2006).

WAELDE, CHARLOTTE, 'Copyright, Corporate Power and Human Rights: Reality and Rhetoric' in Fiona MacMillan (ed), New Directions in Copyright Law Volume 2 (Cheltenham, Edward Elgar, 2006).

WHITTY, NIALL R and VISSER, DANIEL, 'Unjustified Enrichment' in Reinhard Zimmermann, Daniel Visser and Kenneth Reid (eds), Mixed Legal Systems in Comparative Perspective: Property and Obligations in Scotland and South Africa (Oxford, Oxford University Press, 2004).

Articles

ADRIAN, ANGELA, 'What a Lovely Bunch of Coconuts! A Comparison between Louisiana and the United Kingdom with Regards to the Appropriation of Personality' (2004) Entertainment Law Review 212.

ALLEN, ANITA L, 'Surrogacy, Slavery, and the Ownership of Life' (1990) 13 Harvard Journal of Law and Public Policy 139.

ANGELOPOULOS, CHRISTINA J, 'Freedom of Expression and Copyright: the Double Balancing Act' (2008) Intellectual Property Quarterly 328.

APLIN, TANYA, 'The Development of the Action for Breach of Confidence in a Post-HRA Era' (2007) International Property Quarterly 19.

ARMSTRONG, GEORGE M, Jr, 'From the Fetishism of Commodities to the Regulated Market: the Rise and Decline of Property' (1987–1988) 82 Northwestern University Law Review 79.

——, 'The Reification of Celebrity: Persona as Property' (1990–1991) 51 Louisiana Law Review 443.

ARNOLD, RICHARD, 'Confidence in Exclusives: Douglas v Hello! in the House of Lords' (2007) European Intellectual Property Review 339.

BAINS, SAVAN, 'Personality Rights: Should the UK Grant Celebrities a Proprietary Right in their Personality? Part 1' (2007) Entertainment Law Review 164.

——, 'Personality Rights: Should the UK Grant Celebrities a Proprietary Right in their Personality? Part 2' (2007) Entertainment Law Review 205.

——, 'Personality Rights: Should the UK Grant Celebrities a Proprietary Right in their Personality? Part 3' (2007) Entertainment Law Review 237.

BANKOWSKI, ZENON, 'Law, Love and Computers' (1996–1997) 1 Edinburgh Law Review 25.

BEDINGFIELD, DAVID, 'Privacy or Publicity? The Enduring Confusion Surrounding the American Tort of Invasion of Privacy' (1992) 55 *Modern Law Review* 111.

BENTLY, LIONEL, 'Copyright and the Death of the Author in Literature and Law' (1994) 57 *Modern Law Review* 973.

BLACK, GILLIAN (published as Gillian Davies), 'The Cult of Celebrity and Trade Marks: the Next Instalment' (2004) 1:2 *SCRIPT-ed* 230.

——, 'Data Protection Law in Light of *Durant v Financial Services Authority*' (2004) *Juridical Review* 295.

——, 'A New Experience in Contract Damages? Reflections on Experience Hendrix v PPX Enterprises Ltd' (2005) *Juridical Review* 31.

——, 'Editorial: *Douglas v Hello!* – An OK! Result' (2007) 4:2 *SCRIPT-ed* 161.

——, 'OK! for Some: *Douglas v Hello!* in the House of Lords' (2007) 11 *Edinburgh Law Review* 402.

BLACKIE, JOHN, 'Enrichment, Wrongs and Invasion of Rights in Scots Law' (1997) *Acta Juridica* 287.

BLOM-COOPER, LOUIS, 'Press Freedom: Constitutional Right or Cultural Assumption?' (2008) *Public Law* 260.

BOND, DAVID, 'Sport Personalities: Sponsorship and Endorsement deals' (2004) *Entertainment Law Review* 51.

BOYD, STEPHEN and JAY, ROSEMARY, 'Image Rights and the Effect of the Data Protection Act 1998' (2004) *Entertainment Law Review* 159.

BOYD, STEPHEN, 'Does English Law Recognise the Concept of an Image or Personality Rights?' (2002) *Entertainment Law Review* 1.

BOYLE, JAMES, 'Legal Realism and the Social Contract' (1992–1993) 78 *Cornell Law Review* 371.

——, 'The Second Enclosure Movement and the Construction of the Public Domain' (2003) 66 *Law and Contemporary Problems* 33.

BRAZELL, LORNA, 'Confidence, Privacy and Human Rights: English Law in the Twenty-First Century' (2005) *European Intellectual Property Review* 405.

BROWN, ABBE and WAELDE, CHARLOTTE, 'Intellectual Property, Competition and Human Rights: the Past, the Present and the Future' (2005) 2:4 *SCRIPT-ed* 417.

BURLEY, STEPHEN CG, 'Passing Off and Character Merchandising: Should England Lean towards Australia?' (1991) *European Intellectual Property Review* 227.

BUXTON, RICHARD, 'How the Common Law Gets Made: *Hedley Byrne* and Other Cautionary Tales' (2009) 125 *Law Quarterly Review* 60.

CALLAHAN, ELLETTA SANGREY, DWORKIN, MOREHEAD TERRY and LEWIS, DAVID, 'Whistleblowing: Australian, UK, and US Approaches to Disclosure in the Public Interest' (2003–2004) 44 *Virginia Journal of International Law* 879.

CALLERY, CRAIG, 'John Terry: Reflections on Public Image, Sponsorship, and Employment' (2010) *International Sports Law Review* 48.

CAMPBELL, DAVID and WYLIE, PHILLIP, 'Ain't No Telling (Which Circumstances are Exceptional)' (2003) 62 *Cambridge Law Journal* 605.

CARTY, HAZEL, 'Advertising, Publicity Rights and English Law' (2004) *Intellectual Property Quarterly* 209.

——, 'The Common Law and the Quest for the IP Effect' (2007) *Intellectual Property Quarterly* 237.

——, 'An Analysis of the Modern Action for Breach of Commercial Confidence: When is Protection Merited?' (2008) *Intellectual Property Quarterly* 416.

CATANZARITI, THERESE, 'Swimmers, Surfers and Sue Smith – Personality Rights in Australia' (2002) *Entertainment Law Review* 135.

CHESMOND, RHONDA, 'Protection or Privatisation of Culture? The Cultural Dimension of the International Intellectual Property Debate on Geographical Indications of Origin' (2007) *European Intellectual Property Review* 379.

CLIVE, ERIC, 'The Action for Passing Off' (1963) *Juridical Review* 117.

COASE, RONALD H, 'The Problem of Social Cost' (1960) 3 *Journal of Law and Economics* 1.

COOMBE, ROSEMARY J, 'Objects of Property and Subjects of Politics: Intellectual Property Laws and Democratic Dialogue' (1990–1991) 69 *Texas Law Review* 1853.

——, 'Author/izing the Celebrity: Publicity Rights, Postmodern Politics, and Unauthorized Genders' (1991–1992) 10 *Cardozo Arts & Entertainment Law Journal* 365.

——, 'Publicity Rights and Political Aspiration: Mass Culture, Gender Identity, and Democracy' (1991–1992) 26 *New England Law Review* 1221.

——, 'Critical Cultural Legal Studies' (1998) 10 Yale *Journal of Law and the Humanities* 463.

DAWSON, NORMA, 'Famous and Well-Known Trade Marks – "Usurping a Corner of the Giant's Robe"' (1998) *Intellectual Property Quarterly* 350.

DE GRANDPRE, VINCENT M, 'Understanding the Market for Celebrity: An Economic Analysis of the Right of Publicity' (2001–2002) 12 *Fordham Intellectual Property, Media and Entertainment Law Journal* 73.

DELANY, HILARY and MURPHY, CLIODHNA, 'Towards Common Principles Relating to the Protection of Privacy Rights? An Analysis of Recent Developments in England and France and before the European Court of Human Rights' (2007) *European Human Rights Law Review* 568.

EDELMAN, JAMES, 'Restitutionary and Disgorgement Damages' (2000) 8 *Restitution Law Review* 129.

EDITORIAL, 'Case Comment: Article 10 and Publication of Images' (2007) *Communications Law* 26.

EDITORIAL, 'Case Comment: United States: Intellectual Property – Right of Publicity' (2008) *Computer and Telecommunications Law Review* N 207.

FEENSTRA, R, 'Real Rights and their Classification in the 17th Century: The Role of Heinrich Hahn and Gerhard Feltmann' (1982) *Juridical Review* 106.

FELDMAN, DAVID, 'Human Dignity as a Legal Value: Part 1' (1999) *Public Law* 682.

——, 'Human Dignity as a Legal Value: Part 2' (2000) *Public Law* 61.

FISHER, WILLIAM, 'Theories of Intellectual Property', available at http://cyber.law.harvard. edu/people/tfisher/iptheory.pdf and also published in Stephen Munzer (ed), *New Essays in the Legal and Political Theory of Property* (Cambridge, Cambridge University Press, 2001).

FRAZER, TIM, 'Appropriation of Personality – a New Tort?' (1983) 99 *Law Quarterly Review* 281.

FRIED, CHARLES, 'Privacy: Economic and Ethics, a Comment on Posner' (1977–1978) 12 *Georgia Law Review* 423.

FRIEDMANN, DANIEL, 'The Protection of Entitlements Via the Law of Restitution – Expectancies and Privacy' (2005) 121 *Law Quarterly Review* 400.

GARDNER, NICK and BRIMSTED, KATE, 'Confidential Information – Damages' (2005) *European Intellectual Property Review* 190.

GEDDIS, ANDREW, 'Free Speech Martyrs or Unreasonable Threats to Social Peace? – "Insulting" Expression and Section 5 of the Public Order Act 1986' (2004) *Public Law* 853.

GELLER, PAUL E, 'Dissolving Intellectual Property' (2006) *European Intellectual Property Review* 139.

GEROSKI, PA, 'Intellectual Property Rights, Competition Policy and Innovation: Is there a Problem?' (2005) 2:4 *SCRIPT-ed* 423.

GOODENOUGH, OLIVER R, 'The Price of Fame: The Development of the Right of Publicity in the United States: Part 1' (1992) *European Intellectual Property Review* 55.

——, 'The Price of Fame: The Development of the Right of Publicity in the United States: Part 2' (1992) *European Intellectual Property Review* 90.

——, 'A Right to Privacy in the United Kingdom: Why not the Courts?' (1993) *European Intellectual Property Review* 227.

——, 'Re-Theorising Privacy and Publicity' (1997) *Intellectual Property Quarterly* 37.

GORDLEY, JAMES, 'Contract and Delict: Toward a Unified Law of Obligations' (1996–1997) 1 *Edinbugrh Law Review* 345.

GORDON, HAROLD R, 'A Right of Property in Name, Likeness, Personality and History' (1960–1961) 55 *Northwestern University Law Review* 553.

GORDON, WENDY, 'On Owning Information: Intellectual Property and the Restitutionary Impulse' (1992) 78 *Virginia Law Review* 149.

GRADY, MARK F, 'A Positive Economic Theory of the Right of Publicity' (1994) 1 *UCLA Entertainment Law Review* 97.

GRANTHAM, RB and RICKETT, CEF, 'Property Rights as a Legally Significant Event' (2003) 62 *Cambridge Law Journal* 717.

GRETTON, GEORGE, 'Owning Rights and Things' (1997) *Stellenbosch Law Review* 176.

——, 'Ownership and its Objects' (2007) 71 *Rabels Zeitschrift fur Auslandisches und Internationales Privatrecht* 802.

HALPERN, SHELDON W, 'The Right of Publicity: Maturation of an Independent Right Protecting the Associative Value of Personality' (1995) 46 *Hastings Law Journal* 853

——, 'Trafficking in Trademarks: Setting Boundaries for the Uneasy Relationship between "Property Rights' and Trademark and Publicity Rights' (2009) 58 *DePaul Law Review* 1013–1045.

HARRISON, RICHARD, 'Pastiched-Off' (1998) *Entertainment Law Review* 181.

HENNIGAN, JAMES, 'Altered Image Rights' (2003) *Entertainment Law Review* 161.

HOLYOAK, JON, 'United Kingdom Character Rights and Merchandising Rights Today' (1993) *Journal of Business Law* 444.

HOWARTH, D, 'Privacy, Confidentiality and the Cult of Celebrity' (2002) 61 *Cambridge Law Journal* 264.

HUGHES, JUSTIN, 'The Philosophy of Intellectual Property' (1988) 77 *Georgetown Law Journal* 287.

HULL, JOHN, 'The Merchandising of Real and Fictional Characters: an Analysis of Some Recent Developments' (1991) *Entertainment Law Review* 124.

HULL, JOHN and ABBOTT, SARAH, 'Property Rights in Secrets – *Douglas v Hello!* in the Court of Appeal' (2005) *European Intellectual Property Review* 379.

ISAAC, BELINDA, 'Publication Review of *Image, Persona and the Law*, by Simon Smith' (2002) *Entertainment Law Review* 113.

JAFFEY, PETER, 'Merchandising and the Law of Trade Marks' (1998) *Intellectual Property Quarterly* 240.

Bibliography

JOHNSON, PHILLIP, 'The Public Interest: is it Still a Defence to Copyright Infringement' (2005) *Entertainment Law Review* 1.

JONES, VICKY and WILSON, ALASTAIR, 'Photographs, Privacy and Public Places' (2007) *European Intellectual Property Review* 357.

JOOSS, ALEXANDER, 'Life after Death? Post Mortem Protection of Name, Image and Likeness under German Law with Specific Reference to "*Marlene Dietrich*"' (2001) *Entertainment Law Review* 141.

KALVEN, HARRY JR, 'Privacy in Tort Law – were Warren and Brandeis Wrong?' (1966) 31 *Law and Contemporary Problems* 326.

KLINK, JAN, '50 Years of Publicity in the US and the Never-Ending Hassle in Europe' (2003) *Intellectual Property Quarterly* 363.

KORAH, VALENTINE, 'The Interface between Intellectual Property Rights and Competition in Developed Countries' (2005) 2:4 *SCRIPT-ed* 429.

KWALL, ROBERTA ROSENTHAL, 'Preserving Personality and Reputational Interests of Constructed Personas through Moral Rights: a Blueprint for the Twenty-First Century' (2001) *University of Illinois Law Review* 151.

LADDIE, H, 'Copyright: Over Strength, Over-Regulated, Over-Rated' (1996) *European Intellectual Property Review* 253.

LANDES, WILLIAM M and POSNER, R, 'An Economic Analysis of Copyright Law' (1989) 18 *Journal of Legal Studies* 325.

LAURIE, G and WAELDE, C, 'Privacy, Property and Personalities: Whatever Happened to the Public Interest?' (unpublished, copy dated 2004).

LEARMONTH, ALEXANDER, 'Eddie Are You Okay? Product Endorsement and Passing Off' (2002) *Intellectual Property Quarterly* 306.

LEE, CATHERINE, 'Australia: Copyright – Television – Mr Goggomobile and Copyright in Character Recycling in Television Commercials' (2004) *Entertainment Law Review* 1.

LEWIS, DAVID, 'Whistleblowing at Work: On What Principles Should Legislation Be Based?' (2001) *Industrial Law Journal* 169.

LEWIS, MARGARET and ELMSLIE, M, 'Passing Off and Image Marketing in the UK' (1992) *European Intellectual Property Review* 270.

LLEWELLYN, KARL N, 'Some Realism about Realism – Responding to Dean Pound' (1930–1931) 44 *Harvard Law Review* 1222.

LOGEAIS, ELISABETH, 'The French Right to One's Image: a Legal Lure?' (1994) *Entertainment Law Review* 163.

LORD NEUBERGER OF ABBOTSBURY, MASTER OF THE ROLLS, 'Privacy and Freedom of Expression: a Delicate Balance', delivered at Eton, April 2010 and available at www.judiciary.gov.uk.

LORD RODGER OF EARLSFERRY, 'A Very Good Reason for Buying a Slave Woman?' (2007) 123 *Law Quarterly Review* 446.

MACCORMICK, NEIL, 'On the Very Idea of Intellectual Property: an Essay According to the Institutionalist Theory of Law' (2002) *Intellectual Property Quarterly* 227.

——, 'Taking Responsibility Seriously' (2005) 9 *Edinburgh Law Review* 168.

MACGREGOR, LAURA J, 'The Expectation, Reliance and Restitution Interests in Contract Damages' (1996) *Judcial Review* 227.

MACMILLAN, FIONA, 'Striking the Copyright Balance in the Digital Environment' (1999) *International Company and Commercial Law Review* 350.

MACQUEEN, HECTOR L, 'Protecting Privacy' (2004) 8 *Edinburgh Law Review* 248.

——, 'Protecting Privacy' (2004) 8 *Edinburgh Law Review* 420.

——, 'My Tongue is Mine Ain: Copyright, the Spoken Word and Privacy' (2005) 68 *Modern Law Review* 349.

——, 'Towards Utopia or Irreconcilable Tensions? Thoughts on Intellectual Property, Human Rights and Competition Law' (2005) 2:4 *SCRIPT-ed* 452.

——, 'Searching for Privacy in a Mixed Jurisdiction' (2006) 21 *Tulane European & Civil Law Forum* 73.

——, 'Unjustified Enrichment, Subsidiarity and Contract' (forthcoming 2009/2010).

——, 'Intellectual Property in Scotland c.1700–1850' (forthcoming 2009/2010).

MADOW, MICHAEL, 'Private Ownership of Public Image: Popular Culture and Publicity Rights' (1993) 81 *California Law Review* 125.

MANIATIS, SPYRIOS M and CHONG, SEUNG, 'The Teenage Mutant Hero Turtles case: "Zapping" English Law on Character Merchandising Past the "Embryonic" Stage' (1991) *European Intellectual Property Review* 253.

MANIATIS, SPYROS M and GREDLEY, ELLEN, 'Parody: A Fatal Attraction? Part 1: The Nature of Parody and its Treatment in Copyright' (1997) *European Intellectual Property Review* 339.

——, 'Parody: A Fatal Attraction? Part 2: Trade Mark Parodies' (1997) *European Intellectual Property Review* 412.

MANIATIS, SPYROS M, 'Trade Mark Rights – a Justification Based on Property' (2002) *Intellectual Property Quarterly* 123.

MARKESINIS, BS, 'The Calcutt Report Must not be Forgotten' (1992) 55 *Modern Law Review* 118.

MARTUCCELLI, SILVIO, 'An Up-and-Coming Right – the Right of Publicity: its Birth in Italy and its Consideration in the United States' (1993) *Entertainment Law Review* 109.

MASON, JK and LAURIE, GT, 'Personal Autonomy and the Right to Treatment' (2005) 9 *Edinburgh Law Review* 123.

MCCARTHY, J THOMAS, 'Public Personas and Private Property: The Commercialization of Human Identity' (1989) 79 *The Trademark Reporter* 681.

——, 'The Human Persona as Commercial Property: the Right of Publicity' (1995) 19 *Columbia -VLA Journal of Law & the Arts* 129.

MCGEE, A and SCANLAN, G, 'Copyright in Character, Intellectual Property Rights and the Internet: Part 1' (2005) *Entertainment Law Review* 209.

MCINNES, ROSALIND MM, 'Undercover Filming and Corporate Privacy: *Response Handling Ltd v BBC*' (2007) *Scots Law Times* 150.

MCLEAN, ANGUS and MACKEY, CLAIRE, 'Is there a Law of Privacy in the UK? A Consideration of Recent Legal Developments' (2007) *European Intellectual Property Rights* 389.

MEINERS, ROGER E and STAAF, ROBERT J, 'Patents, Copyrights, and Trademarks: Property or Monopoly?' (1990) 13 *Harvard Journal of Law & Public Policy* 911.

MICHALOS, CHRISTINA, 'Image Rights and Privacy: After *Douglas v Hello!*' (2005) *European Intellectual Property Review* 384.

——, '*Douglas v Hello*: The Final Frontier' (2007) *Entertainment Law Review* 241.

MITCHINER, JAMES, 'Intellectual Property in Image – a Mere Inconvenience?' (2003) *Intellectual Property Quarterly* 163.

MOREHAM, NA, 'Privacy in Public Places' (2006) 65 *Cambridge Law Journal* 606.

——, 'Privacy and Horizontality: Relegating the Common Law' (2007) 123 *Law Quarterly Review* 373.

——, 'Publication Review of *New Dimensions in Privacy Law: International and Comparative Perspectives*, edited by Andrew T Kenyon and Megan Richardson' (2007) 66 *Cambridge Law Journal* 231.

——, 'The Right to Respect for Private Life in the European Convention on Human Rights: a Re-Examination' (2008) *European Human Rights Law Review* 44.

MORGAN, JONATHAN, 'Privacy, Confidence and Horizontal Effect: "Hello" Trouble' (2003) 62 *Cambridge Law Journal* 444.

MORRIS, GILLIAN S, 'Fundamental Rights: Exclusion by Agreement?' (2001) *Industrial Law Journal* 30.

MUHONEN, JUKKA V, 'Right of Publicity in Finland' (1997) *Entertainment Law Review* 103.

MULHERON, RACHAEL, 'A Potential Framework for Privacy? A Reply to *Hello!*' (2006) 69 MLR 679.

MUNRO, COLIN R, 'The Value of Commercial Speech' (2003) 62 *Cambridge Law Journal* 134.

NEETHLING, JOHANN, 'Personality Rights: a Comparative Overview' (2005) XXXVIII *Comparative and International Law Journal of South Africa* 210.

NIMMER, MELVILLE B, 'The Right of Publicity' (1954) 19 *Law and Contemporary Problems* 203.

PHILLIPS, JEREMY, 'Life after Death' (1998) *European Intellectual Property Review* 201.

PHILLIPSON, GAVIN and FENWICK, HELEN, 'Breach of Confidence as a Privacy Remedy in the Human Rights Act Era' (2000) 63 *Modern Law Review* 660.

PHILLIPSON, GAVIN, 'Transforming Breach of Confidence? Towards a Common Law Right of Privacy under the Human Rights Act' (2003) 66 *Modern Law Review* 726.

PINTO, TIMOTHY, 'A Private and Confidential Update – Not for Publication" (2007) *Entertainment Law Review* 170.

PORTER, HAMISH, 'Character Merchandising: Does English Law Recognise a Property Right in Name and Likeness?' (1999) *Entertainment Law Review* 180.

PROSSER, WILLIAM L, 'Privacy' (1960) 48 *California Law Review* 383.

RADIN, MARGARET, 'Property and Personhood' (1982) 34 *Stanford Law Review* 957.

REID, ELSPETH, 'Protection for Rights of Personality in Scots Law: a Comparative Evaluation' (2007) *Electronic Journal of Comparative Law* 11.4.

REID, KENNETH GC, 'Obligations and Property: Exploring the Border' (1997) *Acta Juridica* 225.

REITER, ERIC H, 'Personality and Patrimony: Comparative Perspectives on the Right to One's Image' (2001–2002) 76 *Tulane Law Review* 673.

RICHARDSON, MEGAN, 'Trade Marks and Language' (2004) 26 *Sydney Law Review* 193.

RICHARDSON, MEGAN and DUKE, ARLEN, 'Hello! Nike and Kazaa – Bargaining in the Shadow of Intellectual Property Law' (2007) *Entertainment Law Review* 56.

ROBINSON, FELICITY, 'How Image Conscious is English Law?' (2004) *Entertainment Law Review* 151.

RUDDEN, BERNARD, 'Torticles' (1991–1992) 6–7 *Tulane European and Civil Law Forum* 105

RUIJSENAARS, HEIJO E, 'Legal Aspects of Merchandising: the AIPPI Resolution' (1996) *European Intellectual Property Review* 330.

RUTZ, CHRISTIAN, 'Germany: Copyright – Caricature as Fair Use' (2004) *European Intellectual Property Review* 89.

——, 'Parody: a Missed Opportunity?' (2004) *Intellectual Property Quarterly* 284.

SCANLAN, GARY and McGEE, A, 'Phantom Intellectual Property Rights' (2000) *Intellectual Property Quarterly* 264.

SCANLAN, GARY, 'Personality, Endorsement and Everything: The Modern Law of Passing Off and the Myth of the Personality Right' (2003) *European Intellectual Property Review* 563.

SCHREIBER, AYRE, 'Case Comment: *Campbell v MGN Ltd*' (2005) *European Intellectual Property Review* 159.

SHERMAN, BRAD and KAGANAS, FELICITY, 'The Protection of Personality and Image: An Opportunity Lost' (1991) *European Intellectual Property Review* 340.

SIMS, ALEXANDRA, 'The Denial of Copyright Protection on Public Policy Grounds' (2008) *European Intellectual Property Review* 189.

SINGER, JOSEPH WILLIAM and BEERMANN, JACK M, 'The Social Origins of Property' (1993) 6 *Canadian Journal of Law & Jurisprudence* 217.

SMALLDON, MARK, 'Confidential Information: Privacy' (2005) *European Intellectual Property Review* 207.

SMITH, JOEL and BRIMSTED, KATE, 'Case Comment: Confidential Information – Privacy – Confidentiality' (2004) *European Intellectual Property Review* 135.

SPECTOR, HORACIO M, 'An Outline of a Theory Justifying Intellectual and Industrial Property Rights' (1989) *European Intellectual Property Review* 270.

SPENCE, MICHAEL, 'Passing Off and the Misappropriation of Valuable Intangibles' (1996) 112 *Law Quarterly Review* 472.

——, 'Intellectual Property and the Problem of Parody' (1998) 114 *Law Quarterly Review* 594.

STEVEN, ANDREW JM, 'Recompense for Interference in Scots Law' (1996) *Juridical Review* 51.

TETTENBORN, AM, 'Breach of Confidence, Secrecy and the Public Domain' (1982) 11 *Anglo-American Law Review* 273.

THE HONOURABLE LORD KILBRANDON, 'The Law of Privacy in Scotland' (1971) 2 *Cambrian Law Review* 35.

TORREMANS, PAUL, 'Review of *Bagehot on Sponsorship, Merchandising and Endorsement*, ed Hayley Stallard' (2000) *European Intellectual Property Review* 43.

——, 'Review of *Merchandising Intellectual Property*, by John N Adams, Julian Hickey and Guy Tritton' (2007) *European Intellectual Property Review* 474.

TUNNEY, JAMES, 'EU, IP, Indigenous People and the Digital Age: Intersecting Circles' (1998) *European Intellectual Property Review* 335.

VAHRENWALD, ARNOLD, 'Photographs and Privacy in Germany' (1994) *Entertainment Law Review* 205.

——, 'Case Comment: *Kahn v Electronic Arts GmbH Germany*: Personality Rights – Computer Game "FIFA Soccer Championship 2004"' (2004) *Entertainment Law Review* 41.

VAVER, DAVID, 'What's Nine is Not Yours: Commercial Appropriation of Personality under the Privacy Acts of British Columbia, Manitoba and Saskatchewan' (1981) 15 *University of British Columbia Law Review* 241.

——, 'Intellectual Property: the State of the Art' (2000) 116 *Law Quarterly Review* 621.

——, 'Advertising using an Individual's Image: A Comparative Note' (2006) 122 *Law Quarterly Review* 362.

WARREN, SAMUEL D and BRANDEIS, LOUIS D, 'The Right to Privacy' (1890) 4 *Harvard Law Review* 193.

WEBER, OLAF, 'Human Dignity and the Commercial Appropriation of Personality: Towards a Cosmopolitan Consensus in Publicity Rights?' (2004) 1:1 *SCRIPT-ed* 160.

WESTFALL, DAVID and LANDAU, DAVID, 'Publicity Rights as Property Rights' (2005–2006) 23 Cardozo Arts and *Entertainment Law Journal* 71.

WHITTY, NIALL R, 'Rights of Personality, Property Rights and the Human Body in Scots Law' (2005) 9 *Edinburgh Law Review* 194.

——, '*Transco plc v Glasgow City Council*: Developing Enrichment Law after *Shilliday*' (2006) 10 *Edinburgh Law Review* 113.

ZEMER, LIOR, 'On the Value of Copyright Theory' (2006) *Intellectual Property Quarterly* 55.

ZIMMERMAN, DIANE L, 'Requiem for a Heavyweight: A Farewell to Warren and Brandeis's Privacy Tort' (1982–1983) 68 *Cornell Law Review* 291.

——, 'Who Put the Right in the Right of Publicity?' (1998–1999) 9 *DePaul-LCA Journal of Art & Entertainment Law* 35.

ZIMMERMANN, REINHARD, 'Unjustified Enrichment: The Modern Civilian Approach' (1995) 15 *Oxford Journal of Legal Studies* 403.

Reports, Codes of Practice and Discussion Papers

ADELPHI CHARTER, ADOPTED BY THE ROYAL SOCIETY FOR THE ENCOURAGEMENT OF ARTS, MANUFACTURES and COMMERCE ON 13 OCTOBER 2005 (www.rsaadelphicharter.org/)

AHRC PERSONALITY RIGHTS DATABASE (www.personalityrightsdatabase.com/index.php?title=Main_Page).

HOUSE OF COMMONS CULTURE, MEDIA and SPORT COMMITTEE, 'Privacy and Media Intrusion' 2002–2003, 5th Report, HC 458–1.

HOUSE OF COMMONS CULTURE, MEDIA and SPORT COMMITTEE, 'Press Standards, Privacy and Libel' 2009–2010, 2nd Report, HC 362–1.

LAW COMMISSION, 'Report on Breach of Confidence' (Law Com No 110 Cmnd 8368, 1981)

PRESS COMPLAINTS COMMISSION'S CODE OF PRACTICE (www.pcc.org.uk/cop/practice.html).

SCOTTISH LAW COMMISSION, REPORT ON BREACH OF CONFIDENCE (Scot Law Com No 96, 1984).

ADVERTISING STANDARDS AGENCY'S CODES OF PRACTICE (the Non-broadcast Advertising Code: www.asa.org.uk/asa/codes/cap_code/).

RADIO ADVERTISING STANDARDS CODE (Advertising Standards Authority, London: www.asa.org.uk/asa/codes/radio_code/).

TV STANDARDS ADVERTISING CODE (Advertising Standards Authority, London: www.asa.org.uk/asa/codes/tv_code/tv_codes/).

WIPO Intellectual Property Handbook: Law, Policy and Use, 2nd edn (Geneva, WIPO, 2004: www.wipo.int/about-ip/en/iprm/).

Miscellaneous

Hello! issue 1022 (27 May 2008).

Hello! issue 639 (28 November 2000).

OK! issue 595 (30 October 2007).

OK! issue 628 (30 June 2008).

WRITTEN SUBMISSIONS IN *Douglas v Hello!*: 'Case for the Respondents', James Price QC and Giles Fernando, November 2006.

Index

A

ABBA *see Lyngstad v Anabas*
'accidental' heroes 50
ad factum praestandum order 193
Adelphi Charter 125
advertising 3, 4, 32–3, 34
  enhancement advertising use 33, 37
  informational advertising use 33, 34, 37
  see also endorsements
Advertising Standards Agency
  Code of Practice 100n
agency models 52
allegiance use 33, 34
Allen, Woody 50–1
American Apparel 50–1
American Law Institute's Restatements: the
  Restatement of Torts 14, 15, 20
appropriation of personality 19–22, 26, 27
  Canada 20, 27
  character merchandising *see* character
    merchandising
  Common law jurisdictions 22
  defining 21
  English law 21–2
  meaning of 'personality' 19, 22
  proprietary right of publicity 14, 22
  right of publicity distinguished 14
  tort law 20
assignation of rights 168–70
Austria
  post mortem duration 164
authorised use (of publicity rights) 20, 42–3, 59
  Douglas v Hello! 21, 53
  legal rights and legal powers distinguished
    42–3
  licence 56–7
  positive power 59
  remedies 194–5
  subject matter 54, 56, 57
  unauthorised use distinguished 42–3
  see also publicity uses
autonomy and dignity 107–9
  control 111
  denial 112–15
  dignity 107–8
  dwarf-throwing competitions 109, 113
  ECHR, article 8 109–10
  in the economic interest 116–17

free-riding and 128–9
identifying the individual 142–4
image and 109–10
property and 108–9
publicity and 110–12
waiver in persona 117–18

B

Beckham, David 1, 35n, 48, 49, 50, 99
  earnings from image rights 42
  endorsements 36, 37, 92–3
  merchandising 38
  over-consumption of persona 121, 123
Bently, Lionel 157
Best, George 121
Beverley-Smith, Huw 17, 91, 163, 164, 176
  appropriation of personality 20, 21
  dignitarian interests 88–9
  economic interests 88–9
  endorsements 37
  publicity as property 146
  publicity uses 34, 37
  subjective rights 112
Bieffe racing helmets 56, 57
biographical information use 33–4
Boyd, Stephen 26
Brandeis, Louis D 4–5, 20
breach of confidence 25, 27
  Douglas v Hello! 26, 30–1, 63, 71–2
  ECHR, article 8 and 64, 71
  privacy actions 63–4, 67
  United Kingdom 63–4, 67, 71
Brylcreem 92
Byron, Lord 3

C

Campbell v MGN 72, 180–1
  freedom of expression 137
  reasonable expectation of privacy 67, 68
Canada 46
  tort law 20, 27
cartoon characters
  character merchandising 23–4, 41
  copyright 23–4
  Teenage Mutant Ninja Turtles 41, 142
  see also fictional characters

Carty, Hazel 27–8, 82, 87
  celebrity as product 28
  celebrity promotion 37
  economic interests/dignitarian interests 91–2
  endorsements 37
  IP effect 88
  publicity uses 33–4, 36, 37
catchphrases 47
CCTV images 65
celebrity
  as product 28
celebrity image 32, 33–4, 44–5, 48n
character merchandising 22–5, 32
  AIPPI definition 24
  cartoon characters 23–4, 41
  copyright infringement 23–4
  Douglas v Hello! 31
  English case law 22–5
  fictional characters 23n, 24–5, 32, 41, 142
  image merchandising distinguished 24–5
  Kaye v Robertson 31
  Lyngstad v Anabas 40–1, 58
  mementoes 38
  passing off 23, 24, 80n
  personality merchandising distinguished
    24–5
  pure representation 38
  trade marks 23
  utilitarian items 38
  see also appropriation of personality;
    merchandising use
character right 31
Civilian jurisdictions 15, 16, 28
  dignitarian interests 28, 29, 89
  inalienability 147, 168
  patrimonial/non-patrimonial interests 91
  personality rights 16–19, 45
  post mortem duration 163
  publicity as property 145, 146
Clifford, Max 25n, 36n
Coase, Ronald 124
codes of practice
  Advertising Standards Agency 100n
  Press Complaints Commission 66, 175–6
coherence
  as justification 103–6
Colston, Catherine 28, 32, 34, 36, 37
commercial interests *see* economic interests
commercial use 33, 39
  see also publicity uses
commodification 14, 27–8
common field of activity 47
Common law jurisdictions 12, 14, 28
  appropriation of personality 22
  economic interests 28
  publicity as property 145, 146
  remedies 28–9
  tort law 28

communicative use 138–41
consumer protection justification 97, 100–1,
  115n
contract law 13
  dual dignitarian/economic interests 95
contracts for publicity exploitation 53–7
  Douglas v Hello! 53, 54, 59
  pro forma Personality Rights Agreement 53,
    54–5, 57
control *see* autonomy and dignity
Coombe, Rosemary 104
  autonomy 111
  balance of rights 126, 140
  celebrity image 44–5, 48n
  cultural communication 176
  labour-desert justification 99
  over-consumption of persona 122
  proprietary right of publicity 14
  social use of persona 120
copyright 44, 148, 150
  additional damages 190
  cartoon characters 23–4
  character merchandising 23–4
  dual dignitarian/economic interests 94–5
  duration 156, 161
  evolution 148–9
  fair dealing 177–8
  freedom of expression and 136
  incentive justification 98
  labour or creativity 156–7
  labour-desert justification 100
  moral rights 16
  performance use 35
  public interest defence 174–5
  registration and 159–60
  Statute of Anne 148–9, 161
Cornish, William 60, 61, 190
creative use 32, 34, 138–41
Crocodile Dundee 23n, 142
cultural communication 115, 122, 138–41, 150,
  165, 176–7, 179, 197

D

damages 64, 66, 184–5
  account of profits 190–1
  additional damages 190
  calculation of award 191–2
  compensation 184
  defamation 190, 192
  dignitarian loss 185, 192
  Douglas v Hello! 40, 42, 130, 183
    account of profits 190–1
    economic loss 185
    notional licence fee award 187, 188, 189
  economic loss 185, 192
  exemplary damages 192–3
  fame and 144, 192

France 186, 193
Germany 17, 19, 186
Irvine v Talksport 40, 183
   notional licence fee award 187, 188
notional licence fee award 17n, 185–9
reputation and 144
vindication of right 184–5, 192
windfalls 192–3
see also solatium
data protection law 26, 39, 40
   meaning of 'publish' 39
De Grandpre, Vincent M 89, 103–4, 119, 123, 124
Dean, James 147, 162
death
   post mortem duration 15, 17–18, 162–7
   post mortem transmission of right 170
Deazley, Ronan 148–9
defamation 136, 176, 178, 180, 181
   damages 190, 192
   palinode 194
Diana, Princess of Wales
   memorabilia 38, 41
Dietrich, Marlene 19, 163
digital images 26
dignitarian interests 15–16, 27, 88–96, 197
   Civilian jurisdictions 28, 29, 89
   contract law 95
   control 92
   copyright 94–5
   defining 89
   Douglas v Hello! 93–4, 189
   duration of right and 162
   economic interests and 16, 17, 18, 19, 28, 88–96
   Germany 19
   Irvine v Talksport 93
   mental distress 89, 90, 93, 94, 185
   misrepresentation 116, 118
   palinode 194
   post mortem duration and 18
   in publicity practice 92–4
   publicity rights as subset of personality rights 17–18
   solatium award 89, 192
dignitarian justification *see* autonomy and dignity
distress *see* mental distress
doctored photographs 40, 49, 56, 137
Douglas v Hello! 1, 34, 39–40, 42, 47, 48, 180, 195
   appropriation of personality 21, 22
   breach of confidence 26, 30–1, 63, 71–2
   character merchandising 31
   character right 31
   commercial exploitation of image 26, 30–1
   contract with OK! 53, 54, 57, 59, 93–4

damages 40, 42, 130, 183
   account of profits 190–1
   economic loss 185
   notional licence fee award 187, 188, 189
   dignitarian interests 93–4, 189
   distress 39, 40, 93, 94
   dual dignitarian/economic interests 93–4
   ECHR, article 8 71–2, 76, 78
   interdict 183
   invasion of privacy 26
   licensing of privacy right 78–81, 93
   media information use 39–40, 47, 48, 58
   publicity as privacy right 26, 72
   re-publication of images 66
   unauthorised use 21, 59
dress 46
dualistic model 18
duration of right 15, 145, 160–1
   copyright 156, 161
   duration in life 145, 161–2
   monopoly 161–2
   patents 161, 162, 166n, 167
   post mortem duration 15, 17–18, 162–7
   Statute of Anne 161
   trade marks 161, 162, 167
dwarf-throwing competitions 109, 113

E

economic efficiency justification 119
   balance of rights 125–6
   identifying social asset 120–1
   net positive externalities 124–5
   over-consumption of persona 119, 121–4
   transaction costs 124
economic interests 16, 18, 19, 27, 88–96, 197
   autonomy and dignity in 116–17
   Common law jurisdictions 28
   contract law 95
   control 92
   copyright 94–5
   defining 89
   dignitarian interests and 16, 18, 19, 28, 88–96
   Douglas v Hello! 93–4
   duration of right and 162
   Germany 19, 91, 163–4
   Irvine v Talksport 93
   in publicity practice 92–4
endorsements 3–4, 32, 33, 36–7, 41, 55, 100
   Beckham, David 36, 37, 92–3
   informational advertising 33, 34, 37
   'non-tools' endorsement 37
   'tools of the trade' endorsement 36–7
   types 36–7
enhancement advertising use 33, 37
European Convention on Human Rights (ECHR) 184
   education (article 2) 112

freedom of expression (article 10) 69, 71,
   134–8, 140, 171–2, 181
freedom of thought, etc. (article 9) 112
right to privacy (article 8) 25, 26, 62, 63, 64,
   65, 69, 71, 112
   autonomy and 109–10
   dignity and 108
   waiver 76–8

F

fair comment 181
fair dealing 177–8
fame 99, 115, 129
   damages and 144, 192
   reputation and 36, 45, 48, 49, 50, 52, 53,
      143
Fenwick, Helen 67
Ferrari 53, 55–6, 170
   see also Irvine v Talksport
fictional characters 23n, 24–5, 32, 41, 142
   see also cartoon characters; character
      merchandising
formalities 156
   labour or creativity 156–7
   registration 157–60
France
   case law 50, 90
   damages 186, 193
   dwarf-throwing competitions 109
   fame 50
   franc symbolique award 193
   inalienability 168
   personality rights 18–19, 91, 164
   post mortem duration 163, 164
   reasonable expectation of privacy 68
   remedies 193
   right to the image 18–19, 115
   right over the image 18–19
   transfer of rights 168
Frazer, Tim 20, 21, 62, 90, 123
free-riding
   argument from 127–9
   definition 127–8
   dignitarian objection 128
   unfair competition and 128
   WIPO and 127–8
freedom of expression 69–71, 75, 76, 134–8
   balance of rights 137–8
   copyright and 136
   ECHR, article 10 69, 71, 134–8, 140, 171–2,
      181
   intellectual property rights and 136
   permitted uses of persona 171–2
   United Kingdom 135–6
   United States 69, 135

G

Garland, Judy 120, 138
Germany
   damages 17, 19, 186
   dignitarian interests 19
   economic interests 19, 91, 163–4
   inalienability 168
   non-economic interests 163–4
   personality right 19, 91
   post mortem duration 163–4
   reasonable expectation of privacy 68
   remedies 193
   subjective rights 112
   transfer of rights 168
   unjust enrichment 52
Goodenough, Oliver 15, 51, 131–2
   endorsements 37
   freedom of expression 135
   performance use 33, 34, 35
   publicity uses 32, 33, 35, 37, 38
goodwill
   passing off and 49–50
Gordon, Wendy 127
gossip 4, 36
Grable, Betty 46
Grady, Mark F 119, 121, 123–4
Gredley, Ellen 178–9

H

Halpern, Sheldon W 25, 135n
Hello! *see Douglas v Hello!*
Hilfiger 55–6, 57
Hogan, Paul 23n, 142
Holyoak, Jon 31, 48–9
Howkins, John 125, 126–7, 140
Hughes, Justin 106, 136–7
human dignity *see* dignitarian issues
Human Rights Act 1998 5, 25, 27, 61, 62,
   63n
Hume, David 148, 150

I

icon use 33, 34
identifying the individual 142–4
identity
   concept 13–14, 45, 46
   control 111
   defining 45
   right 114–15
image merchandising
   character merchandising distinguished
      24–5
image use 33–4
   allegiance use 33

biographical information use 33–4
enhancement advertising use 33, 37
informational advertising use 33, 34, 37
inalienability 145–7, 168, 169, 197
incentive justification 97–8
individual
  identifying 142–4
informational advertising use 33, 34, 37
informational use 32, 34, 36
Ingram, Major Charles 50n
injunction 64, 66, 76, 93, 123, 183
  see also interdict
  balance of convenience test 183
  interim injunction 182–3
  super-injunctions 183–4
intellectual property rights
  economic arguments 119
  evolution 148–9
  freedom of expression and 136
  as monopoly rights 148–9
  publicity as 14
  see also copyright; patents; trade marks
interdict 47, 64, 182, 183
  see also injunction
International Association for the Protection of
  Intellectual Property (AIPPI) 24
IP effect 34n, 88
Irvine, Eddie 114
  contract with Ferrari 53, 55–6, 57, 170
  promotion deals 54, 55–6
  see also Irvine v Talksport
Irvine v Talksport 30–1, 40, 47, 114, 142, 180
  confidential relationship 73
  damages 40, 183
    notional licence fee award 187, 188
  doctored photographs 40, 49, 56, 137
  dual dignitarian/economic interests 93
  goodwill 49–50
  merchandising use 38
  over-consumption of persona 123
  passing off 30–1, 40, 41, 49–50
  promotion use 38, 40, 58
  reasonable expectation of privacy 73
  reputation 49–50

J

Jackson, Michael 162–3
Jay, Rosemary 26
Jones, Catherine Zeta *see Douglas v Hello!*

K

Kaye v Robertson
  character merchandising 31
Klink, Jan 15
Kwall, Roberta Rosenthal 16, 111

L

labour-desert justification 97, 98–100
Landau, David 13, 15, 105, 146, 164
Landes, William M 161, 162, 164
Leybourne, George 3
libel *see* defamation
licensing 14, 168–70
  privacy right 78–81
  remedies 194–5
Llewellyn, David 60, 61, 190
Locke, John 98, 149
Logeais, Elisabeth 18, 45–6, 50, 115, 143
look-alikes 47
Lopez, Jennifer 48, 49
Lyngstad v Anabas 40–1, 47
  character merchandising 31
  confidential relationship 73
  merchandising use 40–1, 58
  passing off 40
  reasonable expectation of privacy 73

M

McCarthy, J Thomas 15, 44, 103, 113, 144, 145,
  191
  economic harms/dignitarian harms 91
  freedom of expression 135
  incentive justification 97
  performance use 35
  publicity right as inherent right of identity
    13, 111, 143, 158
  universal right 143
  wealth distribution 131
MacCormick, Neil 2, 42, 43, 61, 107, 145
Macleans' Revalenta Food 199
MacMillan, Fiona 140
MacQueen, Hector 148, 156, 168
Madonna 100
Madow, Michael 15, 105, 115, 124, 132, 144
  consumer protection justification 100
  creative and communicative use 139
  economic interests/dignitarian interests 86–7,
    94, 116
  free-riding, argument from 127
  incentive justification 97
  labour-desert justification 99
  misrepresentation 115
  over-consumption of persona 121–2, 123
  publicity uses 32, 34
  reputation 51–2
  transfer of rights 169
  wealth distribution 129–31
magazines
  publicity use 35–6
  see also Douglas v Hello!
Maniatis, Spyros 178–9
mass markets/marketing 3

media blackout 183–4
media information use 36, 38, 48, 58
  Douglas v Hello! 39–40, 47, 48, 58
medical issues 67, 108, 173, 174, 175
mental distress
  dignitarian interest 89, 90, 93, 94, 185
  Douglas v Hello! 39, 40, 93, 94
  solatium 185
merchandising use 37–8, 40–1, 58
  Irvine v Talksport 38
  Lyngstad v Anabas 40–1, 58
  see also character merchandising
Michalos, Christina 81
Middleton, Kirsty 28, 32, 34, 36, 37
Milligan, Andy 92–3, 99, 121
Minogue, Kylie 120–1, 138, 177
misrepresentation
  dignitarian issues 116, 118
  passing off and 40, 49n, 105n, 114, 115, 136, 158
'Miss Shaw' 199
models 52
monopolies
  duration 161–2
  likelihood of legislation 150–1
  publicity as a monopoly 147–50, 170
Monroe, Marilyn 18, 99, 100, 147, 162
moral rights 16
Moreham, NA 108
Mosley, Max
  exemplary damages 192–3
  see also Mosley v News Group Newspapers Ltd
Mosley v News Group Newspapers Ltd
  breach of confidence 64, 67, 74
  damages 190
  dignity 108
  disclosure of personal information 74
  freedom of expression 70
  public interest 173–4
  reasonable expectation of privacy 66, 67
Moss, Kate 50n

N

natural rights of property 111
Neethling, Johann 17, 91, 111–12, 114, 158, 164
newspapers
  advertising 3, 4
  press intrusion 4
  publicity use 35–6
Nimmer, Melville B 12–13, 143, 144
  on Brandeis and Warren 4n, 5n
  economic interests/dignitarian interests 90, 91
non-famous individuals 51–2
notional licence fee award 17n, 185–9

O

OK! magazine *see Douglas v Hello!*
Oliver, Jamie 36
order *ad factum praestandum* 193

P

palinode 194
paparazzo photographs 39, 65, 94
parody 33, 115, 140, 178–80
passing off 21, 49–50, 80
  character merchandising 23, 24, 80n
  goodwill 49–50
  Irvine v Talksport 30–1, 40, 41, 49–50
  Lyngstad v Anabas 40–1
  misrepresentation 40, 49n, 105n, 114, 115, 136, 158
  reputation 49–50
patents 130, 148, 150
  alienation 169
  duration 161, 162, 167
  notional licence fee 186
  post mortem duration 167
  registration 156, 157–8, 159, 160
People Magazine 48, 49
Pepsi 37, 49, 92
performance use 33, 34, 35
performance values 35
perjury 136
persona
  control 113–15, 116–17
  defining 59
  economic efficiency justification 120–1
  identifying the individual 142–4
  inalienability 145–7
  over-consumption 121–4
  permitted uses 171
    communicative use 138–41
    creative use 32, 34, 138–41
    fair comment 181
    fair dealing 177–8
    false or misleading use 100–1
    freedom of expression 134–8, 140, 171–2
    parody 178–80
    private use 171
    public interest 173–7
    public policy 172
    'setting the record straight' 180–1
  reputation *see* reputation
  as social asset 120–1
  as subject matter 44, 58, 59
personal endorsements *see* endorsements
personal right 103, 116, 143, 148n
personality
  appropriation *see* appropriation of personality
  defining 19, 22, 30

personality merchandising
  character merchandising distinguished 24–5
personality rights 14
  Civilian jurisdictions 16–19
  France 18–19, 91, 164
  Germany 19, 91
  non-transferable 17–18
  post mortem protection 18–19
  publicity as subset of 16–19
Phillipson, Gavin 67
photographs
  doctored 40, 49, 56, 137
  paparazzo photographs 39, 65, 94
  publicity value 13
  taken in private places 65–6
Police sunglasses 48, 49, 92–3
Posner, Richard 119, 161, 162, 164
post mortem duration 15, 17–18, 162–7
post mortem transmission of right 170
Presley, Elvis 18, 38
Press Complaints Commission
  Code of Practice 66, 175–6
privacy 2, 13, 19, 25, 60–1
  breach of confidence *see* breach of
    confidence
  children 68
  concept 61–2
  control of privacy 61–2
  data protection 26
  defences to privacy infringements 75–6
  defining 61–2
  dissemination of private information 75
  ECHR, article 8 25, 26, 62, 63, 64, 65, 69, 71,
    112
    autonomy and 109–10
    dignity and 108
    waiver of right 76–8
  four Restatement rights 15
  freedom of expression 69–71, 75, 76
  Human Rights Act 1998 5, 25, 27, 61, 62, 63n
  licensing of privacy right 78–81
  publicity as privacy right 25–7, 72
    confidential relationship 73
    defences to privacy infringements 75–6
    Douglas v Hello! 26, 72
    invasion vs dissemination 73–5
    licensing of privacy right 78–81
    positive exploitation 76–8
    private information 73–5
    reasonable expectation of privacy 73
    waiving right to privacy 76–8
  re-publication of images 66
  reasonable expectation of privacy 64–9, 73
    CCTV images 65
    children 68
    ECHR, article 8 65, 69
    France 68
    Germany 68

nature of information 67–8
  paparazzo photographs 65
  photographs taken in private places 65–6
  prior conduct of claimant 68
  United Kingdom 64–9
  widely-available information 66
seclusion and 62
tort law 20
United Kingdom 4, 5, 21, 25, 61–2, 71–2
  breach of confidence 63–4, 67, 71
  development of practice 2–3
  freedom of expression 69–71
  Human Rights Act 1998 5, 25, 27, 61, 62,
    63n
  re-publication of images 66
  reasonable expectation of privacy 64–9
United States 4
waiver of right 76–8
pro forma Personality Rights Agreement 53,
  54–5, 57
product
  celebrity as 28
promotion use 4, 37, 38, 58
  Irvine v Talksport 38, 40, 58
property rights
  celebrity as product 28
  name, voice etc. 45
  'publicity as property' 5, 12–16, 22, 28, 30, 90
    inalienability and 145–7
  United States 22, 45, 149, 169
Prosser, William 20, 21, 28, 74–5
public interest defence 70–1, 173–7
  copyright 174–5
public policy 172
public use
  concept 38–9
publicity
  definition 58
publicity uses 32–5
  advertising use 32–3, 34
  allegiance use 33
  authorised *see* authorised use
  biographical information use 33–4
  commercial use 33, 39
  communicative use 32, 34, 138–41
  creative use 32, 34, 138–41
  endorsement use 36–7
  enhancement advertising use 33, 37
  icon use 33, 34
  image use 33–4
  informational advertising use 33, 34, 37
  informational use 32, 34, 36
  legal rights and legal powers distinguished
    42–3
  media information use 36, 38, 39–40, 47, 48,
    58
  merchandising use 37–8, 40–1, 58
  paradigm cases 39–41, 47

performance use 33, 34, 35
promotion use 4, 37, 38, 40, 58
public nature of use 38–9
subject matter *see* subject matter
tripartite classification 35–9
unauthorised *see* unauthorised use

R

Radin, Margaret 108–9
re-publication of images 66
recognisability
    reputation and 46, 48, 49, 52
recognition value 44–5, 48n, 76
registration 157–60
    advantages 157–8
    copyright and 159–60
    costs 159
    disadvantages 158–9
    patents 156, 157–8, 159, 160
    post mortem registration 166–7
    trade marks 156, 157–8, 159, 160
Reiter, Eric H 16, 18, 28, 52, 131, 132
remedies 15, 182
    authorised use 194–5
    Common law jurisdictions 28–9
    damages *see* damages
    franc symbolique award 193
    France 193
    Germany 193
    injunction *see* injunction
    interdict 47, 64, 182, 183
    order *ad factum praestandum* 193
    palinode 194
    preventing unauthorised use 182–4
    solatium 17, 19, 89, 185, 192, 193
reputation 3, 31, 36, 48–53, 56, 57, 58, 59, 143
    agency models 52
    damages and 144
    death and 163
    fame and 36, 45, 48, 49, 50, 52, 53, 143
    free-riding argument 128
    licensing 56–7
    meaning 59
    negative 51
    non-famous individuals 51–2
    passing off 49–50
    recognisability 46, 48, 49, 52
Rowling, JK 100
Ruijsenaars, Heijo E 24
Ryanair 50n

S

Scott, Sir Walter 156
Sherman, Brad 157
Sinatra, Nancy 176

slavery 112n, 129
Smith, Adam 129, 148n, 150, 162
solatium 17, 19, 89, 185, 192, 193
sound-alikes 47
Spence, Michael 113, 114, 118
sponsorship 55, 100
sports clubs
    pro forma Personality Rights Agreement 53, 54–5, 57
Statute of Anne 148–9, 161
subject matter (of publicity rights) 31, 58–9
    authorised use 54, 56, 57
    celebrity image 44–5
    defining 'identity' 45
    elements of the individual 44–8
    identifying 44–8
    image, meaning 59
    indicia, meaning 59
    information, meaning 59
    persona 44, 58, 59
    recognisability 46
    reputation *see* reputation
    unauthorised use 57
super-injunctions 183–4
Switzerland
    post mortem duration 164

T

Talksport *see Irvine v Talksport*
Teenage Mutant Ninja Turtles 41, 142
'tools of the trade' endorsements 36–7
tort law
    American Restatement of Torts 14, 15, 20
    appropriation of personality 20
    Canada 20, 27
    Common law jurisdictions 28
    privacy 20
    see also breach of confidence; passing off
torture 113, 114
trade marks 21, 37–8, 44
    character merchandising 23
    duration 161, 162, 167
    parodies 179
    post mortem duration 167
    re-registration 167
    registration 156, 157–8, 159, 160
    see also passing off
tragedy of the commons 119, 121
transfer and transmission of right 167
    assignation 168–70
    licensing 168–70
    lifetime transfer 168–70
    post mortem transmission 170
    temporary transfer 169

Index

U

unauthorised use (of publicity rights) 20, 21,
  42–3, 59
  authorised use distinguished 42–3
  consumer protection justification 100
  damages *see* damages
  Irvine v Talksport 53
  legal rights and legal powers distinguished
    42–3
  negative right 59
  preventing 182–4
  subject matter 57
  see also publicity uses
'Uncle Mac' 47
unfair competition 13, 14, 105, 106
  free-riding and 128
  WIPO and 127, 128
United States
  assignation and licensing 169
  freedom of expression 69, 134, 135
  post mortem duration 15, 164–7
  privacy law 4
  property rights 22, 45, 149, 169

reputation 50–2
unjust enrichment 19, 52, 88, 186

V

Valleverde footwear 56, 57
Vaver, David 20, 21, 27, 46, 98, 143, 144

W

Waelde, Charlotte 60, 163
Warren, Samuel D 4–5, 20
wealth distribution 129–31
Westfall, David 13, 15, 105, 146, 164
Whitty, Niall 60, 163, 194
Woods, Tiger 50n, 117
World Intellectual Property Organisation
    (WIPO)
  free-riding 127–8

Y

Young, Robert 115

Lightning Source UK Ltd.
Milton Keynes UK
UKOW06n1443250615

254116UK00003B/29/P